THE SOUTH IN BLACK AND WHITE

McKAY JENKINS

The South in Black and White

Race, Sex, and Literature
in the 1940s

The University of North Carolina Press

Chapel Hill and London

Library of Congress Cataloging-in-Publication Data
Jenkins, McKay, 1963– The South in Black and white : race, sex,
and literature in the 1940s / by McKay Jenkins.
p. cm. Includes bibliographical references and index.
ISBN 0-8078-2491-7 (alk. paper).—
ISBN 0-8078-4777-1 (pbk. : alk. paper)
1. American literature—Southern States—History and criticism.
2. Literature and society—Southern States—History—20th
century. 3. Percy, William Alexander, 1885–1942—Political and
social views. 4. Smith, Lillian Eugenia, 1897–1966—Political and
social views. 5. McCullers, Carson, 1917–1967—Political and social
views. 6. Southern States—Race relations—Historiography.
7. Cash, W. J. (Wilbur Joseph), 1900–1941. 8. Afro-Americans in
literature. 9. Race in literature. 10. Sex in literature. I. Title.
PS261.J46 1999 810.9'975'09044—dc21 99-12598 CIP

03 02 01 00 99 5 4 3 2 1

For Katherine

CONTENTS

ACKNOWLEDGMENTS

Throughout the research and writing of this book I have had an exceedingly supportive and encouraging group of mentors and friends. The inspiration for this particular project came initially not from literary sources but from Nell Painter's dynamic engagement with issues of race, gender, and Southern identity in a Princeton graduate seminar on Southern history. Her enthusiasm for and analysis of the difficult issues examined here continue to set an impressive example of interdisciplinary scholarship. Also at Princeton, William Howarth and Arnold Rampersad offered generosity and professionalism from the start and allowed for the peculiar mix of biography, history, and textual analysis found here. I consider myself lucky to have had such sympathetic and eclectic readers. John McPhee, who has had little to do with my scholarship but a great deal to do with my desire to be a writer, remains, in his discipline and commitment to the craft, a mentor of the highest order.

The best testament to the writers and scholars whose work has inspired me is found within these pages, but some deserve special mention. Toni Morrison's book *Playing in the Dark* served as something of a personal watershed for its insight into American literary race relations. Likewise, the work of Richard King, Bertram Wyatt-Brown, Henry Louis Gates Jr., John Egerton, Taylor Branch, Edward Ayers, Cornel West, Patricia Williams, Daniel Singal, Morton Sosna, and Nicholas Lemann stands out as the foundation on which this book is built.

Closer to home, Ben Yagoda continues to inspire with his work and good humor. Wes Davis, Pete Balaam, Robert Worth, Laura Sayre, Kevin Hicks, Tom Pinneo, and Jim Yardley have all, in their own ways, helped shape the ideas found here.

Deep thanks to Wahneema Lubiano and Louise Westling for their thorough and insightful readings of early drafts. At the University of North Carolina Press, Sian Hunter, Mary Caviness, and Paula Wald have been patient and professional editors. Thanks also to the Association of Princeton Graduate Alumni for a grant to conduct research in William Alexander Percy's hometown of Greenville, Mississippi, and to the English Department at the University of Delaware for providing the time and support necessary to complete this project.

Finally, thanks to Katherine, Satch, and Ella for their patience and love. Jag alskar dig.

THE SOUTH IN BLACK AND WHITE

Whatever Else the True American Is, He Is Also Somehow Black

Even for a region long accustomed to racial violence as an emblem of its struggle for self-definition, the South in the 1940s was a place where race remained the name attached to issues that had little overt connection with skin color. Economic, political, and gender discourse often hinged on the rhetorical manipulation of race and the myriad places that whiteness and blackness defined each other. The way people spoke of themselves, their ancestors, their wives, their jobs, all inexorably turned on notions of race, long a particularly malleable metaphor for human difference. If, as the historian Joel Williamson writes, the white South had become in the early part of the century "in both its mind and body, what it had been seeking to be since the 1830s, a relatively solid, unitary, most-together place," it began in the 1940s to see how illusory this unity was in fact becoming. "The profound fissures that had existed in the South before those years—between black and white, between the slaveholding elite and the nonslaveholding masses and, subsequently, the social heirs of each, Conservative Democrats and Radical Populists, between racial Conservatives and racial Radicals, and between men and women, were not dissolved, but they were covered over by a heavy plastering of myth, troweled smoothly on by an elite determined to make it seem that there were no cracks in the structure that was their world and never really had been" (459).

Finding the "cracks in the structure" of white Southern identity is the object of this book. How did white writers in the 1940s construct images of race and race relations as they put together narratives that professed to have little, if anything, to "do" with race? In what ways did images of race bubble to the surface in these texts, even those with apparently few, if any, black characters? Upon even cursory examination it becomes apparent that race and gender not only were *not* peripheral to a culture constructed predominantly by whites, they were at the very heart of the culture. The Swedish social economist Gunnar Myrdal wrote in 1944 that

> white Americans can, of course, keep the Negro problem out of their minds to a greater extent and, in addition, they have good selfish reasons for keeping it below the level of consciousness. To be sure, the investigator is frequently told that there is "no Negro problem" in America. Everything is quiet on the racial front. Ne- groes are all right in their place; and they, for their part, do not want things changed. In fact, they are the happiest lot on earth. Just look at them: how they laugh and enjoy themselves; how they sing and praise the Lord.
>
> This attitude is met most frequently and expressed most em- phatically in the Deep South. But it is not true. The contrary state- ment, that the white South is constantly concerned with the Negro problem, that it has allowed the Negro problem to rule its politics and its business, fetter its intelligence and human liberties, and ham- per its progress in all directions, would be nearer the truth. In the South, statements that there is "no Negro problem" cover doubt, disagreement, concern and anxiety, moral tension, and a need for escape and defense. To furnish such a covering is, from a psycho- logical point of view, the "function" of such statements. (Rose, 13)[1]

The doubts, disagreements, concerns, anxieties, moral tensions, and needs for escape and defense are exactly what I seek to uncover by a close look at the "function" of statements about race, particularly as they are expressed in a given body of literature. My central desire is to pick apart a cultural discourse that I believe had accrued over a period of decades for a precise purpose: to replace physical shackles with rhetori- cal ones. I agree fully with the historian Grace Elizabeth Hale's com- ment that whites "responded to this increasing diversity and this rising black middle class with fear, violent reprisals, and state legislation— their floundering attempts to build a new racial order. Whites created the culture of segregation in large part to counter black success, to make a myth of absolute racial difference, to stop the rising" (21). The desire for the impossible, be it for a nation free of blacks, a time of sexual in- nocence, or a return to an era of chivalric yeoman farmers, runs deep in the texts I examine, in vastly different ways. My method is to weave to- gether a number of threads—cultural and literary history; biographical narratives and commentary; and contemporary racial and cultural theory—to create a picture of an era that remains underexplored and is in many ways instructive for our own times of troubled race relations. I explore what Ralph Ellison meant when he wrote in "What America Would Be Like Without Blacks":

> Since the beginning of the nation, white Americans have suffered from a deep inner uncertainty as to who they really are. One of the ways that has been used to simplify the answer has been to seize upon the presence of black Americans and use them as a marker, a symbol of limits, a metaphor for the "outsider." Many whites could look at the social position of blacks and feel that color formed an easy and reliable gauge for determining to what extent one was or was not American. Perhaps that is why one of the first epithets that many European immigrants learned when they got off the boat was the term "nigger"—it made them feel instantly American. But this is tricky magic. Despite his racial difference and social status, something indisputably American about Negroes not only raised doubts about the white man's value system but aroused the troubling suspicion that whatever else the true American is, he is also somehow black. (*Territory*, 111)

It is Ellison's notion of "tricky magic" with which I am concerned: the ways a region that devoted so much rhetorical energy to defining itself as homogeneous revealed itself in fact to be organically dependent on the very categories of identity it most loathed and repressed. Indeed, it is nothing so much as the "troubling suspicions" that reveal the South's rhetorical fault lines. In precisely the places that rhetoric, be it personal or cultural, insists on its own solidity or cohesiveness can be found its most interesting cracks and fissures. Indeed, in many cases, the masking capacity of racial rhetoric was apparent even to those who voiced it. "It is the fate of the Southerner to be involved in his region, always to feel himself held by it," wrote Ralph McGill, the longtime editor of the *Atlanta Constitution*. "He may never have believed the myths. The often cruel injustices of the rigid formula of race may have offended him and aroused him to open opposition. The cost of parochialism and injustice, not merely to the Negro, but to the material and spiritual welfare of his own people, may have been long on his conscience. But nonetheless, he is a part of what he has met, and been. And the past, in tales of his parents, his great-aunts and uncles, has been in his ears since birth" (Sosna, vii).

The influence of history, in regional, racial, and literary terms, is deeply woven into the works discussed here. The 1940s were the mid-point of the Southern Renaissance, still influenced by the populism of Erskine Caldwell and James Agee, the agrarianism of the Fugitives, and the high modernism of Faulkner. But the period was also lurching toward an engagement with the fundamental tenets of postmodernity: fractured identity, blurring regional boundaries, and ethnic multiplicity that would arrive with the work of, among others, Flannery O'Connor, Richard Wright, and Walker Percy. Throughout this book, I examine this period of literary and cultural transition to explore how a group of writers wrestled with issues that defined both themselves and their region.

The foundations of this project are the writings—fiction and non-fiction, histories, memoirs, letters, and journalism—of four white writers: Wilbur J. Cash, William Alexander Percy, Lillian Smith, and Carson McCullers. The four represent a geographical arc that marks important differences in their imaginative framework. Although they both claimed Georgia as home, Smith and McCullers came from very different places. McCullers spent much of her life in the Northeast but was born in Columbus, a piedmont town near the Chattahoochee River that forms the border with Alabama; Lillian Smith was born in Florida but spent most of her life in the mountains of north Georgia near the borders of Tennessee and North Carolina. Percy lived most of his life in the Mississippi Delta town of Greenville, where he inherited and ran a cotton plantation even as he became the region's most renowned poet. Cash was born into a poor millworking family in Gaffney, South Carolina, and spent the bulk of his adult life working as a newspaper man in Charlotte, North Carolina. The regional differences are important to keep in mind, for they carry with them a specificity that shows up clearly in the literature at hand. Smith, for example, although she lived her adult life in the mountains, often relied on swamp imagery to describe her fictional towns and the (frequently) black characters that emerged from them; she'd grown up in Jasper, Florida, close to the Okefenokee Swamp, known to Native Americans as the "land of trembling earth" for its unstable, shifting ground. Percy writes a long chapter about the catastrophic Mississippi River flood of 1927 in which he was put in charge of the relief for thousands of local black farmhands. Cash's obsession with Nazi Germany can in part be traced to the violent, white supremacist rhetoric that emerged from the piedmont mill towns of North and South Carolina he knew even as a child. McCullers consistently returns to images of small-town "freaks" and descriptions of the state insane asylum, located in Milledgeville, Georgia—appropriately enough the hometown of McCullers's literary heir, Flannery O'Connor. Place defines writers as much as time, and in each chapter I try to mark the influence of geography on the writerly imagination as well as that of politics and literature.

As important as region was to the formation of these writers' racial imaginations, another factor must be considered at least as important: sexuality. All four were deeply ambivalent about their own sexuality: Smith was a lesbian; Percy was effeminate and cast himself, publicly at least, as essentially sexless; McCullers was perhaps best described as androgynous (she was drawn to members of both sexes but was terrified by physical sexuality); and Cash, who did not marry until he was forty and killed himself one year later, struggled for much of his adult life with impotence. The link between sexual alienation and an engagement with racial segregation, then, are tightly linked in all four writers and reveal much about the energy behind each writer's struggle with identity and repression. There can be little question of the role that sexual isolation played in the minds of all four writers, particularly as it allowed them to occupy a space between their own privileged whiteness and the alienation of blackness. Eve Kosofsky Sedgwick has noted that the gay rhetorical position can be useful in taking apart notions of stable identity: "The most important work in destabilizing 'essentialist' rhetoric is that of dealing with the far less permissible, vastly more necessary project of recognizing and validating the creativity and heroism of the effeminate boy or tommish girl of the fifties (or sixties or seventies or eighties) whose sense of constituting precisely a *gap* in the discursive fabric of the given has not yet been done justice" (43).

If effeminate boys and "tommish" girls were forced underground in the 1950s, 1960s, or 1970s, they were far more so in the decade to be discussed here. Cash, Percy, Smith, and McCullers were each troubled by the sexual roles they were expected to play, and could not. As Sedgwick writes, "For many gay people [isolation] is still the fundamental feature of social life; and there can be few gay people, however courageous and forthright by habit, however fortunate in the support of their immediate communities, in whose lives the closet is not still a shaping presence. . . . The most obvious fact about this history of judicial formulations is that it codifies an excruciating system of double binds, systematically oppressing gay people, identities, and acts by undermining through contradictory constraints on discourse the grounds of their very being" (68–70).

If being a racial liberal carried a heavy price in the South of the 1940s, being an "out" homosexual would have been unthinkable. This fact necessarily limited some of the avenues of expression for these writers and goes some distance to explain why each one may have looked to images of race to help understand the workings of human passions and politics.

In this study, Chapter 1 sketches a historical overview of the 1940s and of some of its important political, racial, and literary underpinnings, as well as an outline of the roots of Southern racial politics and rhetoric that informed these writers. It looks backward, as all studies of Southern literature must, to the Civil War and Reconstruction, and looks forward, to the civil rights movement that immediately followed the period this book examines. Such an overview, I hope, will relieve any reader's anxieties about why the particular decade of the 1940s was chosen: by placing it squarely in the sweep of history, I hope to show that my choice of periods was both arbitrary, in the sense that any delimitations on history are arbitrary, and worthwhile, since so much attention has been paid to the period both preceding and following the one looked at here. Before such works as John Egerton's impressive *Speak Now Against the Day: The Generation Before the Civil Rights Movement*, contemporary writers of racial history—to say nothing of university students—have tended to pay attention to the more dramatic 1860s and 1960s and leave what came between untouched. I hope to prove that the cultural soil of the late 1930s and 1940s is fertile indeed for the study of Southern literary history, and is ultimately as representative of the country's racial struggles writ large as any other time.

Chapter 2 focuses on Cash's *The Mind of the South*, published in 1941, and the ways it manipulates and conflates images of race, class, and, frequently, violence, to create what at the time was considered one of the most perceptive and "accurate" portrayals of the South ever written. Thought by many of his contemporaries to be the greatest analyst of Southern mythology, even as it accreted around race, Cash considered his most potent influence to be Thomas Dixon. Like Dixon, Cash had a flair for exceedingly rich rhetoric: he could, with pathos, describe the tragic plight of Southern blacks at the same time that he could call lynching a white man's "frolic." But like the other writers discussed here, Cash also grappled with issues that moved beneath the surface of his rhetoric. He was a man plagued from his youth by sexual insecurity and seemed to take an almost sadistic pleasure in describing the violence done to blacks who dared to engage in a physical sexuality of which he himself seemed incapable.

Chapter 3 looks at Percy's 1941 memoir, *Lanterns on the Levee*, as a paean to a mythical past that may never have existed, and at the ways racial metaphors served to complicate such wistfulness. One of the mid-century's most well-known Southern aesthetes, Percy was a model of both sophistication and complexity. He was the son of a powerful U.S. senator and a highly sensitive poet; a devoted apologist of aristocracy and a relative racial progressive; a plantation owner and a fighter of the Ku Klux Klan. Like many wealthy Southerners of his day and throughout history, Percy was in large part raised by black nannies and black friends, and his adult writings are deeply ambivalent about the turning point in a white child's life when he is told to reject the people to whom he feels most emotionally connected. Percy's narrative also expresses deep ambivalences about his own sexual identity and the place of his aristocratic culture in Southern history; like Smith and McCullers, his empathies with blacks can be read as a direct outgrowth of his own sense of sexual alienation.

In Chapter 4 I examine the work of Lillian Smith, particularly her 1944 novel, *Strange Fruit*, and 1949 collection of essays, *Killers of the Dream*, to consider her provocative thinking about the psychological damage racist ideology inflicts on all members of a community, white as well as black. In her lifetime, Smith was known as much for her political activism as for her fiction, a fact that tormented her but left a legacy of some of the decade's most influential writings on race. She was a regular correspondent with Walter White, the executive secretary of the National Association for the Advancement of Colored People (NAACP), and a constant source of irritation to Ralph McGill, whom she mocked as a progressive poseur. Her primary project, I argue, was to show the link between racial and sexual segregation as parallel emblems of cultural schizophrenia. For Smith, in *Killers of the Dream*, black bodies served as objects to be explored, like one's sexual body, only at great moral risk.

By the time we were five years old we had learned, without hearing the words, that masturbation is wrong and segregation is right, and each had become a dread taboo that must never be broken, for we believed God, whom we feared and tried desperately to love, had made the rules concerning not only Him and our parents, but our bodies and Negroes. Therefore when we as small children crept over the race line and ate and played with Negroes or broke other segregation customs known to us, we felt the same dread fear of consequences, the same overwhelming guilt we felt when we crept over the sex line and played with our body, or thought thoughts about God or our parents that we knew we must not think. Each was a "sin," each "deserved punishment," each would receive it in this world or the next. Each was tied up with the other and all were tied close to God.

These were our first lessons. . . . We believed certain acts were so wrong that they must never be committed and then we committed them and denied to ourselves that we had done so. It worked very well. Our minds had split: hardly more than a crack at first, but we began in those early years a two-level existence which we have since managed quite smoothly. (84)

The "splitting" of the Southern mind, from the intersecting forces of sexual repression and racial segregation, was central to Smith's writing. Indeed, her conception of a "two-level existence" that whites lived under is not unlike the public/private "double-consciousness" that W. E. B. Du Bois wrote of as the burden of blacks. Like McCullers, too, Smith was most interested in exploring the fissures in Southern minds, and the racialized rhetoric that often accompanied these psychological breaks.

Chapter 5 examines McCullers's early works, especially *The Heart Is a Lonely Hunter*, *The Member of the Wedding*, "The Ballad of the Sad Café," and *Reflections in a Golden Eye*, as texts that set out to confuse images of race and gender in an effort to undermine entrenched boundaries of Southern identity and social position. Like Lillian Smith, McCullers was acutely aware of the intricate interweavings of race and gender; virtually every character in her novels is identifiable largely through characteristics of their "opposite." Her novels are full of freak shows, carnivals, and prisons that the main characters find fascinating, familiar, and oddly comforting. Like several of her Southern contemporaries, notably Erskine Caldwell and Flannery O'Connor, McCullers's most evocative metaphor for expressing the malleability of identity was the use of the internally conflicted and externally grotesque, a category that included blacks and other nonwhites as often as it did the sexually or physically aberrant. In *The Heart Is a Lonely Hunter*, the black Doctor Copeland, the novel's most educated character, speaks in Oxonian English and lectures incessantly about the Protestant work ethic. By contrast, the drunken, white labor agitator Jake Blount, "with his thick nostrils and the rolling whites of his eyes," describes himself as "part nigger myself. I'm part nigger and wop and bohunk and chink. All of those." Mick Kelly, a twelve-year-old girl, dresses and acts like a boy; and Biff Brannon, the owner of the New York Café, wears his wife's perfume, spends his time knitting, and entertains fantasies about Blount as a naked Inca warrior. Such explorations of loneliness and alienation, I argue, have their roots in the "crossing" of racial and gender boundaries.

All four of these writers were controversial best-sellers in their day, and all four have largely fallen out of fashion in contemporary literary circles. All four considered themselves alienated by the cultural mainstream; while their views on race varied tremendously, from Smith's radicalism to Percy's benign paternalism, all were and still are largely considered to have been racially progressive, especially when their particular period and region is taken into consideration. Regardless of their personal politics, there is, I think, much to be said for a close-hauled look at writers in the same "racial" category who nonetheless had sharp differences in class, gender, and sexual orientation. Indeed, the larger hope of this project is to discover the roots of white racialized thinking, to explore some of the cultural and psychological foundations upon which a generation built its often dehumanizing racial rhetoric. This hope was shared by the writers explored here, as well as by some of their contemporaries. Gunnar Myrdal, for example, condemned "the stern look on even educated people when they repeat these trite and worn stupidities, inherited through the generations, as if they were something new and tremendously important and also to watch their confusion when one tries to disturb their ways of thinking by 'outlandish' questions" (Rose, 17–18). It was certainly one function of the literature studied here to ask these "outlandish questions." The exploration and articulation of these questions is the primary objective of this book.

The conclusion attempts to take the ambivalences and anxieties of the 1940s and project them forward, to examine how contemporary writers about and scholars of race continue to digest and rework perceptions of race even as they unfold. Most important, the conclusion —like the rest of the book—hopes to cement the notion that understanding *whiteness* is as valid and fruitful an intellectual endeavor as understanding *blackness*, a field of study that has received a far more vibrant burst of scholarly attention over the last twenty years. Looking to African American writers and scholars particularly, the conclusion attempts to add the 1990s to the viewfinder of history, to explore how our own ideas of racialized rhetoric compare to that expressed fifty years before.

In the end, then, this book sets out to explore the thicket of meaning behind comments like one made recently by a "moderate white lawyer," recounted by the contemporary white Southern writer Willie Morris in his 1997 book *The Ghosts of Medgar Evers*: "If it wasn't for the Negroes . . . people around here wouldn't have nothin' to talk about."

CHAPTER ONE

Moving among the Living as Ghosts

A Historical Overview

How can one idea like segregation become so hypnotic a thing that it binds a whole people together, good, bad, strong, weak, ignorant and learned, sensitive, obtuse, psychotic and sane, making them one as only a common worship or a deeply shared fear can do? Why has the word taken on the terrors of taboo and the sanctity of religion? What makes it so important to us that men will keep themselves poor to sustain it, out of jobs to defend it? Why is it so sacred that the church has let it eat the heart out of religion? Why will not Christian ministers in the South—with the exception of a valiant handful— preach against it? Why is it that newspaper editors will not write editorials opposing it? The answer is surely worth searching for.

LILLIAN SMITH, *Killers of the Dream*

At the 1968 meeting of the Southern Historical Association, Ralph Ellison was quoted as saying:

I can't, here in New Orleans, fail to point out that so much of American history has turned upon the racial situation in the country. . . . Our written history has been as "official" as any produced in any communist country—only in a democratic way: individuals write it instead of committees. Written history is to social conduct and social arrangements in this country very much like the relationship between myth and ritual. And myth justifies and "explains" facts. . . . But too often history has been an official statement, and it has danced attendant to political arrangements. (Stone, 6)

To understand the South, Ellison argued, one must not only explore "the racial situation" but also the fine line between myth and history that so many white writers had managed to occlude. For those who grew up in the South in the mid-twentieth century, this was not always an easy task. In the 1920s, Walter Hines Page declared that the survivors of the Civil War, and those who continued to perpetuate the legends handed down to them, "unwittingly did us a greater hurt than the war itself. It gave every one of them the intensest experience of his life and ever afterward he referred every other experience to this. Thus it stopped the thought of most of them as an earthquake stops a clock. The fierce blows of battle paralyzed the mind. Their speech was a vocabulary of war, their loyalties were loyalties, not to living ideas or duties, but to old commanders and to distorted traditions. They were dead men, most of them, moving among the living as ghosts; and yet, as ghosts in a play, they held the stage" (Rubin, 149).

As pressured as it was in the early part of the century, the South had become fertile ground for the re-evaluation and reconstruction of cultural mythology. A region always possessed by its past found itself seriously challenged by hard demographic and economic change. The prospect of racial confrontation moved many politicians and writers to build, or build upon, a tradition of deep and encompassing cultural nostalgia that supplanted any engagement with ongoing cultural change or racial equality. Reluctant to bend with the tide of change that was upon them, many white Southerners only held tighter to images of a past they considered to be uncomplicated and glorious. Iconographic repetition in the South—from the image of dead war heroes hanging in the plantation hall galleries to the actual re-enactments of Civil War battles that continue to this day—are at the heart of the twentieth-century Southern experience. Thomas Dixon called for a return to a South cleansed of black blood; the Agrarians yearned for a pre-industrial society; Faulkner wrote wistfully, in *Intruder in the Dust*, of the moment

for every Southern boy fourteen years old, not once but whenever he wants it, there is the instant when its still not yet two o'clock on that July afternoon in 1863, the brigades are in position behind the rail fence, the guns are laid and ready in the woods and Pickett himself with his long oiled ringlets and his hat in one hand probably and his sword in the other looking up the hill waiting for Longstreet to give the word and it's all in the balance, it hasn't happened yet, it hasn't even begun yet, it not only hasn't begun yet but there is still time for it not to begin against that position and those circumstances which made more men than Garnett and Kemper and

Armistead and Wilcox look grave yet it's going to begin, we all know that, we have come too far with too much at stake and that moment doesn't need even a fourteen-year-old boy to think *This time. Maybe this time* with all this much to lose and all this much to gain. (194)

Each of these images represent a backward craning of the neck, a strained yearning for what has long been dead, a manifestation of what Hannah Arendt has called the culturally "fantastic": the layers of sentiment, romance, and mythology that mask, obscure, and even replace both historical fact and contemporary racial and political upheaval. "In the late nineteenth-century South, history seemed more the cousin of prophecy than the sibling of science," writes the historian Grace Elizabeth Hale. "'The undead past,' Robert Penn Warren's later phrase for the twisted temporality of his region, still lived because white southerners' historical imaginations became the cards in which they read their racial future" (43). These sentimental layers are often as not unconscious expressions pointing both to images of the writers' own troubled identities and to the cracking and repositioning of cultural identity writ large. "So while the world I know is crashing to bits," William Alexander Percy wrote in the 1941 foreword to *Lanterns on the Levee*, "and what with the noise and the cryings-out, no man could hear a trumpet blast, much less an idle evening reverie, I will indulge a heart beginning to be fretful by repeating to it the stories it knows and loves of my own country and my own people" (xx). In addition to such writers as T. S. Eliot and Henry Adams, Southerners like Percy can be usefully described as "Catonists," writers pessimistic about the future and longing for a past heroic age. Catonism, Richard King writes, is

the ideological response of a landed upper-class (and its spokesmen) which is economically, socially and politically on the defensive. The Catonist fears the encroachment of alien values and impersonal commercial forces which disrupt an aristocratic and organic order cemented by ties of family, status, tradition, and, sometimes, race or nationality. The Catonist also fears the "people" politically, though he may often celebrate the organic, cultural linkages that constitute hierarchical unity. . . . The Catonist takes the collapse of his specific world for the end of virtue and order generally. In cultural-psychological terms the Catonist manifests "wholeness hunger," the yearning for an earlier time before the dissociation of sensibility. And the Catonist's historical consciousness is "monumentalist": it seeks to resurrect the past and to revivify a former, more heroic ethos in the present. (51–52)

White denial and white fantasies of nineteenth-century heroism were vividly apparent to Gunnar Myrdal, who by 1944 was writing that nowhere was this reliance on myth so keen as in the denial of the very existence of black life. Although masked, re-invented as Sambos, Jezebels, and Mammies, or ignored by whites altogether, blacks had always in fact been an inextricable and necessary component of white culture, he wrote.

> In the more formal life of the community the Negro problem and the Negro himself are almost completely avoided. In the school it will be avoided, like sex. The press, with few exceptions, ignores the Negroes, except for their crimes. The public affairs of the states and cities are ordinarily discussed as if Negroes were not part of the population. The strange unreality of this situation becomes clear when one realizes that for generations hardly any issue has been free of the race issue, and that the entire culture of the region—its religion, literature, art, music, dance, its politics and education, its language and cooking—are partly to be explained by positive or negative influences from the Negro. (Rose, 16)[1]

The "strange unreality" of racial imaging that Myrdal described was hardly new. One can look back at least as far as Jefferson's 1782 *Notes on Virginia* to find roots for the ways images of blacks are constructed: "Comparing them by their faculties of memory, reason, and imagination, it appears to me, that in memory they are equal to the whites, in reason much inferior, as I think one could scarcely be found capable of tracing and comprehending the investigations of Euclid, and that in imagination they are dull, tasteless and anomalous. Never yet could I find that a black had uttered a thought above the level of plain narration; never see even an elementary trait of painting or sculpture" (139–40). Fixing a racial label to the underpinning of the Civil War, Abraham Lincoln gathered a delegation of black leaders at the White House and told them that "there is an unwillingness on the part of our people, harsh as it may be, for you free colored people to remain with us," he said. "But even when you cease to be slaves, you are yet far removed from being placed on an equality with the white race. . . . The aspiration of men is to enjoy equality with the best when free, but on the broad continent not a single man of your race is made the equal of a single man of ours. . . .

I cannot alter it if I would. It is a fact. . . . It is better for us both, therefore, to be separated" (Woodward, *Burden*, 81).

In the wake of the withdrawal of federal troops in 1877, enforced segregation began to close a grip on the South that would last eighty years.
Beginning in 1890 with Mississippi, Southern states began passing a series of measures—the poll tax, the grandfather clause, literacy and understanding tests, property qualifications, and the white primary—that
constitutionally disenfranchised blacks and a significant number of poor
whites as well. The Supreme Court's 1896 *Plessy v. Ferguson* decision,
which made legal "separate but equal" facilities on interstate rail travel,
gave segregation the legal blessing of the nation's highest court. In the
dissenting opinion to that decision, Justice John Marshall Harlan wrote:

> The white race deems itself to be the dominant race in this coun-
> try. And so it is, in prestige, in achievements, in education, in wealth
> and in power. So, I doubt not that it will continue to be for all time,
> if it remains true to its great heritage and holds fast to the princi-
> ples of constitutional liberty. But in view of the Constitution, in
> the eye of the law, there is in this country no superior, dominant
> ruling class of citizens. There is no caste here. Our Constitution is
> color blind, and neither knows, nor tolerates classes among citi-
> zens. In respect of civil rights, all citizens are equal before the law.
> (Gaines, xiii)

Even in dissent, Harlan "regarded white dominance as axiomatic and
eternal," the historian Kevin Gaines writes. "Without evident irony, he
believed that white supremacy would be upheld by 'principles of constitutional liberty,' a profound, if unintended, indictment of the original
intentions of the framers, for whom African slavery was evidently es-
sential to liberty for white men" (xiii).[2]

In the South in particular such a univocal discourse of power gave
segregationists not only disproportionate power in national affairs but a
vast and pervasive source of cultural rhetoric that effectively denied the
political existence of blacks, Harry Ashmore writes.

> Legal segregation, as had the predecessor slavery, remained a pe-
> culiar Southern institution, and their identification with it denied
> Southern Democrats national office; but, as they had demonstrated
> in the case of Al Smith in 1928, no Northern Democrat could be
> elected if the party leaders overrode the Southerners' veto on the
> nomination. Yet, in the face of this controlling political reality,

the Southern leaders insisted that there was, in fact, no race issue—that the region, in the spirit of noblesse oblige, had repaired the havoc wrought by the misguided social experiment of its conquerors, creating in place of slavery a separate-but-equal accommodation necessary to protect disadvantaged blacks against naturally superior and sometimes predatory whites. (*Hearts*, 9)

"Protection" was certainly one of the legacies of segregation, but what was mostly protected was an economic and political structure that allowed whites to continue to dominate virtually all of the South's natural and human resources. Such an ideology certainly lay behind both the white supremacist rhetoric with which Cash was so entranced and the paternalism of the Percy family, which "protected" blacks from the raging floodwaters of the Mississippi not just so the blacks would not drown, but so that the white plantation owners would not lose their cheap labor.

To be sure, the white Southern racial imagination evolved right along with the history it mirrored. Whites "'even segregated days of the week,' Mamie Garvin Fields recalled of growing up in South Carolina. White people stayed away from town on Saturday afternoons, setting aside that time for blacks from the countryside to shop and meet. 'Those white folks didn't want you to come to town in the weekday at all. . . . Really, certain whites didn't like to think you had leisure to do anything but pick cotton and work in the field'" (Ayers, 132).

Three separate but related branches of white racial engagement emerged at the turn of the century, Richard King writes. The first, articulated by Hinton Helper, called for ridding the South of its black people by colonization; for obvious economic reasons such a plan was never adopted. The second position, proposed by Helper's ideological opposite, George Fitzhugh, called for a position of "integrated subservience." It assumed continuing black docility and subservience, while Helper's assumed black defiance and considered close contact with blacks as "impure and revolting." The third position came as a compromise between the two. As articulated by Tennessee politician Parson Brownlow and others, it sought to keep the docile, "good" blacks at hand and somehow to isolate or get rid of defiant, "uppity" ones. Behind these plans "lay the perennial racist dichotomy between the Negro as child and the Negro as beast" (King, 33).

Southern newspapers continued to be obsessed with reports of black violence and went some distance to justify lynchings as a way to control black aggression, Ayers writes.

Virtually every issue of every Southern newspaper contained an account of black wrongdoing; if no episode from nearby could be found, episodes were imported from as far away as necessary; black crimes perpetrated in the North were especially attractive. "The longer I am here, the more I dread and fear the nigger," a white woman from Massachusetts wrote from her new home in Louisiana. "They have no regard for their own lives, and seem to have no feeling. Consequently if they have some fancied wrong to avenge, the first thing they think of is to kill. You rarely hear of them fighting fist fights. It is always a razor or knife or revolver." (153)

In the first two decades of the century, Southern prisons began to swell with black inmates, as state after state passed laws to curb black mobility, Ayers writes. As the prisons filled up, blacks were leased out to road and railroad crews. "Not surprisingly, such a system bred inhumane travesties. In some of the most forbidding landscapes of the New South terrible scenes of inhumanity were played out: mass sickness, brutal whippings, discarded bodies, near starvation, rape. Time after time, word leaked out about what was happening in the camps in the swamps or the piney woods; time after time, investigations lamely concluded that something would have to be done; time after time the deaths and exploitations went on." The violence inflicted on blacks in the decades after Reconstruction "was a way for white people to reconcile weak governments with a demand for an impossibly high level of racial mastery, a way to terrorize blacks into acquiescence by brutally killing those who intentionally or accidentally stepped over some invisible and shifting line of permissible behavior" (Ayers, 152, 156).

By the 1920s, New South ideologues had set forth a quasi-paternalistic racial ideal, in which whites claimed responsibility for black moral guidance and education while at the same time urging black self-help and self-reliance. They were caught somewhere between an aristocratic paternalism of the Fitzhugh sort and a bourgeois paternalism of moral and educational "uplift," King writes. Their ideological heirs were the Southern moderates of the Progressive period, who also stressed the "benevolent" paternalism of the educated and enlightened middle-class Southerner. Horrified by lynching and egregious forms of racial domination, these moderates were still firmly committed to separate but equal development and to the idea of black inferiority.

But alongside this moderate paternalism, a new, more brutal motif appeared in racial thought around the turn of the century—the

Negro as "beast" or the "diseased Negro." Always lurking behind the earlier racial paternalism, this form of racism flourished in the 1890s and during the first decades of this century. The black man was seen less as the perennial child or docile old uncle who offered ease to the frantic strivings of whites and more as the barely tamed savage, the oversexed rapist, and/or the carrier of polluting disease which threatened the health, indeed the very survival of the pure white race. The logic of this position was eventual black extinction by natural selection. In the meantime, blacks were kept in line by both legal and extra-legal means. (King, 32−33)[3]

These images, molded as they were from the heat of economic distress, solidified in the region's literature and political rhetoric. Thomas Nelson Page had used the happy old "darkie" to lament mythic days of yore; Margaret Mitchell, Faulkner, and McCullers were just the best-known writers who invoked black nannies in their fiction; Joel Chandler Harris used folktales to portray Southern blacks as happy storytellers. But the remarkable shift from Thomas Dixon's "brute Negro" in 1905 to William Styron's prophetic Nat Turner in 1967 "has been one of the most remarkable indicators of social change in the South," Nancy Tichsler writes (Ferris and Wilson, 171). In the interim, during the height of Jim Crow "the introduction of race into any discussion sent most Southern whites into pig-headed denial, as they performed extraordinary (and often unconscious) mental gymnastics to excuse the immobilization and oppression of a large portion of the Southern working class," Nell Painter writes. "White supremacists gained a wide audience in the South that seldom challenged their fantasies, which so often included sex: an insistence on racial purity that ignored white men's abuse of black women; a confusion of voting rights with miscegenation; a stigmatization of black women for their supposed lack of feminine virtues; and hysteria over black male autonomy and sexuality" (in Escott, 45−46).[4]

The important thing to remember, here and throughout this book, is the link between historic, economic, and political events and the metaphorical images they create; just as Nazi Germany ratcheted up its "dirty Jew" rhetoric as that country fell into economic peril in the 1930s, so did whites heat up their antiblack rhetoric as the South's economy worsened and blacks began either to yearn for more autonomy or to leave the South altogether. Between 1940 and 1960 the region, which once enjoyed a labor surplus, saw a decline in farm labor of almost 60 percent.

"After 1920 most of the old rural institutions were caught in a web of failure. The system of sharecropping and tenant farming that had flourished from 1865 to 1920 was on the brink of abject failure. No longer could the South survive this waste of human energy and souls. Both black and white tenants deserted the farm by hundreds of thousands, driven away by biting poverty" (Ferris and Wilson, 12).

The crash of the Southern economy in the 1910s and 1920s and its attendant racial and demographic tensions were epitomized by the fate of one of the most cherished icons of the South: cotton. In 1919, a golden year of postwar prosperity, John Egerton writes, cotton soared to thirty-five cents a pound on a big crop of about 15 million bales; the following year, "plummeting demand and a huge stockpiled surplus sent prices crashing to 14 cents and triggered a major agricultural depression nine years before the Big One. The bottom dropped out of the tobacco market, too, and the price of prime cultivated land fell to ten dollars an acre or less" (22).

Cotton was more than just the primary source of employment in the South; it "used up people and land, consumed and then discarded them," Egerton writes. "The big planters were like gamblers, betting their soil and their seed and their field hands against the weather, the weevils, the market, the foreign competition. Historically, through the slavery era and beyond, the planters had won more often than not, and won big— but times were changing, and the signs were everywhere that they were headed for a fall" (22). Such economic and racial pressures began to eat away at some of the most cherished of Southern myths, Woodward wrote in his 1960 study, *The Burden of Southern History*.

Every self-conscious group of any size fabricates myths about its past: about its origins, its mission, its righteousness, its benevolence, its general superiority. But few groups in the New World have had their myths subjected to such destructive analysis as those of the South have undergone in recent years.

The Cavalier Legend as the myth of origin was one of the earlier victims. The Plantation Legend of ante-bellum grace and elegance has not been left wholly intact. The pleasant image of a benevolent and paternalistic slavery system as a school for civilizing savages has suffered damage that is probably beyond repair. Even the consoling security of Reconstruction as the common historic grievance, the infallible myth of unity, has been rendered somewhat less secure by detached investigation. And finally, rude

hands have been laid upon the hallowed memory of the Re-
deemers who did in the Carpetbaggers, and doubt has been cast
upon the antiquity of segregation folkways. These faded historical
myths have become weak material for buttressing Southern de-
fenses, for time has dealt as roughly with them as with agrarianism
and racism. (12–13)

Part of the country's literary response to this economic hardship—
and the racial tensions that accompanied it—began in the form of the
"proletarian novel," with rising interest in the novels of the 1920s and
the 1930s fiction of Caldwell, Steinbeck, and Dos Passos, and drama by
Clifford Odets. George Tindall writes,

The image may be rather nebulous and the ultimate ends unclear,
but the fact of change is written inescapably across the Southern
[literary] scene. The consciousness of change has been present so
long as to become in itself one of the abiding facts of Southern life.
As far back as the twenties it was the consciousness of change that
quickened the imagination of a cultivated and sensitive minority,
giving us the Southern renaissance in literature. The peculiar historical consciousness of the Southern writer, Allen Tate has suggested, "made possible the curious burst of intelligence that we get
at the crossing of the ways, not unlike, on an infinitesimal scale, the
outburst of poetic genius at the end of the sixteenth century, when
commercial England had already begun to crush feudal England.
Trace it through modern Southern writing, and at the center—in
Ellen Glasgow, in Faulkner, Wolfe, Caldwell, the Fugitive-Agrarian
poets, and all the others—there is the consciousness of change, of
suspension between two worlds, a double focus looking both backward and forward." (qtd. in Grantham, 18)

Tate and the rest of the Agrarians had, in the 1930 collection *I'll Take
My Stand*, done their part to revive the myth of a pastoral, anti-industrial
region, apart from Yankee acquisitiveness and racial mixing, but even
this was being criticized as so much mythology. "Its proposition that the
Southern way stands or falls with the agrarian way would seem to have
been championing a second lost cause," Woodward writes. "If they were
right, then our questions would have been answered, for the Southerner
as a distinctive species of American would have been doomed, his tradition bereft of root and soil. The agrarian way contains no promise of
continuity and endurance for the Southern tradition" (*Burden*, 9).[5]

In the 1940s, William Alexander Percy wrote at length about the economic troubles that departing black labor had on his family farm, and W. J. Cash saw clearly the connection between race and the rage of poor white millworkers. Smith too recognized the connection between a slumping rural economy, a growing sense of autonomy among blacks, especially those returning from the front, and spiraling racial resentment. "He heard somebody say the rains had delayed the picking," she wrote of Tracy Deen in *Strange Fruit*. "He saw crowds of colored folks with lint in their hair and clothes, waiting to be paid off. A commissary. General merchandise stores with sheds piled with cotton. Somebody weighing bales. No feeling. The South was a picture full of things, people, smells, deeds, sounds. But no feeling. Things have changed, folks said. You won't know the place. Niggers all going North. Hard to get help. Everybody biggety. War's ruined 'em. Won't work. Cotton slumping. Boll weevil been terrible" (53). If the "proletarian" tradition was in full swing by the 1940s, more mainstream literature and history about the South and the Civil War continued to be a growth industry as well. *Gone with the Wind* won the Pulitzer Prize for fiction in 1937; it sold a million copies in the first six months of publication, surpassing another book about the South, *Uncle Tom's Cabin*. Paul Herman Buck's *Road to Reunion, 1865–1900* won the award for history in 1938, the same year Marquis James won for his biography of *Andrew Jackson*; Robert Sherwood's play *Lincoln in Illinois* won the Pulitzer for drama in 1939; Carl Sandburg's biography, *Abraham Lincoln: The War Years*, won for history in 1940. Arthur Schlesinger's *The Age of Jackson* won for history in 1946; Robert Penn Warren won for fiction with *All the King's Men* in 1947; and *A Streetcar Named Desire* won for drama in 1948. The decade closed with Faulkner winning the Nobel Prize in 1950 and the film version of *All the King's Men* winning the Academy Award for best picture. With Faulkner and Warren as the obvious exceptions, these works were on the whole notable for *not* engaging with the economic crises of the moment.

The decline of the kingdom of cotton did little to alleviate the intensity of racial hatred; quite the contrary. A new wave of "exodusting" blacks, escaping racial and economic oppression to the North, were pegged as contributing to the South's agricultural decline. The decline of the cotton industry and the black migrations that followed meant that both traditional ways of making a living and traditional ways of experiencing life were no longer possible. Between 1910 and 1970 six and a half million blacks moved from the South to the North; five million of them, Nicholas Lemann writes, moved after 1940, during the shift to mechanized farming (6). Such hard demographic movements had a profoundly troubling impact on one of the most cherished of Southern myths, that of the aristocratic Southern planter. Always dependent on black labor to make plantations productive, after World War I white agricultural barons found themselves with fewer and fewer black serfs. If they'd remained, the argument went, crops would somehow have turned around. Moreover, the black migration reinforced some of the oldest white stereotypes. David Cohn, the Mississippi writer and contemporary of Percy, wrote: "The coming problem of agricultural displacement in the Delta and the whole South is of huge proportions and must concern the entire nation. The time to prepare for it is now, but since we as a nation rarely act until catastrophe is upon us, it is likely that we shall muddle along until it is too late. The country is upon the brink of a process of change as great as any that has occurred since the Industrial Revolution. . . . There is an enormous tragedy in the making unless the United States acts, and acts promptly, upon a problem that affects millions of people and the whole social structure of the nation" (*Born*, 329–30).

Even in 1944, Lemann writes, white plantation owners were beginning to sense that the black population shift would have long and dire consequences. He quotes a letter written to the local cotton industry association by Richard Hopson, who ran the Hopson plantation in the Mississippi Delta: "I am confident that you are aware of the acute shortage of labor which now exists in the Delta and the difficult problem which we expect to have in attempting to harvest a cotton crop this fall and for several years to come. I am confident that you are aware of the serious racial problem which confronts us at this time and which may become more serious as time passes. I strongly advocate the farmers of the Mississippi Delta changing as rapidly as possible from the old tenant or sharecropping system of farming to complete mechanized farming" (49).

The continuation of racism after cotton was no longer "king," Myrdal wrote, "is an example of the sociological principle that ideologies continue after the conditions that give rise to them no longer exist" (Rose, xviii). Indeed, with the economy faltering and the end of the First World War in sight, rumors spread that returning black soldiers would not be content with their former status and were purchasing all available arms in preparation for a race war. Not all destitute whites chose to escape the South, of course, and many of those who stayed took out their economic frustrations on blacks. There is a reason that the Ku Klux Klan had made itself felt most acutely in the post-Reconstruction era and in the 1920s—both periods followed hard on the heels of economic uncertainty and dramatic increases in black expressions of autonomy. According to Peter Bergman's *Chronological History of the Negro in America,* Klan membership went from 100,000 in 1920 to 4.5 million in 1924—the same year in which a federal Immigration Act excluded blacks of African descent from entering the country. The Klan did not experience as large a gain until the period following the *Brown v. Board of Education* decision thirty years later, when 100,000 new members joined between 1954 and 1958 (397, 411, 556).

As was the case in the reaction to the feared revolts of Denmark Vesey and Gabriel Prosser a hundred years before, white reaction to the black presence was both physically violent and rhetorically charged. Sixty-five years after the Civil War, the South, "far from exhibiting a desire to be free from the burden of history . . . seemed instead to cling obsessively to its past, to relive it and even rewrite it," Egerton writes. "The glorious Lost Cause had instilled a sense of pride and honor and moral superiority in many whites, but the hard truth was that in the 1930s the South was itself a lost cause, a downtrodden region haplessly nursing wounds that were as much self-inflicted as administered from without" (24). More than three-fourths of all Southerners had a standard of living in the fall of 1932 that would certainly qualify them as paupers, Egerton writes. Two-thirds of them lived on farms or in small villages, and close to two-thirds of the farmers were sharecroppers or tenants. The average gross income of farm families did not reach $1,000 a year in nine Southern states, casting them to the bottom of the agricultural heap; yet to be a sharecropper or a tenant farmer in the South in 1932 was to be caught up in an existence that often was nothing more than peonage or forced labor—just one step removed from slavery. "But lest you think those were the poorest of the poor, keep in mind that they at least were employed and had a bare minimum of food and clothing and shelter to sustain them; millions of others were vagabonds with no resources at all. Almost nobody had money. The South could count a quarter of the nation's population but only a tenth of its wealth. No more than five hundred people in the entire region had incomes of $100,000 or more in 1929, and three years later that list was reduced to a handful; probably no more than a hundred or so people per state earned even $10,000 or more in 1932" (Egerton, 20).[6]

The black migration changed the face of the North as well. The black population of Chicago alone grew from 44,000 in 1910, to 109,000 in 1920, to 234,000 in 1930. During the 1940s the city's black population grew by 77 percent, from 278,000 to 492,000; in the 1950s, it grew another 65 percent, to 813,000, and by 1960 Chicago had more than half a million more blacks than it had just twenty years earlier (Lemann, 16, 70). As black Southerners moved North, however, they were rarely met with welcoming arms. In 1935, a race riot in Harlem over rumors of police brutality caused $200 million in property damage; E. Franklin Frazier wrote that the riot was caused by "resentments against racial discrimination and poverty in the midst of plenty" (Bergman, 471). Seven years later, 1,200 people armed with knives, rifles, and shotguns gathered in Detroit to prevent three black families from entering the 200-unit Sojourner Truth housing project set up by the U.S. Housing Authority; the *New York Times* reported that scores of black and white people were injured, and it was not until two months later that 800 state troopers were able to escort twelve families into the project.

In 1943, also in Detroit, 26,000 white workers went on strike at a Packard Motor plant to protest the employment of blacks. When rioting broke out, thirty-four people died, including seventeen blacks who were killed by police. At Walter White's request, President Roosevelt declared a federal state of emergency and sent in 6,000 troops. That same year, race riots broke out in Mobile, Atlanta, and Beaumont, Texas; in the latter, martial law was ordered in the wake of the rape of a young white mother. In Harlem that year, a riot erupted after a black soldier objected to a white police officer's treatment of a black woman. It took 8,000 state troops, 1,500 civilian volunteers, and 6,600 city police to quell the uprising. Five people were killed and 400 injured; all of the dead and all but forty of the wounded were black. All this domestic violence transpired while the United States was fighting a two-front global war, which in both the Asian and European theaters had violent racist overtones.

If race riots were the most dramatic manifestation of Northern racial violence, lynching provided the South with its own particularly disturbing practice. According to *The Chronological History of the Negro in America*, 1,400 blacks were lynched between the years 1882 and 1892, 1,100 between 1900 and 1915, and 292 during the 1920s. In 1922, the *History* points out, 30 of the 51 lynchings took place after the suspect had already been apprehended by the police. In the 1930s, 119 blacks were lynched; the number declined to 44 between 1940 and 1962. *The Encyclopedia of Southern Culture* reports that the total number of people lynched between 1882 and the early 1950s was probably closer to 6,000, about 82 percent of them in the South. Nationally, 72 percent of all victims were black; in the South, 84 percent were black (175).[7] Not all executions during the period were carried out by lynch mobs. Between 1940 and 1949, the national total of executions carried out under civil authority was 1,284. Of these, 458 whites and 595 blacks were executed for murder. Of greater interest: 19 whites were executed for rape, compared to 179 blacks (Bergman, 489).[8]

Rich with overtones of violence, revenge, and political and sexual domination, lynching was a powerful tool for writers and activists on both sides of the race issue. W. J. Cash wrote,

Negro apologists and others bent on damning the South at any cost have, during the last decade or two, so constantly and vociferously associated the presentation of figures designed to show that no rape menace exists or ever has existed in the Southern country, with the conclusion that the rape complex is therefore a fraud, a hypocritical pretext behind which the South has always cynically and knowingly hidden mere sadism and economic interest, as to have got it very widely accepted. Nonetheless (and Walter White's nearly explicit contention to the contrary notwithstanding) there were genuine cases of rape. There were other and more numerous cases of attempted rape. There were Yankee fools and scoundrels —and not all of them low-placed Yankees—to talk provocatively about the coming of a day when Negroes would take the daughters of their late masters for concubines; seeming to Southern ears to be deliberately inciting the former bondsmen to wholesale outrage. There was a real fear, and in some districts even terror, on the part of white women themselves. And there were neurotic old maids and wives, hysterical young girls, to react to all this in a fashion well enough understood now, but understood by almost nobody then.

Hence, if the actual danger was small, it was nevertheless the most natural thing in the world for the South to see it as great, to believe in it, fully and in all honesty, as a menace requiring the most desperate measures if it was to be held off. (117–18)

Cash's language, here as elsewhere, seems oddly apologetic for the evils that arose from what in his text seem inexorable social forces; lynching may have been horrible, he seems to be saying, but its perpetrators, who believed in lynching "fully and in all honesty," could hardly be blamed. He brims over with rhetorical enthusiasm for the circumstances surrounding lynching: white sons fighting to keep their bloodlines pure; their "sincere" justification for violence toward blacks as re-

venge for the rape of white women. Cash, in fact, only mirrored the political rhetoric he had encountered, as in South Carolina governor Cole
Blease's famous opposition to federal lynch law: "Whenever the Constitution comes between me and the virtue of the white women of the
South, I say to hell with the Constitution!" (Ashmore, *Hearts*, 23).[9] Cash
did go to some lengths to undo the myth that only poor whites carried
out lynchings, but he did not exhibit the abject horror that was central to
the rhetoric of Lillian Smith, for whom lynching was also a central
theme.

> One day, sometime during your childhood or adolescence, a Negro
> was lynched in your county or the one next to yours. A human
> being was burned or hanged from a tree and you knew it had hap-
> pened. But no one publicly condemned it and always the murderer
> went free. And afterward, maybe weeks or months or years after-
> ward, you sat casually in the drugstore with one of those murder-
> ers and drank the Coke he usually paid for. A "nice white girl"
> could do that but she would have been run out of town or perhaps
> killed if she had drunk a Coke with the young Negro doctor who
> was devoting his life in service to his people. So Southern Tradition
> taught her bleak routines with flashes of lightning to quicken our
> steps. (*Killers*, 97–98)[10]

Lynching gave rise to a powerful new form of sociological scholarship that would reverberate throughout the fiction and politics of the
era. With the assistance of three black scholars, John Hope of More-
house, Robert Moton of Tuskegee, and Charles S. Johnson of Fisk,
Arthur Raper published *The Tragedy of Lynching* in 1933. The book documented what many people suspected: Southern blacks were usually
lynched for reasons other than sexual assaults on white women. Raper
gave vivid accounts of the torture, mutilation, and burning of black
lynch victims.

> "One is forced to the conviction," he wrote, "that their [the lynch-
> ers] deeper motivation is a desire not for the just punishment of
> the accused so much as for an opportunity to participate in the
> protected brutalities." In one case he found a county judge who
> called those who had removed an accused black murderer from jail
> and hanged him an "orderly" group of "high class" people. Raper
> presented every conceivable argument against lynching—ethical,
> economic, practical and political. Walter White, the executive sec-

retary of the NAACP and a tireless campaigner against lynching who was often at odds with Southern liberals, congratulated Raper and said the book would do "a tremendous amount of good . . . because it was the New South itself speaking." (Sosna, 33)[11]

Throughout the 1920s and 1930s, the old image of the Solid South was also being battered by a new sociological regionalism, led by Howard W. Odum and Rupert B. Vance at the University of North Carolina. They presented neither the image of the Savage South nor that of industrial progress, but rather a concept of an economically troubled "Problem South." Through the students and colleagues of Vance and Odum, together with the federal agencies set up to carry out the New Deal, this wave of scholarship ushered in a new series of programs for economic reform and social development.[12]

Political rhetoric, always running at a high pitch in disadvantaged regions and hard times, became rich with racial vitriol in the South of the late 1930s. In 1939, a year in which only 99 of 774 Southern public libraries were open to blacks, the Greenville, South Carolina, chapter of the Ku Klux Klan broadcast that "the Klan will ride again if Greenville Negroes register to vote." That same year, crosses and Negroes in effigy were burned in Miami to warn off voters; Mississippi senator Theodore Bilbo introduced a Back to Africa bill in the Senate; and Secretary of State Harold Ickes was forced to arrange for Marian Anderson to sing an Easter concert on the steps of Lincoln Memorial because officials from the Daughters of the American Revolution refused to allow her to appear at Constitution Hall, which they owned. Harry Ashmore recounts the details of South Carolina's U.S. senator "Cotton Ed" Smith's infamous 1938 "Philadelphia Story," about how, and why, he had walked out of the Democratic National Convention two years before.

> First, he said, he thought he had gotten into the wrong hall and fallen among Republicans when he found the convention floor sprinkled with black delegates. Then, sitting in the blessed lily-white sanctuary that was the South Carolina delegation, he had received the ultimate shock when a black preacher—in Cotton Ed's lexicon a "slew-footed, blue-gummed, kinky-headed Senegambian"—walked out on the platform to deliver the invocation. "And he started praying and I started walking," went the peroration. "And as I pushed through those great doors, and walked across that vast rotunda, it seemed to me old John Calhoun leaned down

from his mansion in the sky and whispered in my ear, 'you did right, Ed. . . .' " (*Hearts*, 21)

Cotton Ed's speech just continued the Southern tradition of ceaseless invocation of ancestors and mythology. The invocation of John Calhoun, the ultimate ghost of the Southern rebel, is plainly representative of a culture in the final stages of ideological collapse. Like a person whose neurotic self-image leads to psychological breakdown, Richard King writes, the South's "fantasy" could no longer sustain itself because it no longer "worked":

> Though the question of when a culture becomes fantastic is terribly complicated, not least because all cultures are based upon certain fantasies, a provisional answer might apply the pragmatic criterion: when it no longer "works." Themes and motifs split off and become isolated from the whole; they are spun out into whole visions. One might say, following Freud, that in fantasy there is a refusal to acknowledge that we must die, that we have a body that imposes certain limits on us, and that we must live in a world with other people. In cultures grown fantastic, the regressive or reactionary form of memory is dominant. Time is denied. (17)

As the 1940s dawned, of course, it was not just economic and racial distress that imperiled Southern mythology. The onset of World War II brought another powerful source of anxiety, and this, too, showed up in Southern writing. "It was the year when Frankie thought about the world," McCullers wrote in *The Member of the Wedding*. "And she did not see it as a round school globe, with the countries neat and different-colored. She thought of the world as huge and cracked and loose and turning a thousand miles an hour. The geography book at school was out of date; the countries of the world had changed" (20).

The entry of the United States into the war sent powerful ripples throughout the South; not only was the economy hamstrung by changing demands, but much of its labor force, white and black, either left for the front or migrated to jobs in munitions factories in the West, Midwest, and North. A transient, mobile American workforce was in the making, and none were more eager to change locales than Southern blacks. Many of them, according to Sosna, agreed that the "greater the outside danger to the safety of this country, the more abundant the gains for the Negro are likely to be." Indeed, the war offered black activists an unprecedented opportunity to demand equal treatment. The black trade unionist A. Philip Randolph of the Brotherhood of Sleeping Car Porters and Walter White of the NAACP pushed for the desegregation of the armed services in 1940 by presenting a seven-point plan to President Roosevelt. In October, Roosevelt agreed to admit blacks, but only in proportion to their percentage of the country's population, running close to 10 percent. Blacks, however, were not allowed to share regiments because that would "produce situations destructive to morale and detrimental to the preparation of national defense." By November 30, there were 98,000 blacks in the U.S. Army. Randolph had also organized a massive march on Washington to protest racial discrimination in defense industries. The march, scheduled for July 1, 1941, never took place, but it held the promise of mobilizing an unprecedented number of blacks and was canceled only after President Roosevelt issued an executive order establishing a Fair Employment Practices Committee (Bergman, 490).[13]

Once the war was over, one of the most trying political and demographic pressures was brought to bear by black soldiers returning from the front. Many of them had fought side by side with white soldiers against enemies committed to racial extermination; working together to dismantle a racist regime abroad, as Lemann has written, could only have inspired returning black soldiers to seek to do the same at home. He quotes Horace Busby, a longtime aide to then-senator Lyndon Johnson: "The Negro fought in the war, and now that he's back here with his family he's not gonna keep taking this shit we're dishing out. We're in a race with time. If we don't act, we're gonna have blood in the streets." Johnson made the same speech to David Ginsburg, one of his New Deal friends in Washington. "I remember him always making the point over and over of the need to avert a crisis," Ginsburg said. "The issue had to be obliterated from our society. Blacks had fought in the war. They'd manned the factories. You couldn't treat them as second-class citizens" (Lemann, 136).

For the first time, the entire nature of the Jim Crow South received national attention as America's "leading domestic problem," Sosna writes. "During the depression it had been possible to lose perspective on Jim Crow amid the poverty of the Deep South. The boom generated by the war, however, made it clear that rising prosperity alone would not alleviate racial discrimination. Segregation, the issue dreaded by most white Southern liberals, was now becoming the test of their commitment to the struggle for Negro rights" (120).

The end of the war also forced the South to return its attention to its own mercurial economy. The cotton industry had suffered a crisis, losing almost all of its foreign markets. Although the federal government would commit over $10 billion to the South for defense factories as compensation for its loss of cotton and tobacco markets, this radically altered the economic landscape. The stimulation that the war had brought to the depressed South in the form of military bases and defense industries had to be converted to the peacetime creation of consumer goods and services. Per capita income in the region was still under $400 a year (closer to $200 for blacks), and that was barely half the national average. One out of every three adults had left school by the end of the sixth grade. Millions of men and women, white and black, would be returning from the military or from wartime jobs in the North; they would need education and job training, employment, housing, and medical and legal help (Egerton, 40).

In the 1940s, when urbanization was growing rapidly in the country as a whole, the cities of the South's fifty-three metropolitan areas grew more than three times as fast as comparable cities in the rest of the country, at a rate of 33.1 percent as compared with 10.3 percent elsewhere. For every three city dwellers in the South at the beginning of the decade there were four at the end, and for every five farm residents, there were only four. An overwhelmingly rural South in 1930 had 5.5 million employed in agriculture; by 1950 only 3.2 million. A considerable proportion of these Southerners were moving directly from country to suburb, following the path of the bulldozer to "rurbanization" and skipping the phase of urbanization entirely. Rural blacks, the most mobile and impoverished of all Southerners, were more likely to move into the heart of the urban areas abandoned by the suburban dwellers. In the 1940s alone, the South experienced a one-third reduction in its rural-farm Negro population. The effect of the black exodus on white-run agriculture was not lost on white writers, particularly those like William Alexander Percy, whose family owned one of central Mississippi's largest plantations. But white anxiety about black demographic shifts dated back at least to the turn of the century. In Charles Chesnutt's novel *The Marrow of Tradition*, Major Carteret, an effete aristocrat plotting a race riot, muses over the influx into his North Carolina town of job-seeking blacks: "Only this very morning, while passing the city hall, on his way to the office, he had seen the steps of that noble building disfigured by a fringe of job-hunting negroes, for all the world—to use a local simile—like a string of buzzards sitting on a rail, awaiting their opportunity to batten upon the helpless corpse of a moribund city" (31).

The new postwar prosperity, it turns out, was especially beneficial to blacks, Myrdal wrote. While measures varied, the rise of average real income among Negroes after 1940 was two to three times that among whites, although practically all of that improvement occurred before the economic recession of 1955 (Rose, xix). For the first time in its history, the NAACP began to attract a mass following, in part because of the mass migration northward. From 355 branches and a membership of 50,556 in 1940, the association increased to 1,073 branches and a membership of over 450,000 by 1946. "There never was a time in the history of the United States," noted the black Virginia newspaper editor P. B. Young, "when Negroes were more united concerning the impact of segregation on their lives" (Sosna, 106). In fiction, it seems, postwar prosperity extended even to black fictional characters. The literature examined in the following chapters is full of middle-class Southern black characters, notably the black doctors in Lillian Smith's *Strange Fruit* and Carson McCullers's *The Heart Is a Lonely Hunter*. While professional black characters were hardly unknown in American literature to this time, most had been created in the north beginning with the Harlem Renaissance.

The shifting of black populations continued to have a strong impact on federal civil rights policy. Throughout the 1940s, the Supreme Court handed down watershed decisions that pushed the country toward desegregation. In 1944, in *Smith v. Alwright*, the Court declared that Texas's all-white primaries were unconstitutional. The number of registered black voters jumped almost immediately from 5 percent to 12 percent; two years after the 1954 *Brown v. Board of Education* decision, that number had risen to 25 percent. In 1946, in *Morgan v. Commonwealth of Virginia*, the NAACP successfully argued against the segregation of interstate buses. In *United Public Workers v. Mitchell* (1947), the Court opposed discrimination against federal civil service employees. By 1948, in *Sipuel v. Board of Regents*, the Court demanded the provision of "equal protection" for Ada Lois Sipuel, who had tried to gain entry into the University of Oklahoma Law School since no black school was available. To get around the decision, the university set up a law school for blacks, but Sipuel refused to attend. Two years later, in *Sweatt v. Painter*, the Court ordered the admission of a black student to the University of Texas Law

School on the grounds that the black school was insufficient. An important judicial decision at the state level was made in 1947, in a case argued by Thurgood Marshall, in which the South Carolina federal district judge J. Waties Waring upheld the right of blacks to vote in the state's Democratic primaries.

In 1946, President Truman issued Executive Order 9808 creating the Presidential Committee on Civil Rights to study existing federal protections; a year later, the commission issued *To Secure These Rights* recommending that the Civil Rights section of the Justice Department be expanded to a full division and that Congress establish a permanent Federal Employment Practices Act, federal laws against lynching, and equal enforcement of law. By this time, 200,000 blacks had joined the federal payroll, compared to just 50,000 in 1933.

Political rhetoric at the national level in the 1940s mirrored these changes. For the first time in the twentieth century, blacks were mentioned by name by the Democratic National platform in 1940:

> Our Negro citizens have participated actively in the economic and social advances launched by this Administration, including fair labor standards, social security benefits, . . . work relief prospects . . . decent housing. . . . We have aided more than half a million Negro youths in vocational training, education and employment. . . . We shall continue to strive for complete legislative safeguards against discrimination in Government service and benefits, and in national defense forces. We pledge to uphold due process and the equal protection of laws for every citizen regardless of race, creed, or color. (Bergman, 491)

The Republican platform, by comparison, said: "We pledge that our American citizens of Negro descent shall be given a square deal in the economic and political life of this nation. Discrimination must cease. To enjoy the full benefits of life, liberty, and the pursuit of happiness, universal suffrage must be made effective for the Negro citizen. Mob violence shocks the conscience of the nation and legislation to curb this evil should be enacted" (Bergman, 491).[14]

In the 1944 election, after a meeting in New York attended by the leaders of twenty-five black organizations, an open letter written on behalf of 6.5 million black Americans was sent to both Democrats and Republicans. Politicians seeking black votes were told they must be committed to eliminating the poll tax, passing antilynching legislation, integrating the armed forces, and establishing a federal com-

A HISTORICAL OVERVIEW

mittee on fair employment practices and "a foreign policy of international cooperation that promotes economic and political security for all peoples."

Beyond such generic demands, the letter also addressed in more pointed language the ongoing struggles at home:

> We are opposed to any negotiated peace as advocated by the Hitler-like forces within our country. Victory must crush Hitlerism at home as well as abroad. . . . We insist upon the right to vote in every state, unrestricted by poll taxes, white primaries, or lily-white party conventions, the gerrymandering of districts, or any other device designed to disenfranchise Negroes and other voters. . . . The ever-serious evil of lynching and mob violence has become more critical as a result of unrestrained violence against Negroes in the armed services. No national administration can merit the support of Negroes unless it is committed to a legislative and administrative program for the elimination of this national disgrace." (Walter White, 263–64)

The proposals were greeted with little support by either party, although the Republicans did include a pledge to form a federal Fair Employment Practices Committee. Four years later, the Democratic Party platform did call for Congress to support President Truman in full and to support equal protection, equal employment opportunity, and the right of equal treatment in the armed services. In response, thirty-five delegates of Southern states walked out of the convention and formed the Dixiecrats, or States Rights Democrats, a splinter group that then met in Birmingham and nominated Gov. Strom Thurmond, of South Carolina, and Gov. Fielding L. Wright, of Mississippi, for their own presidential ticket. Their platform stated:

> We stand for segregation of the races, and racial integrity of each race; the constitutional right to choose one's associates; to accept private employment without governmental interference, and to earn one's living in any lawful way. We oppose the elimination of segregation in employment by Federal bureaucrats called for by the misnamed civil rights program. We favor home rule, local self-government and a minimum interference with individual rights. We oppose and condemn the action of the Democratic convention in sponsoring a civil rights program calling for the elimination of segregation, social equality by Federal fiat, repudiation of pri-

vate employment practices, voting and local law enforcement. We affirm that the effective enforcement of such a program would be utterly destructive of the social, economic, and political life of the Southern people. (Bergman, 518)[15]

Partially because of this brand of rhetoric, black voter registration efforts in the South during this period met with predictable white resistance. In 1946, Macio Snipes, a veteran, was shot and killed by four whites after he voted in Taylor County, Georgia. "The first nigger to vote will never vote again" said a sign posted on a black church (Bergman, 511). In 1948, another black, Robert Mallard, was lynched after voting in Vidalia, Georgia. Indeed, after the war, liberal white journalists and activists were roundly criticized by black leaders for abandoning their earlier energies and leaving blacks to fend for themselves. Walter White complained that "the highest casualty rate of the war seems to be that of Southern white liberals. For various reasons they are taking cover at an alarming rate—fleeing before the onslaught of the professional Southern bigots" (Loveland, 46).

Before the United States entered the war, white liberals had been active in movements against lynching, the poll tax, and educational inequity. Now, with blacks directly attacking segregation, some white liberals criticized them for making excessive demands that they said only invited racial violence. The white writer David Cohn believed that although it would be possible for Southern blacks to gain voting rights, justice in the courts, and equitable shares of tax money for health, education, and public services, on segregation there could be no compromise. Yet Cohn insisted that if the federal government interceded to end segregation, "every Southern white man would spring to arms and the country would be swept by civil war."

Even Hodding Carter, who won a Pulitzer Prize for his editorials against white supremacy as editor of the *Greenville (Miss.) Delta Democrat-Times*, wrote in 1948 that "[t]he white South is as united as 30,000,000 people can be in its insistence upon segregation. Federal action cannot change them. It will be tragic for the South, the Negro, and the nation itself if the government should enact and attempt to enforce any laws or Supreme Court decisions that would open the South's public schools and public gathering places to the Negro."[16]

Some Southern liberals were not so ambivalent. In a February 1942 letter to Walter White, Lillian Smith wrote with uncharacteristic optimism:

It is so apparent that the world's stage is set for a magnificent act on the part of the Anglo-Saxons! If the British people would give India her freedom, if Mr. Roosevelt by a proclamation justified by war would give the Negro in America his full status of citizenship, it would cause a mighty exaltation to sweep over the face of the earth. Mr. Roosevelt is afraid. He has no reason to be. Beneath the South's terrible dullness and prejudice is a deep sense of guilt. I believe white southerners would draw in a deep breath and thank God for what he had done. I believe this. And I know my South. (Gladney, 56)

The struggles of Southern writers in the 1940s, then, simply mirrored the struggle of the region around them to navigate a period deeply marked by turmoil and transition. The 1940s brought powerful, if ambivalent, racial feelings to a head, and set the stage for the fledgling civil rights movement that was just one generation away.

CHAPTER TWO

Private Violence Desirable

Race, Sex, and Sadism in Wilbur J. Cash's

The Mind of the South

It is reported from reliable sources that the little children, some of them mere
tots, who lived in the Greenwood neighborhood, waited with sharpened
sticks for the return of Neal's body and that when it rolled in the dust on the
road that awful night these little children drove their weapons deep into the
flesh of the dead man.

From Howard Kester's report on the
Marianna, Florida, lynching

In a chapter of *The Mind of the South* dedicated to explaining the resur-
gence of lynching in the South of the 1920s, W. J. Cash writes of the way
certain blacks, "with a bolder lift to their heads," had returned home
after the First World War and were met with violent white resistance.
These blacks, he argued, had in the previous decade learned a new sophistication both in Europe and in Harlem, from which they often returned South with a "jazziness" that enraged Southern whites. Within
this otherwise sharply barbed attack on white racism, Cash goes into a
two-paragraph aside about one group of "new" Negroes that he considered to be particularly responsible for provoking white rage: black
bellboys.

Once the suppression of red-light houses and the streetwalker had
turned most Southern hotels into public stews, these bellboys had
also acquired a virtual monopoly of the trade of pander and pimp,
and demanded and secured from the white prostitutes they served
all the traditional prerogatives of the pimp, including not only a

large share of their earnings but also and above all the right of sexual intercourse—often enforced against the most reluctant of the women, again under threat of betrayal to the police.

The result was the rise of a horde of raffish blacks, full of secret, contemptuous knowledge of the split in the psyche of the shamefaced Southern whites, the gulf between their Puritanical professions and their hedonistic practices—scarcely troubling to hide their grinning contempt for their clients under the thinnest veil of subservient politeness and, in the case of the bellboys, hugging to themselves with cackling joy their knowledge of the white man's women. (320–21)

In this passage are subtleties far more interesting than Cash's surface outrage over racial violence, which he no doubt sincerely felt. Cash's choice of scenes on which to construct his argument, in which black boys not only have sexual intercourse with white women but with "grinning contempt" mock "the split in the psyche of the shamefaced Southern whites," reveals as much about Cash and the "mind" of Southern racism as anything he might have set out to write. It was not only white women that these "cackling" blacks knew, it was the sexual impotence of the white men. Black bellboys, in other words, provoked white rage not because they had sex with white women but because they revealed white male sexual anxiety for what it was: contemptible, shameful, and weak. Also within this passage, as we shall see, are traces of Cash's own history that mark him as a writer grappling with issues far more complex than mere political outrage; he was a man plagued from his youth by a sexual insecurity that often found a voice in his writing about race. Blacks, for Cash, became convenient vessels into which he poured the dark waters of his own soul.

To dismiss Cash as a dissembling racist, in other words, is to miss a larger point. What is interesting, and useful for an understanding of the South—and racialized thinking in general—is the way Cash imagined blackness *as a part of,* or *as an influence on,* the construction of the "mind" of whiteness. In this respect we can take Cash at his word: if he concedes that blacks "influenced every gesture, every word, every emotion and idea, every attitude" of whites, then we must try to understand how Cash conceived this process happening, how he imagined blackness itself as the missing center of the white "man at the center." It is my contention that Cash's own life, particularly the deeply ambivalent perceptions he had of his own sexuality, will reveal much of the torment that found expression in his rhetoric of race. What I hope to show is the complex way that race serves as a repository for complex and often violent discourses that on the surface may seem to have "nothing to do with" race itself. When Cash conflates the experiences of poor white millworkers and former slaves, he becomes increasingly aware of the parallels in class between the two groups, parallels that in his mind fought to overcome received notions of racial differences. When Cash describes a particularly gruesome lynching, his language reflects his own eroticization of violence.

It should be said from the outset that I do not purport to read *The Mind of the South* as a piece of Southern history but rather as a piece of cultural analysis as well as a kind of self-portrait. Published in 1941 after more than a decade of tortured writing, *The Mind of the South* became for nearly twenty-five years the era's most talked-about book on Southern culture. It sold about 1,400 copies in its first two months of publication, and for the next nineteen years thousands more circulated among colleges and libraries. Dewey Grantham, on the book's twentieth anniversary, called *The Mind of the South* "perhaps the most brilliant essay ever written on the Southern character"; Cash's first biographer, Joseph L. Morrison, wrote in 1967 that Cash's "man at the center" strategy was an "ingenious literary device." The book received a new groundswell of interest during the 1960s, as the civil rights movement brought renewed interest to the exploration of race and Southern culture (Jack Temple Kirby, in Escott, 208–9).

Cash has been handled in recent years more roughly for his unusual rhetorical style, which in virtually every case chooses anecdote over document and grandiloquence over fact. Most critical attention has been paid to Cash's insights into class relationships between rich and poor whites; until recently, very little had been written about his rhetorical relationship to race other than to admonish the book for caricaturing black life. Yet for a book that claims from its outset to be about "the man at the center," *The Mind of the South* has long been recognized as a book with a *missing* center. If the book purports to chronicle "the mysteries of the common brotherhood of white men," then it does so only as it records the reactions white men have to their black neighbors. Indeed, black *people* are virtually nonexistent in this text; they are mentioned only indirectly as whites worry about them, employ them, sleep with them, lynch them. At some level Cash was aware of this; he points to the relationship between whites and blacks as "nothing less than organic. Negro entered into white man as profoundly as white man entered into Negro—subtly influencing every gesture, every word, every emotion and idea, every attitude." Yet he still avoided almost completely any engagement with a black "mind." Female slaves were simply "to be had for the taking"; as a race, Negroes were "in the main . . . a creature of grandiloquent imagination, of facile emotion, and, above everything else under heaven, of enjoyment" (King, 162–63). Indeed, at no point does he attempt to portray the life or imagination of the blacks with whom he grew up, or whom he imagined living side by side with his regional forebears.

Joel Williamson's 1984 book *The Crucible of Race* posits that the

flowering of the Old South in the New—including Wilbur Cash, William Faulkner *et al.*—was the direct result of the black presence, that it was in fact the tangible fruit of a tri-generational and complex interplay of black and white reaching a new plateau in the decades after World War I and deployed upon new ground. Ironically, each of these thinking Southerners knew as Cash did that somehow the Negro was at the center of things. They all worried about the edges of the problem, but none was able to transcend his times, drive to the core, and perceive that racial thinking in the minds of white Southerners had been vari-parted and evolutionary, and that they themselves had been shaped by coming of age at a peculiar juncture in the culture resulting from that process. (4)

Other critics give Cash credit for admitting up front that blacks are to him an utter mystery. Cash writes: "Even the most unreflecting must sometimes feel suddenly, in dealing with them, that they were looking at a blank wall, that behind that grinning face a veil was drawn into which no white man might certainly know he had ever penetrated. What was back there, hidden? What whispering, stealthy, fateful thing might they be framing out there in the palpitant darkness?" (326–27).[1] But as Gunnar Myrdal would write three years after *The Mind of the South* was published, the place of "the Negro" in white thinking reveals all too much about the white mind: "If the Negro is shunned in formal conversation, he enters all informal life to a great extent," Myrdal writes. "He is the standard joke. It is interesting to note the great pleasure white people in all classes take in these stereotyped jokes and in indulging in discussions about the Negro and what he does, says, and thinks. The stories and the jokes give release to a troubled people. When people are up against great inconsistencies in their creed and behavior, which they cannot or do not want to account for rationally, humor is a way out. To the whites, the

RACE, SEX, AND SADISM

Negro jokes serve the function of 'proving' the inferiority of the Negro" (Rose, 16).

In Cash's case, nervous humor is replaced by a caustic irony, particularly when he is describing racial violence. In "The War in the South," a piece written for H. L. Mencken's *American Mercury* in February 1930, Cash wrote that "the single best weapon for putting down the 'invader' and the 'renegade' is Ku Kluxery—the repressed sadism, the native blood-lust, the horrible mob instinct, which smolder among the brutal and the ignorant everywhere in the South, and, above all, and ironically, among the mill-workers themselves." As we shall see, repressed sadism was not just to be found in millworkers, but in Cash himself.

In Cash's hands, lynching becomes something more than racial violence; it becomes infused with psychological obsessions and personal confessions that reveal as much about the writer himself as they do about the culture of which he is inarguably critical. "I do not think it is true, as the South-haters have sometimes broadly insinuated, that anybody was ever lynched in the land simply because the Southerners counted it capital fun," he wrote in *The Mind of the South*. "But it is true that, from the Civil War forward, the old frolic tendency was more and more centered here, that enjoyment grew apace with practice in the business, that it figured with rising force as a very model of heroic activity, and that this feeling played a constantly expanding role in the complex" (125).[2]

It is true that Cash's ironic treatment of white Southern rituals — including lynching—was most often intended to ridicule such barbarity. But there is nonetheless something uneasy in characterizing lynching as "the old frolic" or "a very model of heroic activity." It is too easy to dismiss such writing as merely ironic; it must, it seems to me, also be read as the language of someone *conflicted*, not just irreverent, about racial violence. As Edward Ayers has written about Cash's empathy for both blacks and poor whites,

> Perhaps Cash felt entitled to this kind of mind-reading, this useful ventriloquism. He had, after all, put in hours in steamy cotton mills during his college summers; he had watched his parents suffer in the depression; he had worn cardboard in his shoes; he had written his book in a freezing room lit by a single light bulb while neighborhood boys tossed gravel at the window, mocking this strange man who sponged off his parents well into his thirties. Maybe his words grew out of pain and empathy.

The problem is his words don't sound like it. Cash did not voice the sympathy for the oppressed that has marked, in varying degrees, virtually every book of New South history published since World War II. Fortunately for Cash's reputation today, he was also contemptuous of the South's planters, businessmen, and politicians, fair game throughout the intervening half century and into the foreseeable future. Yet, by today's standards, Cash would have to be considered racist, sexist, and elitist. (qtd. in Eagles, 120)

For all his rage against elitist mill owners, political demagogues, and the white supremacist poor who most frequently carried out lynchings, and for all his rhetorical gestures in support of the downtrodden, Cash's words, don't, in fact, "sound like it." His language unfailingly returns to the visceral, the unconscious, and it is in these gestures that so much can be read. On July 24, 1940, he wrote an editorial in the *Charlotte News* under the headline "Suicide Surge" in which he mused over new statistics indicating that more than twice as many people died by their own hand in 1938 as in 1920. The editorial ran only six paragraphs and ascribed the higher rate to "the difficulty of the times," particularly "the year when Hitler really heaved up on the American horizon." But after reporting that South Carolina had the lowest suicide rate in the country, Cash made an odd turn in the penultimate paragraph. "The large Negro population explains a good deal of it, of course; Negroes rarely commit suicide," he wrote. "But it obviously doesn't explain all of it, since other states have an even larger proportion of Negroes than South Carolina. And considering cotton prices, Cotton Ed Smith and other tribulations, all cannot be complete joy in South Carolina" (qtd. in Joseph Morrison, 268).[3]

Given his own tragic life story, the violent place and time in which he lived, and the florid rhetoric of *The Mind of the South*, Cash's move from a discussion of suicide to an aside about race is as revealing as it is odd. As a reporter, editorialist, and regional historian, Cash was intimately aware of the lynchings of blacks from Reconstruction to his own time; indeed, much of his most vitriolic prose was reserved for the condemnation of the organized violence of "Ku Kluckers." But there is something troubling about his irreverence about absent "joy" in South Carolina, as though an intricate web of rage and despair lay below Cash's famous irony. Equally disturbing, just forty-nine weeks after writing these lines, and at a time that most people considered to be the emotional high point of his life, Cash, after an acute bout of psychotic delu-

RACE, SEX, AND SADISM

sions in which he imagined himself being hunted by murderous Nazis, hanged himself in a hotel room in Mexico City.

Lillian Smith, who published *Killers of the Dream* eight years after *The Mind of the South*, was acutely aware of the tortured connection between white male sexual neurosis and the racial violence that often resulted from it; perhaps because she was a woman, and a lesbian, she had a critical distance that Cash could not achieve. She writes,

> Only a few of our people are killers; only a handful would take a man's life so greedily. But there have been too many lynchings in the South of this nature where the Negro—a stranger to the mob who lynched him—has not only been shot but his body riddled with bullets (each person in the group killing his lifeless body again and again and again), for us not to understand that the lynched Negro becomes *not an object that must die* but a receptacle for every man's dammed up hate, and a receptacle for every man's forbidden feelings. Sex and hate, cohabitating in the darkness of minds too long, pour out their progeny of cruelty on anything that can serve as a symbol of an unnamed relationship that in his heart each man wants to befoul. That, sometimes, the lynchers do cut off genitals of the lynched and divide them into bits to be distributed to participants as souvenirs is no more than a coda to this composition of hate and guilt and sex and fear, created by our way of life. (163)

Cash's own curiosity about racial violence served as an outlet for his own sexual and political anxieties. His rhetoric is that of an abused or neglected child, who creates fantastic horror stories both to vent and to mask anxieties about his own frailty and fears. He was not unlike the evangelists described by Smith, who also linked the power of racial rhetoric with religious fervor and used both to mask a more powerful, visceral dread. "Nothing but a lynching or a political race-hate campaign could tear a town's composure into as many dirty little rags or give as many curious satisfactions," she wrote in *Killers of the Dream*. "The revivalists I knew . . . were ambivalent men who had healed themselves by walling off one segment of their life and who kept many doors open in their personality by keeping one door securely locked. And they were men whose powerful instincts of sex and hate were woven together into a sadism that would have devastated their lives and broken their minds had they acknowledged it for what it was. Instead, they bound it into verbal energy and with this power of the tongue they drove men in herds toward heaven, lashing out at them cruelly when they seemed to be stampeding" (103–4).

It is this frenzy, this sadism, that I want to explore in Cash, to look at how his rhetoric unconsciously represents, in Toni Morrison's words, "both a way of talking about and a way of policing matters of class, sexual license, and repression, formations and exercise of power, and meditations on ethics and accountability. Through the simple expedient of demonizing and reifying the range of color on a palette, African-Americanism makes it possible to say and not say, to inscribe and erase, to escape and engage, to act out and act on, to historicize and render timeless. It provides a way of contemplating chaos and civilization, desire and fear, and a mechanism for testing the problems and blessings of freedom" (7).

Important as it may be to examine Cash's explorations of violence, it seems only intellectually honest to remain clear-eyed about the historical *fact* of lynching, and not allow it to become merely a rich literary image, for him or for us. Confronting the horror of lynching directly, it is hoped, will provide us with a more thorough understanding of the literary texts, particularly those written by Cash and Lillian Smith, that later depended on the grim material. A singularly dramatic case will serve as a representative example. The 1934 lynching of Claude Neal in Marianna, Florida, which became one of the most notorious lynchings in the United States, occurred just a few years before Cash wrote his book and must surely have colored his imagination as it did that of the rest of the country. The Neal case is also useful in that it became one of the more thoroughly documented lynching investigations; the correspondence between Walter White and Howard Kester, a white lynching investigator, includes descriptions of the lynching that are almost too graphic to read. For this reason as much as any other, given the graphic nature of Cash's own rhetoric, Kester's language has been included here. The narrative of the Neal case has been compiled from Kester's report and letters found in the NAACP Papers at the Library of Congress as well as from James McGovern's thorough history, *Anatomy of a Lynching: The Killing of Claude Neal.*

From the time he was a little boy, Claude Neal had played with the children of a local white family named Cannidy, and when he grew strong enough to work, he helped out on the Cannidy's farm in Marianna, Florida, a rural village tucked in the panhandle just miles from the Alabama and Georgia lines. As time passed, Neal and one of the Cannidy children, Lola, began spending more and more time together and eventually became intimate. "For some months and possibly for a period of years," it would be later be reported, "Claude Neal and Lola Cannidy had been having intimate relations with each other. The nature of their relationship was common knowledge in the Negro community. Some of his friends advised him of the danger of the relationship and had asked him not to continue it."

When Lola's body was found in a field in the fall of 1934, suspicion immediately focused on the twenty-three-year-old Neal, but other rumors abounded. One of the most plausible centered on a white man, who had recently dropped off a set of blood-stained clothes to Neal's mother to be washed. "These may or may not be facts but they deserve investigation," a black minister wrote to an investigator. "Living here as I do where it is dangerous for me or any other man of color to write or say too much . . . I am giving you a hint of some things being said here."

Word of the killing left blacks in Neal's hometown terrified. In a letter to the local newspaper written while Neal was still held in Alabama, eight black citizens, including the principal of a local black high school, wrote, "We trust that the brutal act supposed to have been committed by one of our Race will not break that friendly and mutual relationship that exists among the white and colored citizens of Jackson County, one of the best counties in the State. We have the uttermost confidence in the best white citizens of the county, and trust you have the same in us. We shall ever strive and teach our Race to never betray that trust. We pray that you will get the guilty brutes and protect the innocent."

The letter was signed "Your humble citizens." Another black man named John Curry expressed even more fear in his letter to the paper:

To the White Citizens of Jackson County:

Just a few lines to let you all know that we good colored citizens of Jackson County don't feel no sympathy toward the nigger that ————the white lady and killed her. No! We haven't felt he did right because he should stay in his place, and since he did such as he did, we are not feeling that we have a right to plead to you all for mercy.

It makes us chagrined and feel that he has ruined the good colored people that try to behave themselves and work for an honest living.

I feel very bad over it myself to see that we have such a fellow in the Race and I am among the good colored people that feel just like I do toward him. I talked with them, and they can't see how they can have sympathy for him.

But I am writing to let you know that we leave it to you all to do what you all see fit to do to him. But still asking you all not to be hard on your good servants that have been honest and faithful for the time that we have been working with you for the other fellow. Because we good colored people want to thank you all for the favors and the chance that you will have given us to let us have schools for our children and teachers to teach them and jobs for us to work and get bread for them that they can have a chance. Also we thank you all for making it easy.

Because if it wasn't for the good white citizens, we realize that many of our girls and boys would have been mobbed for nothing they done but for the brutal act that was done. I also thank the sheriff for working so faithfully to get the right man.

Your faithful servant,

John Curry

still pleading for a chance for the better class of colored people and not to punish us for him, because if he do wrong he is wrong, and we have no sympathy for him!

Even before a coroner's jury had charged Neal after its one-day review of the evidence, lynch mobs began swarming into Marianna from all over the region. Descriptions of the burial of Lola Cannidy in local newspapers added to the fury. On Saturday, October 30, a column in the Marianna newspaper, under the headline "You Can't Know How it Hurts Unless This Happens to You," Lola's father was quoted as saying,

Lord, but you can't know how it hurts unless you had something like this happen to someone you loved. . . . The bunch have promised me that they will give me first chance at him when they bring him back and I'll be ready. We'll put those two logs on him and ease him off by degrees. I can't get the picture of Lola out of my mind when we found her. Her throat was bruised and scratched where he had choked her so she couldn't cry out. My son was in the field about a quarter of a mile away when he saw someone talking with her at the pump, but he thought it was just one of the local boys and didn't pay much attention. He was right there in the field when she was being killed. Her head was beat in and she had been choked so hard her eyes were coming out of their sockets, her arms were broken and she was all beat up. When I get my hands on that nigger, there isn't any telling what I'll do.

Lola's sister was given equal time in another front-page article, headed "I Wish Every Resident of Jackson County Could See the Body of Lola."

When I viewed the body of my sister I was horrified. Whoever killed her—well I don't believe any form of punishment could fit the crime. I can hardly believe that such a horrible thing could happen to my sister. If I have to be killed I hope it won't be in the manner she met death. I know that there never has been anything in Jackson County that was so brutal. I'd like to see the man who did this just once. I can't understand what the motive was for this brutal deed. To think that Claude Neal, who had been raised with my sister and me and worked for us all his life, could do such a thing—it is unbelievable. I only wish that every resident of Jackson County could view the body of my sister. If they could, they wouldn't rest until the murderer was caught and justice meted out.

As it happened, no investigation was completed, and no trial was held. At first, the Marianna sheriff agreed to hide Neal in one jail and his sister and mother in another, but a lynch mob that grew to 300 people began searching all the jails within seventy-five miles of Marianna, threatening at one point to dynamite the jail holding the two women unless they were surrendered to the mob. On Saturday, October 21, a group of men with acetylene torches came again to the jail; the sheriff somehow managed to hide the women on the floor of his car and drive them to Pensacola. Neal was transported from the jail in Panama City to one in Pensacola, and finally to another prison across the border in Brewton, Alabama, where he signed a confession to the crime. The final move and the confession put Neal's life at great risk; Sheriff Herbert E. Gandy of Escambia County reputedly declared that he "never wanted to kill a negro so bad in his life." Word of Neal's once-secret hiding place quickly leaked out, and a lynch mob rapidly formed. While one group decoyed the sheriff holding Neal into following them away from the jail, another group broke in, told the jailer they would blow the place up if he did not stand aside, and dragged Neal into a car. The terrified jailer recalled hearing one of the kidnappers tell Neal, "If he had any talking to do to the Lord he had better do it now because he didn't have long to live."

Bound by plow rope in the back seat of the car, Neal was driven back to Marianna.

Enraged whites used the capture of Neal as a flame to ignite an anger that for many white Southerners had been smoldering since the end of the Civil War. A crowd of sightseers gathered at the Cannidy home, where they were met by the bereaved family. That Friday afternoon, October 26, an article appeared in the Dothan, Alabama, newspaper stating: "Florida to Burn Negro at Stake: Sex Criminal Seized from Brewton Jail, Will Be Mutilated, Set Afire in Extra-Legal Vengeance for Deed." The story carried the high-pitched rhetoric of its animated reporter: "For hours as word of the jail storming and seizure spread, the grapevines and telephones of Northwest Florida buzzed and grim faced farmers prepared to make the Cannidy home their rendezvous. They know what was to happen: that was freely bruited and the Negro bound securely at the stake waited. The mobsmen and the citizens of Northwest Florida waited for nightfall when the Negro is destined to pay the extra-legal penalty for his crimes—the murder and outraging of the white girl. . . . The Negro is to be carried to the spot where he committed the crime a week ago."

By 3 P.M. that day, the Associated Press put the word of the pending lynching on its national wire. In New York, the dispatch was picked up by Walter White. White wired Florida governor David Sholtz, asking him to intervene, but since Florida law prohibited the calling of the National Guard unless it was requested by a county sheriff, Sholtz could only notify Marianna sheriff Chambliss that the guard would be made available if he desired its help. Chambliss declined.

As evening settled in over this little Florida town, upwards of 2,000 spectators gathered for the coming spectacle. Although a number of small-town newspaper accounts exist to tell the tale of what happened next, the lynching of Neal is most intimately and horrifically described by a young white Southerner named Howard Kester, who was hired as an investigator days after the lynching by Walter White. White wired Kester in early November. "We would like to get all the gruesome details possible together with any photographs of the body, crowd, etc. and as much evidence as is possible as to the identity of the leaders and members of the mob," White's telegram read. "As the capacity of the American people for indignation is great, but short lived, get the facts to us as soon as possible."

What Kester discovered upon reaching Marianna has become the stuff of legend. In a firsthand report to White and the NAACP that ran to some sixteen pages, Kester's descriptions of what he found in Florida have become signature documents of American racial history. "I was told by several people that Neal was tortured for ten or twelve hours," Kester wrote. "It is almost impossible to believe that a human being could stand such unspeakable torture for such a long period."

After interviewing one member of the lynch mob, Kester reported what remains one of the most horrifying racial crimes ever committed. "The story of the actual lynching as related to me and later corroborated by others is as follows," Kester wrote.

"After taking the nigger to the woods about four miles from Greenwood, they cut off his penis. He was made to eat it. Then they cut off his testicles and made him eat them and say he liked it." (I gathered that this barbarous act consumed considerable time and that other means of torture were used from time to time on Neal.) "Then they sliced his sides and stomach with knives and every now and then somebody would cut off a finger or toe. Red hot irons were use on the nigger to burn him from top to bottom." From time to time during the torture a rope would be tied around Neal's neck and he was pulled up over a limb and held there until he almost choked to death when he would be let down and the torture begin all over again. After several hours of this unspeakable torture, "they decided just to kill him."

Even after Neal died, his body continued to be subjected to unfathomable atrocities, Kester wrote.

Neal's body was tied to a rope on the rear of an automobile and dragged over the highway to the Cannidy house. Here a mob estimated to number somewhere between 3,000 and 7,000 from eleven southern states were excitedly waiting his arrival. When the car which was dragging Neal's body came in front of the Cannidy house, a man who was riding the rear bumper cut the rope. Mrs. Cannidy came out, and drove a butcher knife through his heart. Then the crowd came by and some kicked him and drove their cars over him.

Men, women and children were numbered in the vast throng that came to witness the lynching. It is reported from reliable sources that the little children, some of them mere tots, who lived in the Greenwood neighborhood, waited with sharpened sticks for the return of Neil's body and that when it rolled in the dust on the road that awful night these little children drove their weapons deep into the flesh of the dead man.

The body, which by this time was horribly mutilated, was taken by the mob to Marianna, a distance of ten or eleven miles, where it was hung to a tree on the northeast corner of the courthouse square. Pictures were taken of the mutilated form and hundreds of photographs were sold for fifty cents each. Scores of citizens viewed the body as it hung from the square. The body was perfectly nude until the early morning when someone had the decency to hang a burlap sack over the middle of the body. The body was cut down about eight-thirty Saturday morning, October 27, 1934.

Fingers and toes from Neal's body have been exhibited as souvenirs in Marianna where one man offered to divide the finger which he had with a friend as "a special favor." Another man has one of the fingers preserved in alcohol.

Despite the horrific and extremely public nature of the lynching, the town of Marianna returned to a kind of stunned calm after the event. Kester reported that "on the whole the lynching was accepted . . . as a righteous act." Marianna's mayor blamed the lynching on crowds from Alabama and Georgia and said his office had done all it could by "holding them back as well as they could." Ministers, politicians, and the local press did little to condemn the act; indeed, a number of editorials from nearby papers endorsed the lynching. Under a headline that declared the lynching was "Avenging an Insult," the *Panama City Pilot* editorialized that "[h]ere is just cause why a community was stirred and maddened with grim determination to avenge the insult to womanhood. This was the real reason why hundreds of men left their work and joined in the hunt, with only one object in view—to hunt the criminal, find him if it consumed all of a year, and mete unmerciful torture to him, as he did to a young girl."

In discussions of Cash's engagement with race and racial violence, most observers describe him as a man who went from being a "racial paternalist" in his young adulthood to a relative progressive whose editorializing about the horrors of lynching were in step with some of the more enlightened white writing about race of the time. But pegging Cash as a racial liberal or conservative is less useful than examining his language itself, to see what it reveals about the way he envisioned his region's past and present.

Although Cash is traditionally read as being ironic or sarcastic about the racial violence performed by his historical forebears, it is more fruitful for our purposes to take him at his word, to look at the *way* he invokes race and racial violence. In other words, if Cash describes lynching as a "white man's frolic," we should ask why Cash would have chosen to use such language, what psychological and political impulses may lie behind it. Cash was a man plagued throughout his youth and adulthood by severe psychological and physical breakdowns; what I find curious is the way these breakdowns found voice in his writing about race. Like William Alexander Percy, Cash was quick to acknowledge the influence blacks had on him as a child. If his failure to fully engage with actual black lives reveals a compromised imagination, his language is nonetheless revealing for its awareness of the mysterious ways that black lives colored his own.

In the early part of the century in small towns like Gaffney, South Carolina, racial violence was "as much a part of life as religion," Cash's biographer Bruce Clayton writes. When Wilbur Cash was six years old, a black man was lynched in nearby Greenwood County. A mob of more than a thousand whites took the accused rapist from jail, tied him to a tree, and riddled his body with bullets. "The Negro's head was literally shot into pulp," the local paper reported, "his brains covering his hat and face." Governor Duncan Clinch Heyward was in attendance at the lynching; he convinced "a humane man" to pull "the doomed Negro's hat over his face before the crowd started shooting" (14–15).

Growing up, Cash often heard that Thomas Dixon, from nearby Shelby, North Carolina, was the highest exemplar of Southern patriotism. "All of us learned to read on 'The Three Little Confederates,'" he wrote in *The Mind of the South*. "All of us framed our hero-ideal on Stuart and Pickett and Forrest—on the dragoon and the lancer—ten thousand times, in our dreams, rammed home the flag in the cannon's mouth after the manner of the heroes of the Reverend Tom Dixon, ten thousand times stepped into the breach at the critical moment on that reeking slope at Gettysburg, and with our tremendous swords, and in defiance of chronology, then and there won the Civil War" (King, 156).[4]

Even here, in his descriptions of reading about the war, Cash's sexual imagery is unmistakable; unlike Percy, whose descriptions of war ran to the chivalric and the decorous, Cash uses the phallic imagery of "tremendous swords" and flags that are "rammed home" in the cannon's "mouth." Masculinity and regional pride are inextricably mixed. Dixon was the author of the best-selling, racist novel *The Clansman*, which Cash, although he would change his mind, admitted was his favorite childhood book. Dixon loomed over Cash's authorial ego as a writer who had won enormous fame. Yet even in his adult role as newspaper editor, Cash remembered seeing D. W. Griffith's film version, *The Birth of a Nation* and "watching the Rev. Tom Dixon's Ku Kluckers do execution of uppity coons and low-down carpetbaggers, and alternately bawling hysterically and shouting my fool head off" (Joseph Morrison, 13).

Cash's father, John William, who lived some twenty-five years longer than his son, was a charter member of the Gaffney Cherokee Avenue Baptist Church. His mother, Nannie Lutitia, was more devout but better humored than her husband. Born Joseph Wilbur on May 2, 1900, in Gaffney, Cash disliked both his given names and reversed them to differentiate his initials from his father's, and later adopted a byline made up only by his initials.[5] He was known as Wilbur to his family, Jack to his newspaper colleagues, and Sleepy to his schoolmates. This last he acquired during high school, when he showed up one day with a bruise on his face; he explained that he'd read himself to sleep on the porch one Sunday morning and had tumbled into the yard (Joseph Morrison, 7). The conservative society of Cash's childhood was reflected by the legally sanctioned white supremacist governance of "Pitchfork Ben" Tillman and Cole Blease as much as it was by Dixon's fiction. Indeed, as the architect of South Carolina's white supremacist political apparatus, Tillman claimed to have personally given Dixon the story that led to the writing of *The Clansman*. Tillman once shouted that he had three daughters, "but so help me God I had rather find either one of them killed by a tiger or a bear and gather up her bones and bury them, conscious that she had died in the purity of her maidenhood, than to have her crawl to me and tell me the horrid story that she had been robbed of the jewel of her womanhood by a black fiend" (Clayton, 17). Tillman and Blease won office, Joseph Morrison writes, as "paladins of white-supremacy politics, which meant nothing more or less than winning political place by shouting 'nigger' louder than one's opponent" (14).[6] Blease boasted that he'd "planted" the finger of a black lynching victim in his garden; he was later quoted ranting that "when a nigger laid his hand on a white woman the quicker he was placed under six feet of dirt, the better" (Clayton, 14–15).

Tillman and Blease got to the governor's mansion, in other words, by appealing primarily to poor white workers, to whom they promised economic relief but delivered little more than a feeling of racial solidarity. Poor and white had for generations defined most of Cash's family. His paternal grandfather, James Henry, and great grandfather, Sidney Cash, worked in the Confederate munitions plant at Hurricane Shoals, later the site of the Clifton Cotton Mills No. 1, on the Pacolet River. The mill was part of the South Carolina Manufacturing Company, which owned more than 25,000 acres between the Pacolet and the Broad Rivers. The principal fuel at Hurricane Shoals was charcoal, and the company's tramway, on which cordwood was hauled, was operated by the Cashes with about a dozen flatcars. After the war, James Henry helped build and operate a sawmill on the property. His sons John William and Ed grew up poor in a family of ten; Ed learned to be a master mechanic, and was later invited to manage the mill in Gaffney. Cash's mother's side of the family, the Hamricks, was also largely of Scotch-Irish descent, but the original Hamrick, Hans Georg, was a German who arrived in Philadelphia in 1731. His sons migrated south to Cleveland County, North Carolina, to farm.

Gaffney, where part of Cash's family had lived since the early eighteenth century, was a typical mill town in the South Carolina piedmont. The family lived on Railroad Avenue, about midway between the mill and the rows of identical cottages occupied by the factory hands; from the beginning of his life, Cash was exposed to the difficulties of life for underpaid poor white laborers. The horrid working conditions for poor whites in the 1920s and 1930s could not have failed to remind mill hands of the parallels between their plight and that of black slaves. As James Roark has pointed out, the economic decline of the white Southern worker after the Civil War left them as a class almost as destitute as blacks. "Made up of new men, this elite had not the slightest intention of enshrining the Old South in a textile mill," Roark writes. "The industrialists' chief resemblance to the ante-bellum planter class lay in their willingness to squeeze labor until labor bled. By the end of the century the number of white sharecroppers approached that of black sharecroppers, and it prove difficult to distinguish the treatment of white and black workers" (qtd. in Eagles, 98).

In other words, wealthy plantation and textile magnates had a vested interested in keeping poor whites and blacks involved in a race war; white and black laborers, after all, had more in common economically with each other than with their overseers, and perpetuating racial discord served to distract workers from the economic disparities between workers and their bosses. It was the investment in racist discourse, then, that kept poor whites invested in a system that exploited them as well as it exploited blacks, and left racial solidarity as a cultural mask covering up economic inequities.

Throughout *The Mind of the South*, Cash links poor whites to blacks in the mistreatment they suffered at the hands of their masters. If blacks suffered the brand during slavery, white workers in the modern era were being "made into a sort of automaton, to be stood over by a taskmaster with a stop-watch in his hand . . . to be everlastingly hazed on to greater exertion by curt commands and sneers, and to have to stand periodically and take a dressing down with a white face, just as though one were a nigger, under the ever-present threat of being summarily dismissed" (353). Cash was hardly alone in this conflation of race and class; although she was far more concerned with issues of race than class, Lillian Smith also wrote piercingly of the political rhetoric that masked its own racism behind appeals to white brotherhood. In a letter to Hoke Norris, the editor of the *Chicago Sun-Times*, Smith wrote that poor whites did not hate blacks so much as "they hate us: they hate the upper-class whites of the South who fed them the drug of 'whiteness' until they destroyed themselves spiritually. They hate us because they, too, are segregated: segregated as rigidly socially from the Big Wheels and their families as are Negroes. This never-talked-about segregation which must be like a white fog around poor whites is the thing that makes them hate Negroes with a psychotic violence; it isn't their competition for jobs— that is a rational fear; this other thing is deep, sick, psychotic" (Loveland, 240).

Cash, to be sure, recognized this psychotic link between political rhetoric and race-baiting. As Daniel Singal has observed, Cash's work dealt a "knockout blow" to the cavalier myth of the "yeoman" farmer as some form of medieval knight whose very destitution receded in the shadow of racial superiority: "The final impression left was not that of a civilized society, but rather one governed, to use Cash's own phrase, by a 'savage ideal' " (373). Indeed, the reason some contemporary critics absolve Cash of his racial rhetoric is because he spreads out his vitriol so evenly among all races and classes. He uses some of his most florid prose to paint the class he in many ways held most dear: poor whites. "By 1900 the cotton-mill worker was a pretty distinct physical type in the South; a type in some respects perhaps even inferior to the old poor white, which in general had been his to begin with," Cash writes. "A dead-white skin, a sunken chest, and stooping shoulders were the earmarks of the breed. Chinless faces, microcephalic foreheads, rabbit teeth, gog-

gling dead-fish eyes, rickety limbs, and stunted bodies abounded—
over and beyond the limit of their prevalence in the countryside. The
women were characteristically stringy-haired and limp of breast at
twenty, and shrunken hags at thirty or forty" (204).

This language comes more from Erskine Caldwell than from Faulkner, although by this time caricatures of poor whites had become a sta-
ple of Southern fiction. As Sylvia Jenkins Cook has written in her study
From Tobacco Road to Route 66: The Southern Poor White in Fiction, poor
whites became for many writers of the early twentieth century physical
embodiments of Southern economic hardship:

> The grotesque reputation of the poor white suited neither the pro-
> ponents of the New South nor the sentimentalists of the Old, but
> in the twentieth century his propensities for extreme behavior and
> shocking conditions were no longer such obstacles. The 1920s and
> 30s revival of southern fiction was accompanied by a national in-
> terest in the possibilities of an American radical literature and also
> an expansion of documentary techniques that grew concomitantly
> with the extraordinary experiences of the depression. All of these
> focused interest once again on the poor white and the challenge he
> presented to conventional ways of viewing southern society and
> culture. (56)

For Cash the writer, poor whites occupied a position also long held by
blacks: as metaphors for the damage done by a highly destructive economic system, be it based on cotton and slave labor or textiles and poor
white labor. Indeed, Cash's text is at its most lucid and insightful as it
documents the cultural history that allowed such class exploitation to
exist. In a newspaper article entitled "North Carolina Faces the Facts,"
published August 29, 1935, in the *Baltimore Evening Sun,* Cash made what
was at the time a dramatic gesture against the common thinking of the
time. "The fact is overwhelmingly plain," he wrote. "The hands which
actually manipulated rope and trigger at Louisburg may very well have
been those of degraded poor whites. The hands which actually manip-
ulate rope and trigger—or kerosene can and brand—in Southern
lynchings generally are very often those of degraded poor whites,
though not always. But the force which really lynched at Louisburg—
the force which really lynches everywhere in the South—was and is the
force of public opinion. And when one says public opinion, one shifts
the ultimate responsibility straight back upon the 'best people'—the ruling class" (Joseph Morrison, 217).[7]

Cash's examination of the "force" of public opinion is similar in kind to the equally subtle thinking found in Charles Chesnutt's landmark novel *The Marrow of Tradition*, published forty years beforehand. Describing a plot to exterminate blacks from a North Carolina town, Chesnutt wrote that

> public sentiment all over the country became every day more favorable to the views of the conspirators. The nation was rushing forward with giant strides toward colossal wealth and world-domination, before the exigencies of which mere abstract ethical theories must not be permitted to stand. The same argument that justified the conquest of an inferior nation could not be denied to those who sought the suppression of an inferior race. In the South, an obscure jealousy of the negro's progress, an obscure fear of the very equality so jealously denied, furnished a rich soil for successful agitation. Statistics of crime, ingeniously manipulated, were made to present a fearful showing against the negro. Vital statistics were made to prove that he had degenerated from an imaginary standard of physical excellence which had existed under the benign influence of slavery. Constant lynchings emphasized his impotence, and bred everywhere a growing contempt for his rights. (238)

As Anne Goodwyn Jones has pointed out in her perceptive essay "The Cash Nexus," Cash's position also follows Antonio Gramsci's notion of the formation of political hegemony. Poor whites carried out acts of violence against blacks because, invested in a myth of racial solidarity, they perceived blacks as both an economic and a cultural enemy. Wealthy whites, both Cash and Gramsci knew, were ultimately the ones who benefited from this war; poor whites, in other words, carried out campaigns of racial terror as gestures of solidarity with them. During Reconstruction "the most superior men, with the exception of an occasional Robert E. Lee or Benjamin H. Hill, seeing their late slave strutting about full of grotesque assertions, cheap whiskey, and lying dreams, feeling his elbow in their ribs, hearing his guffaw in high places, came increasingly to feel toward him very much as any cracker felt; felt increasingly under the sway of the same hunger to have their hands on him, and ease the intolerable agony of anger and fear and shaken pride in his screams" (116–17).

Cash, then, is at once aware of his own relative position of vulnerability to the economic power of the South's elite, and aware of his own capacity to displace rage onto the only class that lies below him, blacks.[8] Cash sees the position of the poor white as both a victim of physical and economic violence and as a channel through which racial violence flows. Not only do the owners of the "gentle houses" live on the distressed labor of their white employees, they use poor whites to physically enforce racial fear. The racial rhetoric of white demagogues received some of Cash's sharpest barbs. Blacks are the objects of a rage that even the South's most cherished self-perception—gentility—could not control. There are a number of possible readings of this, of course: did blacks, by their very "blackness," somehow "cause" this rage, which would have otherwise gone unexperienced and therefore unexpressed? That certainly seems to be the argument of writers like Dixon. But as Lillian Smith so insightfully showed in her 1944 novel *Strange Fruit*, such finger-pointing was inevitably transparent. In the novel, the local newspaper editor, Prentiss Reid, muses over the lynching of a black man who had been (falsely) accused of killing the novel's main character, Tracy Deen:

Prentiss Reid lit another cigarette; stared into the wall, shrugged, wrote rapidly for a few minutes.

". . . but what's done now is done. Bad, yes. Lawlessness and violence are always bad. And this particular form smacks of the Dark Ages. It hurts business, it hurts the town, it hurts the county, it hurts everybody in it. But it's time now to get our minds on our work, go back to our jobs, quit this talking. Those who participated in the lynching were a lawless bunch of hoodlums. We don't know who they are. They ought to be punished. But who are they? No one seems to know. A prominent white citizen was killed. Justice had to be satisfied. The case should have been carried to the courts. This black should have been brought to trial. Every law-abiding citizen believes that. But the war sent back a new kind of Negro whom the South doesn't like. And Northern labor agents have made things worse with promises they have no intention of keeping. All Northern industry will do is lure our black folks away and when they no longer need them, leave the simple creatures to starve. There won't be any back-door handouts in Chicago, either—as our colored folks will soon find out. These efforts to interfere with our Southern way of doing things have made some folks nervous, too quick on the trigger. And it has made the black man forget his place. The South will never let him forget that. As long as the North interferes in our affairs, ignorant hoodlums down here will interfere with the law." (367)

Prentiss Reid blames the lynching not on Southern racism but on the "new kind of Negro"—one who learned something of the world while fighting in First World War—and the Northern industrialists who caused Southern labor strife because they offered blacks better wages and working conditions. Moreover, the repetition of the notion that "we don't know who they are" is precisely what Smith and Cash were writing against. Whites in positions of power—particularly in small towns—could hardly have not known who the lynchers were. More important, as Cash points out, powerful whites had very tangible things to gain from such violence: if poor whites carried out campaigns of terror against blacks, it only served to distract them from the economic realities that sapped their wallets, if not their sense of racial identity.

In an early draft of *Mind* Cash had included a paragraph that read: "Given their enormous power over the minds of the common people, I do not believe there has been a single ten-year period since 1910 in which, if the master group of every local area in the South or even the master group of each state as a whole had set themselves to the purpose, lynching could not have been fully extinguished in the entire region" (Joseph Morrison, 102). His published version is consistently astute in its dissection of the rhetoric that bound poor whites to rich whites despite the deep economic disparity between them. "As we know, race feeling had nothing directly to do with the tendency to mob action in the Old South," Cash writes in *Mind*. "So long as the Negro had been property, worth from five hundred dollars on up, he had been taboo—safer from rope and faggot than any common white man, and perhaps even safer than his master himself. But with the abolition of legal slavery his immunity vanished. The economic interest of his former protectors, the master class, now stood the other way about—required that he should be promptly confirmed in his ancient docility. And so the road stood all but wide open to the ignoble hate and cruel itch to take him in hand which for so long had been festering impotently in the poor whites" (116).

Racial violence, then, and lynching in particular, became a way of both enforcing class distinctions and creating the image of a unified sense of white authority. "Publicly resolving the race, gender, and class ambiguities at the very center of the culture of segregation, spectacle lynchings brutally conjured a collective, all-powerful whiteness ever as they made the color line seem modern, civilized, and sane," Grace Elizabeth Hale writes. "Spectacle lynchings were about making racial difference in the new South, about ensuring the separation of all southern life into whiteness and blackness even as the very material things that made up southern life were rapidly changing" (203).

Early on in *The Mind of the South*, Cash describes the roots of the psychosocial bond between rich and poor whites, the mythology that grew up around this relationship, and the economic disparities that this mythology masked:

> If the plantation had introduced distinctions of wealth and rank among the men of the old backcountry, and, in doing so, had perhaps offended against the ego of the common white, it had also, you will remember, introduced that other vastly ego-warming and ego-expanding distinction between the white man and the black. Robbing him and degrading in so many ways, it yet, by singular irony, had simultaneously elevated this common white to a position comparable to that of, say, the Doric knight of ancient Sparta. Not only was he not exploited directly, he was himself made by extension a member of the dominant class—was lodged solidly on a tremendous superiority, which, however much the blacks in the "big house" might sneer at him, and however much their masters might privately agree with them, he could never publicly lose. Come what might, he would always be a white man. And before this vast and capacious distinction, all others were foreshortened, dwarfed, and all but obliterated. (40–41)

This is the class-aware rhetoric for which Cash has always been justly admired. Like Lillian Smith, he was able, through his rhetoric, to capture the visceral, "obliterating" racial rage that was such a recognizable part of the Southern mind. But there is more to it than that. Bertram Wyatt-Brown writes that Cash's "obsession with Nazi encroachments was part of the problem—a projection of his own feelings of violence that had to be exorcised or transferred" (in Escott, 50). Toward the end of his life, Clayton notes, Cash became increasingly obsessed with Hitler and "would begin to scream epithets: Hitler was a madman, a maniac, a Ku Kluxer, white trash" (156). The rage of the white supremacist, then, either at home or abroad, came to represent something viscerally terrifying to Cash, perhaps as much from his own sense of failed masculinity as anything else. But his conflation of poor whites with blacks must be read as a personal connection between his own humble heritage and that of the blacks around him.

As two biographies and several biographical essays have indicated, Cash was predisposed to bouts of depression that may have initially stemmed from repressed rage; neglected by his father, he was also frequently mocked by schoolmates as a weakling, an oddball, or, worse, an intellectual. "Although violence was an objective fact of Southern life, Cash gave it such prominence because of his own personal perspective," Bertram Wyatt-Brown writes. "He knew exactly the consequences of being the object of ridicule. As a child he had experienced the ridicule of his peers. Cursed with a squint from nearsightedness, the bespectacled boy was mocked by his classmates. Once he ran home, defeated, only to be told by his father in good Southern fashion to go back and 'act like a man'" (in Escott, 60). If William Alexander Percy's own childhood neglect turned to a deep melancholia, Cash's edged into anger; emotional emptiness that manifested itself as depression in one man became rage in another. Certainly Cash had a far more mercurial and self-destructive emotional life than Percy, whose own family was famous for its depressions and suicides. For both men, in short, blacks became a frequent repository for their emotional turns of mind. Percy most commonly sentimentalized blacks, particularly the children and women who raised him. Cash, even as he acknowledged the troubling similarities between his own heritage and that of blacks, more often slipped into images of threat and violence.

Cash was fourteen when the First World War began, and he followed as his father went to work in cantonments from Sparrows Point, Maryland, to Jacksonville, Florida. "His first exploration beyond the South brought him the chance, which he seized without question, of bravely asserting the white supremacy on which he had been raised," Joseph Morrison writes. Once, on a railroad coach, "a Negro ventured to sit down next to him, whereupon the intruder got the then-conventional Southern warning to find another seat because Wilbur Cash was not about to 'sit with a nigger'" (21). Indeed, the young Cash was not without his racial pride; particularly early in his life, he liked to dwell on his "Irishness." His fellow newspaper reporter Cameron Shipp recalled Cash "in a moment of happy lubricity rising from his bleacher seat at a Wake Forest football game, announcing himself a descendant of the red Irish kings, and challenging the world to mortal combat" (Joseph Morrison, 9).

Cash briefly attended South Carolina's Wofford College, then dropped out. He then attended Valparaiso University in northern Indiana, which during the early 1920s was to earn international notoriety as the proposed Ku Klux Klan University, but he again dropped out after a semester. Finally, he entered Dixon's alma mater, North Carolina's Wake Forest College. As a student there, "he was as indolent a student as was ever seen, unkempt, usually careless of dress, with all the personal habits usually assumed by the nonconformist and bohemian." When he quit the football team after a brief tryout, he was mocked in the school newspaper: "The gentleman states he is a poet by birth, a dreamer by nature, and a loafer by force of habit. He feared that the rough and tumble game and the violent contact with other members of his race would darken his bright, cheerful view of life. In this case, the poet claims that he would no longer be able to write, with beautiful simplicity, his touching verses on love, maidens, and pastures green. Thus was a good man lost to the cause." His yearbook photo was accompanied by the words "While not the friendliest fellow in college, 'Sleepy' is important in the social life of his chums here" (Joseph Morrison, 30, 34; Clayton, 29).

While a college student, Cash was "probably a racial paternalist," Clayton writes. In an editorial for the Wake Forest *Old Gold and Black*, he advised blacks—few of whom would come across his paper—to avoid the ideas of W. E. B. Du Bois, "whose policy is to wage bitter and aggressive war against the White race and their principles." The editorial stressed that blacks would be given the vote "in time" but should remember that whites do "not intend for political equality to pave the way for social equality" (39). Later, as editor of the twice-weekly *Cleveland (N.C.) Press*, Cash occasionally lapsed into the standard racist rhetoric of many Southern newspapers. He once reported on a black woman who had been arrested and charged with setting fire to the house where her husband slept after they'd quarreled violently. "Minnie Morrow, black, is kind of unfriendly if you get her roiled," Cash wrote. "Elegant funerals are all right, provided—well, it depends on whose funeral it is. No. Minnie ain't got none of the jazz black in her. She ain't no Harlem nigger, either" (Clayton, 73).[9] His usual outrage at racist political rhetoric also occasionally left him; he once reported on a Cole Blease rally: "The picture of black men crowding white women from the street and wantonly insulting them stirred the crowd's fire, and the Senator's promise that such activities in his own state would be greeted by men 'who know how to tie a rope to a tree and to the other end, too' brought laughter and whoops" (Clayton, 74).

But it should not be forgotten that Cash's journalistic instincts most frequently ran to sharp outrage over the conditions under which blacks as well as whites were forced to live; this instinct was to some degree in keeping with progressive journalism of the time. The *Charlotte News* took on the Klan in a number of articles and editorials in the mid-1930s. "Karolina Klan plan to ride tonight, burning crosses, and intimidating innocent blacks" ran one headline in August 1936; in an editorial four years later, the paper called the KKK a "sadistic gang of masked hoodlums." Cash himself frequently wrote progressively about matters of race. As a book critic he encouraged readers to explore the work of Langston Hughes, Claude McKay, Jean Toomer, Countee Cullen, and James Weldon Johnson. As a reporter he wrote on January 15, 1939, of the horrid conditions tuberculosis patients of both races had to live in at the local sanitarium. Thirty-three blacks, many of them waiting to die, shared a single bathroom. Worse, in the tiny isolation ward, "they put the far-gone cases there either to take a change for the better or to die— usually to die. If they die audibly, and they do die audibly nearly always, the other patients hear the rattling gasps, their moans and their mutterings. Most of them see their contorted faces and bodies as they struggle for their last precious breath. The bodies of the dead must be carried out under the eyes of the whole ward. . . . Every year an appalling number of blacks is literally condemned to death by the fact that the hospital has no way to take care of them" (Clayton, 134, 142).

About this time, Cash's conflicted notions of race were subsumed by a more pressing, personal issue: sexuality and a severe attendant anxiety. Due in part to chronic physical ailments that plagued him from early adolescence, including, possibly, hyperthyroidism, the college-aged Cash was known to suffer spasms of choking and at Wake Forest had to wear his collar open because of an incipient goiter. "He was more touchy now, more emotional, apt on occasion to burst into tears," writes Joseph Morrison. "Out of his physical difficulty arose a fear that also plagued him throughout his adult life and that he voiced to a college mate: that he was becoming sexually impotent" (35).

Years of residence at home, Wyatt-Brown writes, along with "oedipal resentment of his unintellectual father and overdependence on his mother, prolonged virginity and late marriage had drastically narrowed the range of his encounters with women." In his early twenties, sexual impotence became, for Cash, an emblem of self-loathing and rage that trickled into much of his later writing. After an abortive year at Wake Forest Law School, Cash accepted a position teaching English at Georgetown College in Kentucky, where he suffered a nervous breakdown, possibly as a result of sexual frustration over a freshman in his class named Peggy Ann. At the end of the school year, Cash and Peggy, an aspiring actress, went for a picnic and moved to consummate their long flirtation. "He had 'thoroughly titillated' her and had her 'panting' for the final act," according to Catherine Grantham (later Rogers), a friend of Cash's. But the young suitor could not perform the final deed (in Eagles, 160). "The failed Don Juan would never be the same again," Clayton writes.

> That disastrous evening haunted him for years; he never com-
> pletely recovered his confidence with women or in himself. For
> years he was plagued by the terrifying fear that his "nervous con-
> dition" was far more serious than anybody knew, that he was sex-
> ually impotent.
> One could hardly imagine a more crushing blow to Cash's sen-
> sitive, romantic psyche. Moreover, in the South, impotence was not
> just a problem, it was an utter disgrace. Someone who was impo-
> tent was not a man. Once the word got out, his impotence might
> even be talked about in polite circles. And in those places where
> menfolk gathered, sexual prowess (admittedly always exaggerated)
> was the mark of a true man. Every Southern boy, even Baptist
> boys, had heard crude jokes and stories about men who could not
> satisfy their women. A disappointed newlywed could count on
> everyone's sympathy, including that of the divorce court judge,
> should her husband prove incapable of performing sexually. So
> great was Cash's shame that he suffered an "incipient nervous
> breakdown." (46)

When he later told his friend Catherine Grantham about the incident, Cash burst into tears; Grantham, however, did not indulge him. "You come out here acting the crucified Christ and treating me as an all-understanding Madonna," she said. "Well, you ain't and I ain't." Despite his woeful rhetoric, she accused Cash of hiding behind the "misogyny" of Mencken, the "virgin worship" of Henry Adams, and the courtly love traditions celebrated by James Branch Cabell. "Strip away the rhyth-mical and high falutin' prose," she told him, and he was "just another sentimental Victorian male, strictly dividing females into just two classes —the all-good and the all-bad and considering only the first class as that from which a self-respecting male could choose a wife." His "crippling" ideas of "honor," she said, would not allow him to "violate the purity" of Peggy Ann (Bertram Wyatt-Brown, in Eagles, 160; Clayton, 46).[10]

By his midtwenties, Cash had begun consulting a urologist in Char-lotte, who found certain "imbalances" in Cash's internal secretions.

Threatened with another "complete nervous collapse," Cash went abroad in 1927, only to return a year later to plead his case to "the only girl" he would ever marry, Peggy Ann, who once again turned him down. "He well knew that his 'first failure' with her would always stand between them," Joseph Morrison writes. "He should have known, however, that his particular brand of woman worship, in which premarital sex with 'decent' women is subconsciously taboo, was the probable cause of that 'first failure.' Instead, he allowed the memory to haunt him" (Joseph Morrison, 46).[11]

The health problems that shadowed Cash were reflected in the terrible trouble he had finishing the manuscript for *The Mind of the South*. He first began speaking of the "mind of the South" during late-night bull sessions at Wake Forest; in any case, Joseph Morrison assures us, he used the expression "well before" Vernon L. Parrington, who used it to open volume 2 of *Main Currents in American Thought*, specifically *The Romantic Revolution in America, 1800–1860* in 1926 (27).[12] H. L. Mencken agreed to publish a magazine-length version of *Mind* in 1929; it was the first of several pieces he would publish, and because the Knopfs shared an office space with Mencken, it was not long before Blanche Knopf invited Cash to send in an outline and a sample chapter. Cash sent a six-page, single-spaced letter outlining the book to the Chapel Hill sociologist Howard Odum, saying, "I want to go into the psychology of the cotton-mill hand, the baron. . . . I'm much interested in the reasons for the prevalence of Ku Kluckery. And I'm even interested in the effect that the negro has had on the thinking of the white man in the South" (Joseph Morrison, 49).

In March 1930, Cash wrote a letter to Mrs. Knopf, laying out his plans. "My thesis is that the Southern Mind represents a very definite culture, or attitude towards life, a heritage, primarily, from the Old South, but greatly modified and extended by conscious and unconscious efforts over the last hundred years to protect itself from the encroachments of three hostile factors: the Yankee Mind, the Modern Mind, and the Negro," he wrote. "In other words, it is a combination of certain orthodoxies and a defense mechanism. On that basis, it seems to me that this book ought probably to fall into some such division as this: Introduction, The Mind of the Old South, The South and the Yankee Mind, the South and the Modern Mind, Conclusion" (Joseph Morrison, 52). It is worth noting that from the outset Cash planned to write about "the Negro," but he never intended to write about a Negro "mind."

But that same spring, Cash suffered a nervous collapse and was or-

RACE, SEX, AND SADISM

dered by doctors, as he recalled later to the Guggenheim Foundation, "to refrain completely from writing and study of any kind, and, indeed, even from reading. For the next two years, these doctors kept me out-doors—riding a bicycle over the countryside, walking, swimming, and cutting wood" (Joseph Morrison, 49, 52).[13] He started the year 1932 by going to urologists at Johns Hopkins Hospital. "At that time," Morrison writes, "the connection between endocrine and psychological disorders was not generally understood. A quarter century after the author's death, his urologist, Dr. Claude B. Squires, stated flatly that had Cash been in the hands of the right psychiatrist during the 1930s, when he suffered in-termittent spells of depression, he would have survived into ripe old age" (56).

Indeed, even with a long string of newspaper pieces published in the *Baltimore Evening Sun*, a series of magazine pieces accepted by Mencken, and the continued interest of the Knopfs in his writing career, Cash could not push through with his book because of his health difficulties, both physical and psychological. In 1932, he destroyed a 60,000–word manuscript and scrapped another version three years later. The first work that would later evolve into *Mind of the South* appeared in the *American Mercury* in May 1935, under the heading "Genesis of the Southern Cracker." Eight months later he forwarded 306 manuscript pages to the Knopfs, promising to complete another 200 pages shortly; ultimately, the book was to spin out to 810 pages. The Knopfs accepted the manu-script on March 2 and agreed to an advance of $250, with $50 at the contract's signing and $50 a month for four months.

A second segment, "The Reign of the Commonplace," appeared in the same fall 1936 issue of Lillian Smith's magazine *Pseudopodia* in which she lambasted Margaret Mitchell's newly published *Gone with the Wind*. Cash's piece was almost word-for-word identical to a section of the book chapter "Of the Frontier the Yankee Made"; an editor's note to the piece said the book would be out by 1937. This was not to be. Cash went back to writing editorials and book reviews for the *Charlotte News*, focusing on foreign affairs, particularly the Nazi war machine. By the fall of 1937, at the age of thirty-seven, he had become a full-time editorial writer for the *News* but was still living at home with his parents. He con-tinued to work on the book; by mid-July 1939, he had cut nearly 15,000 words from the manuscript during four revisions. More delays followed. On September 1, with Hitler launching his blitzkrieg against Poland, Cash penned a long editorial entitled "A Fanatic Menaces Civilization"; later, in a book-page column, he wrote, "I should not like to be a Jew just now, for to be a Jew is a hard thing in this present world. But the thing I should dislike most of all is to be a German and have been exposed to living in the fanatically distorted world Adolf Hitler has made for the moulding of German minds" (Joseph Morrison, 95).[14]

Cash finally delivered the manuscript on August 1. Upon its arrival, Alfred Knopf thanked Cash for his telegram, his letter, "and, God be praised, the manuscript." The book was finally published on February 10, 1941 (Joseph Morrison, 100).

In the meantime, Cash had, in the spring of 1938, met Mary Ross Northrop, a sometime contributor to the *News* book page, who later worked on the Federal Writers Project volume, *These Are Our Lives*, published by the University of North Carolina Press in 1939. She laughingly told her mother the next day that "[l]ast night I met a fat country boy I'm going to marry." Two years later, on Christmas Eve 1940, the two were married; they used their friend Frank McCleneghan's SAE fraternity ring for the ceremony. Cash's impotence apparently was not an issue during his brief marriage (Joseph Morrison, 83, 106, 109).

The publication of *The Mind of the South*, and Cash's marriage to Mary, represented what may have been Cash's happiest days, but they were not to last. He was awarded a $2,000 Guggenheim Fellowship to write a novel, and he decided to take Mary to Mexico to write it. They left North Carolina in May 1941 and stopped off in Texas, where he was to give the commencement address at the state university. On the train from New Orleans to Texas, Cash had a strange bout of anger, stamping a newspaper on the floor and biting his fists. He could not remember what had caused it, but it made Mary nervous.[15]

On the night of June 30, 1941, now in a Mexico City apartment, Cash asked Mary if she could hear voices outside their bedroom. He was afraid, he said, that Nazis were planning to kill one or both of them. It was "a nightmarish moment in which she thought the trouble was with her, not Cash, and not until her husband began pushing furniture against the locked door did she realize that the 'voices' were all in his mind." Later that same evening, Cash grabbed a kitchen knife, before Mary finally calmed him down enough for bed. Once there, Cash picked up a Bible and said to his wife, "Read Ecclesiastes, baby."

The next morning, Mary went upstairs to seek help from some San Antonio people she'd befriended and to ask for advice about psychiatrists and to use their phone; Cash would not let her use their own, fearing it was tapped. When Mary came back to their room, Cash had disappeared. He returned several hours later ashen, shaken, and delusional, having placed all their papers and money in a safe deposit box to secure them from "Nazis." Mary took him to the doctor's office by 2 P.M., but Cash vehemently refused treatment, jerking his arm away from a hypodermic needle. When he finally submitted, he told his wife he was sure the needle contained "poison." Later that night, Cash demanded that he and Mary leave their apartment for a hotel for safety and made her lie on the floor of the taxicab because he feared her red hat would be too visible. After examining four different hotels, Cash finally settled on the Geneva, where he cowered, terrified, in a corner of their room and would not let Mary use the phone, which he was convinced had been tapped. Terrified, Mary ran off to find Ben F. Meyer, the Associated Press correspondent whom she knew; when they returned, Cash had again disappeared. Meyer called the police, who from 4 to 10 P.M. searched the city's hotels. They finally discovered that Cash had taken a room in the Reforma. When they entered his room, they found him hanging by a necktie from bathroom door. He had been dead for several hours. The entire period of delusions lasted just twenty-four hours.

With Cash's death in mind, V. O. Key's 1947 study *Southern Politics in State and Nation* noted that "a depressingly high rate of self-destruction prevails among those who ponder about the South and put down their reflections in books. A fatal frustration seems to come from the struggle to find a way through the unfathomable maze formed by tradition, caste, race, poverty" (664).[16] Indeed, coming less than a year after his marriage, the receipt of a long-desired Guggenheim Fellowship, and the publication of a book he had spent more than ten years writing, the precipitous violence of Cash's death continues to intrigue scholars and biographers to this day. After a life of chronic physical and psychological torment, it has been conjectured, Cash seemed toward the end of his life to have achieved a certain stability; indeed, he had for the first time conquered the two most troubling demons of his adult life, sexual impotence and authorial obscurity.

Some have linked his death to alcoholism, others to the final chapter in a frequently debilitating, mercurial psyche. But a different reading of Cash's death would fit more closely with an examination of his life and close reading of his language. In a newspaper editorial he wrote about lynching, entitled "North Carolina Faces the Facts," Cash concluded with the lines: "I have no illusions. Knowing the tremendous compulsives back of the will to lynching in high and low, I think it is going to be a long time yet before the practice is effectually stamped out in the South." What I find interesting here is the "tremendous compulsiveness" Cash claims is at the "back of the will to lynching." "Compulsiveness" is not a political category, it is an emotional one; saying that lynching is somehow "compulsive" speaks not only to the visceral power such an emblem of white violence has, but also to the eerie allure such violence had for Cash. Even as he excoriated post-Reconstruction era whites for their repeated trips to the hanging tree, his language gives him away as someone fascinated by the violence, intrigued by the destructive power of such atrocities.

Richard King has written compellingly that Cash may have taken on issues of violence and "a cultural regressiveness bordering on a death wish" in order to "master" them. In the end, in a tragic irony, he failed (159).[17] To my mind, Cash's delusions about Nazis, his anxieties about married life, and, most importantly, his choice of suicide—by self-lynching—make a tragic kind of sense given the life that he had experienced and the language that he used to describe it.

For a writer plainly disgusted with the forces that contributed to the South's history of racial violence, Cash nonetheless extended many of the metaphors of old-style Southern racism he undoubtedly hoped to erode. In other words, he was never able to throw off completely the overt racism that had seeped into him since birth; his rhetoric often ran to the flamboyantly, often operatically violent. "A nigger, for example, is either a vile clown or an amiable Uncle Tom," he wrote in the 1929 magazine version of *The Mind of the South*. "If he insists on upsetting things by being something else, he passes, like Elijah, in a chariot of fire, and is wafted to his reward on wings of kerosene" (qtd. in Joseph Morrison, 193). There is irony in the tone here, certainly, and there is a soaring, fictive imagination. But there is something more. There is a macabre engagement with graphic racial violence that marks much of Cash's writing. Early on in *The Mind of the South*, Cash describes the plight of slaves before the Civil War:

> The black man occupied the position of a mere domestic animal, without will or right of his own. The lash lurked always in the background. Its open crackle could often be heard where field hands were quartered. Into the gentlest houses drifted now and then the sound of dragging chains and shackles, the bay of hounds, the report of pistols on the trail of the runaway. And, as the advertisements of the time incontestably prove, mutilation and the mark of the branding iron were pretty common. Just as plain was the fact

RACE, SEX, AND SADISM

that the institution was brutalizing—to white men. Virtually unlimited power acted inevitably to call up, in the coarser sort of master, that sadism which lies concealed in the depths of universal human nature—bred angry impatience and a taste for cruelty for its own sake, with a strength that neither the kindliness I have so often referred to (it continued frequently to exist unimpaired side by side, and in the same man, with this other) nor notions of honor could effectually restrain. And in the common whites it bred a savage and ignoble hate for the Negro, which required only opportunity to break forth in relentless ferocity; for all their rage against the "white trash" epithet concentrated itself on him rather than on the planters. There it stood, then—terrible, revolting, serving as the very school of violence, and lending mordant point to the most hysterical outcries of the Yankee. But the South could not and must not admit it, of course. It must prettify the institution and its own reactions, must begin to boast of its own Great Heart. (85–86)

For Cash, vivid descriptions of racial violence take on an erotic edge, as if the sadism he is describing provides him with his own sexual release. He seems to seek out scenes of graphic violence behind closed doors, both in slave quarters and in the "gentlest houses." His rhetoric seems inescapably tied to erotic fascination, as if his own desire to be on either side of the whip has him transfixed. Cash calls the Gothic world of "chains and shackles," where white men develop a "taste for cruelty for its own sake," a reflection of a "universal" sadism; more accurately, this sadism can be described as Cash's own. In this passage, Cash imagines himself as both the whipper and the whipped. His own history of self-loathing and sexual ambivalence made him at once attracted and repulsed by the violence he sees. He imagines himself being savaged at the same time that he imagines finding release in sadism.

"There they stood, behind the white man's houses, half-hidden in the daytime, dark, mysterious, and ominous in the nighttime," Cash writes. "Out of them the jungle beat of drums; the wild chanting gibberish of nameless congregations packed in unlighted halls; the rhythmic swell of jazz and stomping feet in 'piccolo houses' . . . high floating laughter; sudden screams, rising swiftly from the void and falling abruptly back to it again—all these sometimes rolled up to the white man's ears as he sat with his family in the evening, or snapped him to nightmarish awakening as he slept in the ghostly hours" (326). If there is some of William Alexander Percy in this passage, in the awkward admiration for unselfconscious expression, there is also visceral fear that is more emblematically Cash's own. The jungle drums and wild chants that wake a peaceful white family is not an image that one would find in *Lanterns on the Levee*; Cash here is plainly terrified of the sexually charged, racial unknown.

If such passages are the only pass Cash made at understanding black life—if the only contact with them gives rise to terror—it is easy to see how he can make the jump to physical abstraction when describing the physical violence to which blacks were subjected. Nell Painter links Cash's eroticization of blacks to Freud's essay "On the Universal Tendency to Debasement in the Sphere of Love," in which the psychoanalyst wrote that men often can only become sexually aroused by women of a lower class: "Where such men love they have no desire and where they desire they have no love." Behind the widespread practice of middle- and upper-class men's taking working-class mistresses, Freud wrote, lies a deep-seated feeling that sex is degrading and polluting (in Escott, 95).[18]

Blacks, Cash seems to say, offer white men a glimpse of their own vulnerability, much the way women do. This vulnerability, which in women leads directly to the "rape complex," leads in race relations to what is essentially a "slave complex," an unconscious dread that rich whites are themselves slaves to a Yankee economy and, more viscerally, poor whites are slaves to rich whites. "The rape complex pointed to a proud, boasting, white anxiety-ridden male dominated culture that subconsciously regarded itself as feminine which, from the perspective of the times, meant an inferior, weak culture always in danger of being thrown on its back and ravished," Bruce Clayton writes. "Thus did Cash employ a daring sexual argument, rich in symbols and stunning metaphors, that, ironically and quite unintentionally, re-expressed racist myths and stereotypes" (qtd. in Eagles, 17). Savaging a black body becomes, therefore, a release of the rage and self-loathing that has no other outlet. For someone like Cash, who had himself been beaten up as an alienated, awkward boy, this dynamic takes on extra energy. In "The War in the South," a magazine piece written for Mencken in February 1930, Cash describes a Southern mind that sounds exactly like a mind capable of beating up an introspective boy: "Add something of bewilderment, something more of fear, count in the Southern capacity for florid fancy, and you have the complex which conjures up a Red Peril, which beholds a foe, not to be tolerated, not to be treated with, but to be stamped out, extirpated, without quarter and without squeamishness" (qtd. in Joseph Morrison, 206). It follows that if Cash was aware of the inappropriate physical damage done to blacks, he must at some level have relished the idea of having bodies to which even he could deliver blows. "In aberrant cultural situations the cultural principle in the individual, the super-ego, is more than normally driven by aggressive impulses, guilt (aggression against the self), and over-idealizations," writes Richard King. "Such a 'culture of melancholy' becomes death-dealing: 'the super-ego reveals itself as a pure culture of the death instincts, to the point of suicide.' Rather than enforcing the binding power of Eros, guilt unravels the collective and individual" (17).

At least as a purveyor of the white Southern "mind," Cash certainly was able to see these same impulses in the whites around him. Early on in *The Mind of the South*, Cash describes the admiration young boys in the post-Reconstruction South felt for men "pointed out as having slain five or eight or thirteen Negroes" who still "walked about free." "These lads," Cash wrote, "inevitably tended to see such a scoundrel very much as he saw himself: as a gorgeous *beau sabreur*, hardly less splendid than the most magnificent cavalry captain" (126). If we take a "gorgeous *beau sabreur*" to mean a man who grandly and unflinchingly impales people with his saber, we can glimpse an image of sentimentalized racial violence that is erotic and even homoerotic. In this example, killing Negroes is equated with an ability to penetrate others' bodies, which, at least until the last year of his life, Cash was quite literally unable to do. Indeed, this gives us another way of reading Cash's most famous dictum about the way "Negro entered into white man as profoundly as white man entered into Negro—subtly influencing every gesture, every word, every emotion and idea, every attitude." The notion of a white man "entering" a Negro may be the perfect emblem for Cash; stabbing a Negro with a sword is a way to penetrate the Negro's body and still maintain white sexual and social propriety. Even the notion of men "walking about free" after their murderous exploits seems to speak to this; men who were potently able to perform their masculine duties, who were able to satisfy masculine ideals of what was expected of them, were able to walk about free of the self-consciousness and self-loathing of the man who was impotent. As a man who was physically unable to take his own saber from its scabbard, Cash's admiration of virility is the logical undergirding of such rhetoric.

In a column written for the *Charlotte News*, Cash wrote of Freudian notions of sexuality and repression, noting that highly repressed people can become sexually aroused even by a sermon on "the wages of sin is death." It is also true, "as every good Freudian knows, that these same people may so react to the sight of a shoe, an umbrella, a pail, a dagger"

(Clayton, 59). It is this notion of being sexually aroused by a dagger that is emblematic in Cash; an implement of violence served as a fetish for a writer plainly incapable of realizing his own desires with actual physical bodies. Lillian Smith, for her part, was perhaps more adept at seeing the fetishization of violence for what it was. In *Strange Fruit*, a couple sits discussing a recent lynching:

> Echols laughed. "It was a sight, that nigger! Swingin there. Got what he deserved. What every one of em deserve. But Mollie woulda fainted dead away when she begun to smell."
>
> "Lawd, don't talk about it!" Mollie said, and made a face. With a plump hand she eased up one of her breasts a little where it was chafed.
>
> "Mommy, mommy, mommy, mommy," screamed a child inside the house.
>
> "I declare! J. L.'s havin a nightmare again! That boy bolts his rations so fas he—"
>
> "Mommy, mommy," sobbed the little fellow as he came running out of the house and down the steps, "they'll git me . . . they'll git me . . . I seed em . . ." "Nobody aimin to git ye! Hit's niggers they burn—they ain't agoin to burn you. Get on back with ye to bed, boy." Echols laughed, gave the boy a playful push.
>
> Nobody had ever seen Willie in better spirits, and everybody joined in the laughter as Mollie turned the little fellow around and sent him back. . . .
>
> It did not take them long to get to bed. Nor long for Willie to pull Mollie's big soft body to him.
>
> "My!" Mollie sighed after a time, "my . . . you ain't been like this in a year!"
>
> "Ain't felt like this in a year," Willie laughed and reached for her again. (352)

In this scene, as in much of Smith's work, racial violence is connected directly to white male sexual release; white men become aroused particularly when contemplating the rape of black women or the slaughter of black men. For Cash, the conflation of sex and displaced violence is so alluring that he speaks of the South being "wedded" to lynching:

> At the end of thirty years the South was solidly wedded to Negro-lynching because of the cumulative power of habit, obviously. But it was wedded to it far more because the dominant feeling about it

(the feeling which, in time of stress, would seize control of the best almost as surely as the sorriest cracker) was that, as an act of racial and patriotic expression, an act of chivalry, an act, indeed, having a definitely ritualistic value in respect to the entire Southern sentiment, and as an act which had had, in most concrete cases, the approbation and often the participation of the noblest and wisest of their revered generation of men which was now bending to the grave, it was not wrong but the living bone and flesh of right. . . . Moreover, the same combination of circumstances which had operated to make mob violence socially desirable from the Southern viewpoint operated to make this private violence desirable also. To smash a sassy Negro, to kill him, to do the same to a white "nigger lover"—this was to assert the white man's prerogative as pointedly, in his place, as to lynch. And so, to a very considerable extent, it, too, was felt as an act of patriotism and chivalry. . . . [T]he best men in the South . . . were immensely prone to give consent to the doctrine that a broken head or even death was fair punishment for the sassy nigger (that is, one guilty of any word or deed of assertion) or the "nigger-lover." They were immensely prone, and, for subconscious purposes, maybe even eager to accept the claim, immediately put forward by every offender who was not an utter dolt, that this violence was due to this or that insult offered his women. And, in consequence, they were so honestly blind that it would have been a flagrant case that would move them to do more than merely turn away their eyes. (121–22)

The language in this passage, as elsewhere, is deeply sexualized; calling lynching "the living bone and flesh of right" is to give the act a sexual physicality that is ancillary to the act itself. Moreover, to move from "socially desirable" to "privately desirable" is to leave little doubt about the eroticization of violence. If a socially desirable act of violence can be read as one carried out for the sake of appearance, private violence can only be read as an act that is at some level titillating, arousing, an act of fetishization. For Cash, the fetishization of violence against blacks stood in for the violence he felt directed against himself by the whites around him. Just as Percy, an effeminate man, felt estranged from his Delta community, and Lillian Smith, a lesbian, felt mocked by her North Georgia neighbors, Cash, an odd, impotent, deeply neurotic intellectual, felt out of place in the North Carolina piedmont. And it was in the language of race that he found release.

CHAPTER THREE

Men of Honor and Pygmy Tribes

Metaphors of Race and Cultural Decline

in William Alexander Percy's

Lanterns on the Levee

In our brave new world,

a man of honor is rather like

the Negro—there's

no place for him to go.

WILLIAM ALEXANDER PERCY,

Lanterns on the Levee

The May 7, 1969, edition of the *Greenville (Miss.) Delta Democrat-Times* carried a front-page photograph of a crumbling mansion on the southeast corner of Greenville's South Broadway and Percy Streets. Once the centerpiece of one of the city's most elegant neighborhoods, William Alexander Percy's home, equipped with a library "big enough for a basketball game," had fallen into dramatic disrepair. "The lawns and gardens of the Percy home are overgrown with weeds," the story accompanying the photo read. "Paint is flecked off window frames and massive columns supporting the verandah and portico. The door frame sags in the servant's house, hanging crazily by one hinge. Perhaps to prevent further damage from rocks and other missiles thrown through windows, the front door is permanently unlocked. The door knob has been removed to make entry easy without having to break windows. Vandals have stolen knobs from all bathroom fixtures. Crude obscenities and childish graffiti cover the walls."

Percy's home had once operated as a Delta salon, hosting poetry

readings by Carl Sandburg, Conrad Aiken, and Langston Hughes, con-
versations with Hortense Powdermaker and Hodding Carter, and a tennis match with William Faulkner, who reportedly showed up sockless
and drunk. Percy's young cousin, the future novelist Walker Percy, spent
his adolescence in the house after his father's suicide and his mother's
drowning; it was William who introduced Walker to the young Shelby
Foote. The house had fallen into disrepair after Percy's death in 1942; in
1969, two merchants who were willing to sell the house for $26,500 ac-
knowledged that it needed an additional $100,000 in repairs. There were
no offers, and the house was razed. Today, behind rotting plasterboard
tumbling from a rusting dumpster, behind a low-income housing complex known as the Royal Ridge Apartments, the only sign of the old
Percy mansion is a serpentine brick wall that once guarded the property
from the outside world.

The death of the old house, its replacement with welfare housing,
and the transition of the neighborhood from one of elegance and
grandeur to its present poverty and decay mark changes that William
Alexander Percy dreaded: the collapse of Southern aristocracy, the oblit-
eration of romance, the erasure of gentility, and the inexorable fluidity
of culture and economics. Percy's eloquent, complex memoir, *Lanterns
on the Levee*, published in 1941 just months before his death, is in many
ways an emblem of a time and a culture both dead and still dying; his
language is rife not only with a fixation on his ancestors but with a will
to mythologize, a will to occlude his present with stylized memories of
the past. Percy's narrative also expresses deep ambivalences about his
own identity and the place of his aristocratic culture in Southern history.
Whereas his Agrarian contemporaries hoped to reinstate a past cultural
ethos, based on a rejection of urban industrialism and a return to small
farming communities, Percy had no confidence that the old order could
be restored, nor did he suggest a way of doing so. "He was the melancholic Roman to the end—rarely the joyous and tragic Greek—and
found provisional solace only in the Stoic maxims of Marcus Aurelius
and the ethical precepts of the Gospels," Richard King writes. "And
though he presided over his own small realm in the Delta, he felt no
more sense of freedom in the world at large than that experienced by
another great Stoic, the slave Epictecus" (87).[1]

King's link of Percy to a Roman slave is subtly made. For all his sentiment about the collapse of the genteel world of his ancestors, Percy
consistently returns to metaphors that compare his own status to that of
the blacks around him: misunderstood, misrepresented, misidentified.

For he was more than just the son of a land baron and U.S. senator and the grandson of a Civil War hero; he was also effeminate, and though he was widely loved and admired, he frequently felt alienated from a family and community that he feared considered his talents suspect.[2] As we shall see, this position left him with few whites upon whom he could reflect his own conflicted identity; for all his apparent wealth and status in Greenville, he never perceived himself as anything other than the "queer chicken" he had been dubbed by his overbearing father. He was always the weak, sensitive, melancholic child, and it was to blacks, not to whites, that he looked for spiritual empathy. "I wonder why when the obvious connection between innards and out'ards of red-heads is generally conceded, it is doubted in people of slant eyes and yellow skins and flatly denied in people of kinky hair and black skins," he writes. "Someone's always drawing the color line; now they won't let the Negro's interior be as individual as his exterior. I am told there is no relation between what you see of him and what there is of him: the only difference is a sort of hallucination in the eye of the beholder, he's a white man inside. Very like, very like" (*Lanterns*, 84).

If being a "white man inside" represented a normative cultural and psychological baseline, then Percy, who felt deeply wounded by and isolated from his own white culture, must somehow have felt that he was seen, from the outside at least, as "black." As with Lillian Smith, Percy found himself damaged by traditional discourses of race and sex, even as, on the surface, he occupied positions of significant social power. As we shall see, his writing is frequently conflicted by these two positions; he was at once a patrician and a racial progressive, the owner of what was essentially a feudal plantation and a fighter of the Ku Klux Klan, a man both profoundly ignorant of and deeply connected to the blacks who raised him at least as much as the white parents that birthed him. His racial metaphors swing from anxieties about blacks and lower-class whites replacing his "old order" of aristocratic whites to overly wrought passages of sentiment about blacks representing spiritual and joyous essences that he, as a white, feared he would never enjoy.

What I hope to show here is that these inconsistencies are in fact inherently linked, that blackness, as Toni Morrison insists, can stand in for *both* anxiety and desire, *both* fear and yearning, *both* loss and hope. Percy's work represents an ideal point from which to view these conflicting impulses precisely because he was such an unusual member of a dominant class of Southerner. It was in his yearning for cultural and personal reference points that he arrived at his sentimentalities, both racial and nostalgic; he leaned on images of race just as he leaned on images of his family's past to give himself a sense of place in a world in which he felt deeply ill at ease. Blacks for Percy, like his ancestors, represented both a way in and a way out: a way into his own identity and a way out of confronting the world as it was. For Percy, the man of honor was rather like a Negro because both metaphors did so much work for him; his sweeping, glowing prose is elegant and conflicted; its beauty masks, or tries to mask, turbulent undercurrents of race, class, and cultural upheaval that Percy, as a member of one of the South's wealthiest and most politically powerful families, felt acutely himself.

Upon its publication in 1941, *Lanterns* was praised largely for its evocation of the aristocratic ideal; the book made the best-seller lists, was a finalist for a Pulitzer Prize in biography, and by the end of the year had been reprinted ten times. Southern reviewers, for the most part, praised the book effusively. W. J. Cash, whose *The Mind of the South* had also just appeared, wrote that "Percy is that exceedingly rare thing, a surviving, authentic Southern aristocrat. . . . And his book is a fine one, the merits of which ought not to be obscured by any ideological disputes" (Baker, 172). In Atlanta, Ralph McGill wrote that Percy's picture of the South was far more accurate than that painted by recent sociological studies. The *Charlotte Observer* located the book's appeal in its "beautifully stated defense of the aristocratic ideal" that still survives "in thousands of Southern men and women—men and women no longer a unified band, but scattered like tiny islets through a culture, or lack of it, which they can understand intellectually but not spiritually" (Baker, 170). Images of Southern aristocracy, it is important to note, had only two years before received their most potent polish from the film version of *Gone with the Wind*.

Demurring was James Orrick, who criticized Percy's racial sentiments; in the *Saturday Review of Literature*, he said, "Mr. Percy is so baldly reactionary, arrogant and irrational that it is staggering." Critical also was Lillian Smith, who wrote in her *North Georgia Review* that "those who wear the aura of racial superiority will acknowledge with satisfaction the halo which the author has woven so delicately around his own head." Northern reviewers were more impressed. Carl Sandburg said the book was "among the autobiographies requisite to understanding America." Herschel Brickell, in the *New York Times Book Review*, called *Lanterns* "a paradoxical compact of gentleness and violence" as well as "a work of exceptional merit and importance. The high quality of its prose would entitle it to consideration for a permanent place in our literature. Its real

significance, however, lies in the candor and completeness of the revelation of the Southern aristocracy's point of view. The breed had never
been plentiful and now appears to be dying out, although it has qualities
that may save it from extinction. It is a peculiar breed, not at all easy to
understand, perhaps because its basic principles are protected by an
outer charm which is at once bloom and camouflage."

"Bloom and camouflage" is an apt description for Percy's narrative,
and for his life. It is of little use to remark solely on the racism of Percy's
language. What is compelling is the use to which he puts his racial
metaphors, the ways he, like all the writers considered here, uses images
of blackness to construct, reinforce, or supplement images of his own
whiteness, his own identity; and the ways he masks his own more specifically economic anxieties, and those of his culture writ large, with those
of the more visibly oppressed. It is not racism per se that I am interested
in, but the ways race is *constructed* and the way it is *used*. There need to be,
as Toni Morrison has written, "powerful and persuasive attempts to an-
alyze the origin and fabrication of racism itself, contesting the assumption that it is an inevitable, permanent, and eternal part of all social landscapes. I do not wish to disparage these inquiries. It is precisely because
of them that any progress at all has been accomplished in matters of
racial discourse" (11). Subtitled *Memoirs of a Planter's Son*, Percy's narrative
insists on a weaving of biography and literary analysis; looking at the
culture from which he emerged, and the racial and psychological ambivalence that resulted from it, will move us another step toward understanding the rhetorical roots of his own particular racial discourse. A
brief look at Percy's life will assist in the examination of the ways he
conflated metaphors of race and his own ancestry. This will be followed
by an exploration of the ways his racialized discourse masked pressing
social and economic affairs.

Paul Fussell, among many others, has argued that the Great War
changed everything, that the world, no longer able to abide images of
romance, honor, glory, and chivalry, had become attached to irony and
suspicion. For Percy this was clearly not the case. Percy *needed* sentimentality; like Henry Adams, he was haunted by visions of his family, and his
community, in steep decline. Early on in his memoir, Percy contem-
plates the role played by the men who fought the enforced seating of
black politicians during Reconstruction: "These were the men who, before I was a listener, bore the brunt of the Delta's fight against scala-

waggery and Negro domination during Reconstruction, who stole the ballot-boxes which, honestly counted, would have made every county official a Negro, who had helped shape the Constitution of 1890, which in effect and legally disenfranchised the Negro, who still earlier had sent my grandfather to the legislature to help rid the state of 'old Ames,' the carpetbag governor." He continues:

> These were leaders of the people, not elected or self-elected, but destined, under the compulsion of leadership because of their superior intellect, training, character and opportunity. And the people were willing to be led by them because of their desperate need of leadership in those tragic times, because they recognized their fitness to lead, tested and proved in the series of revealing crises that only began with the war, and because they came from the class which traditionally had led in the South. . . . People steal public funds now, but the public is cynical, no one is horrified, and the accused, guilty or innocent, seldom goes mad. Going mad for honor's sake presupposes honor. In our brave new world a man of honor is rather like a Negro — there's no place for him to go. (69, 72)

For all the racist blundering on the surface here, and for all the apparent homage to the "heroic" actions of the ancestors dismantling the Reconstruction South, there are odd strains to be reckoned with as well. The "desperate" need for leadership that led people to follow imperfect leaders is an image that resonates throughout Percy's work, particularly as it represents deeply ambivalent feelings about his father and the world of Southern character that he embodied for William. But more interesting is Percy's reliance on race to draw lines of distinction between his own time and the fancied days of yore. The "man of honor" in today's world is, like the Negro, alienated, abandoned, homeless, devoid of public support or favor. Percy could simply have said the man of honor has no place to go, but he chooses to link the heir of chivalric duty with the occupant of the lowest social rung. This can only be because Percy himself felt a significant resonance with blacks of his own time, as marginalized, powerless, even anachronistic; if the last moment of political empowerment that blacks could cling to were the dozen chaotic years of Reconstruction, and the last moment Percy can envision is the *end* of Reconstruction, then both parties were left empty in their own time. W. J. Cash wrote with great perception about the dread among aristocrats that accompanied the loss of power and cultural homogeneity. "Flowing with and out of this [decay] came terror, defeatism, apathy, the will to escape," he wrote. "A growing inclination to withdraw themselves altogether from the struggle, from a world grown too dangerous; to shut away the present and abandon the future; here to flee to the inglorious asylum of political sinecure, as likely as not created expressly for the case; there to retreat behind their own barred gates and hold commerce with none save the members of their own caste. A growing tendency to dissociate their standards wholly from reality, and convert them from living principles of action into mere eidolons" (*Mind*, 157–58).[3] Percy set out in *Lanterns on the Levee*, then, to pay homage to his past, and to provide a foil to the uncertain times at hand. "So while the world I know is crashing to bits," he writes, "and what with the noise and the cryings-out no man could hear a trumpet blast, much less an idle evening reverie, I will indulge a heart beginning to be fretful by repeating to it the stories it knows and loves of my own country and my own people" (xx). As Bertram Wyatt-Brown's recent biography of the Percy family makes clear, claims of a gilded genealogy were central to the Percy family. From the time of William the Conqueror, the Percys had ruled Northumberland, a primitive English district on the Scottish border. A succession of earls and dukes perpetuated a fortune in landed wealth that, apart from royalty itself, was scarcely equaled by any other noble family in Great Britain. Henry Percy, the Harry Hotspur whom William Shakespeare immortalized in Henry IV, parts 1 and 2—and, appropriately enough, a figure of disintegrating nobility—figured in the American Percy lore, although incontrovertible proof of ancestry has never been found. "The Percys never questioned the assumption that everyone had an allotted place in the scheme of things and that their own appointed position was among the ruling, propertied ranks" (Wyatt-Brown, 10).[4]

But the family into which Percy was born was also famously tragic. From 1794 to 1929, in every generation except one, at least one family member took his own life. Leroy Pratt Percy, William's uncle and the father of Walker Percy, shot himself in 1929; Walker's grandfather had killed himself in 1917. William's younger brother, Leroy, died of an accidental gunshot wound at the age of eleven, when William was a sophomore in college. The death of the energetic, boyish Leroy, who William wrote "should be representing and perpetuating the name," haunted William for years (Wyatt-Brown, 201). In 1932, Mattie Sue, William's aunt and Walker's mother, drove her Buick off an unrailed bridge into Deer Creek with her son Phinizy; "holding his hand in paralyzing terror,

[she] would not let go, and even held tighter as her fright mounted. Vainly he tried to pull her along with him. Then she suddenly released him. He escaped, scrambled up the bank, and shouted for help. Mattie Sue remained seated in the car." When taken from the car, she was dead but not obviously hurt (274). She had either died of a heart attack or decided not to struggle to escape.

Melancholy, both personal and cultural, seemed to pass along through the Percy bloodlines and went hand in glove with the equally strong images of chivalry. Although he graduated from Harvard Law School, worked in his father's law firm, held important community positions, became a published and widely known poet, traveled broadly through Europe and Japan, and raised three young cousins after the death of his uncle, Will never felt he lived up to his family's romantic standards. "The Southern code of honor by which they lived made the struggle of life all the more trying," Wyatt-Brown writes. "By its rubrics one was expected to live up to almost impossible standards of valor and manhood. The Percys called upon their young to meet exceedingly high expectations both in school and on the playground, in college, marriage, and money-making careers. Early indoctrination under pressure of this kind at times left even the most accomplished of them disappointed by their own performance" (16).[5] No pursuit carried as much cultural weight for the Southerner as a venture into war, and when William finally got his chance, in World War I, he wrote about it with all the flourishes of a Civil War hero. The following is from a letter Percy wrote to his mother and later copied into a *Lanterns* chapter entitled "From the Front."

> *Mother dear:* Just a hurried note. Unless the order is changed we're going into a gorgeous big battle in a few hours, of which you will know the full results long before this reaches you. . . . And for good luck, letters came from you and Father today. I'm glad he liked my little "Squire's Song." It was written at Tours with Frank Gailor in mind as he was going off to the Messines show, but it holds true for any soldier fighting in the great cause. One must be a soldier these days—there is no other part a man may play and be a man. Should anything ever happen to me over here, you and Father must, and I know you will, feel that it was a great privilege to go forth with the heroes. I've had too much and too keen happiness out of this life to want to leave it or to leave it without regret, but this cause is too great to count the cost or speculate on the outcome to the individual.—25 Sept. 1918—9 P.M. (201)

Lanterns on the Levee is marked throughout by such highly personalized sentiment and is likewise always threatened by melancholy and loss. In this, as C. Vann Woodward has written in *The Strange Career of Jim Crow*, Percy's rhetoric is distinctly Southern: "The twilight zone that lies between living memory and written history is one of the favorite breeding places of mythology. This particular twilight zone has been especially prolific in the breeding of legend. The process has been aided by the old prejudices, the deeply stirred emotions, and the sectional animosities that always distort history in any zone, however well illuminated by memory or research" (xii). Percy was known for these sentiments even in his youth; as a student at the University of Mississippi, Faulkner, reviewing Percy's poem *In April Once*, said Percy was "like a little boy closing his eyes against the dark modernity which threatens the bright simplicity and colorful romantic pageantry of the middle ages with which his eyes are full" (Tolson, 77).[6]

Such was Percy's fascination with medieval myth that when his father died in 1929, he hired Malvina Hoffman, the Italian sculptress, to create a $25,000 memorial statue in the form of a brooding medieval knight, which still gazes off into the middle distance in Greenville's cemetery. "The knight was meant to embody Percy's conception of his forebears and his wish that they all—not the senator alone—should be known," Wyatt-Brown writes. "At the same time, the representation helped to obscure the individual, who became lost under the symbol" (3−4).[7] Indeed, as the scion of one of the region's most influential families, Percy never escaped the weight of his vaunted ancestry, even as it tormented him. In the cemetery, William lies beneath a simple granite stone, next to Martha Susan Phinizy, Walker's mother. At one end is a stone with the barely legible name of T. C. Percy, the wife of John Walker Percy, who died in 1894. At the foot of the plot lies a rectangular stone with the name PERCY becoming less and less visible as letters are chipped away by weather and years.

Richard King reads Percy's deeply conflicted relationship to his father as a parallel to the way white Southerners generally respond to their own web of history. "These three stages of historical consciousness present analogies to the unfolding and transformation of memory in psychoanalysis," he writes. "In both instances, the past is problematic: now overpowering, now completely absent from memory, it is debilitating" (18).[8]

It was William's burden, then, to shoulder the twin demons of hardeyed familial expectations and the horrific, if unvoiced, awareness of the consistency of family tragedy; in this, his family mirrors the Southern espousal of doomed desire in general, writhing, in Woodward's words, "in the torments of its own conscience until it plunged into catastrophe to escape. The South's preoccupation was with guilt, not with innocence, with the reality of evil, not with the dream of perfection" (*Burden*, 72). The Percy family, like the Southern aristocracy it represented, was tormented by the shadow of defeat, of catastrophe, of death, and in William Alexander's case in particular, this specter was highly personal; his torturous relationship to his own forebears, particularly his father and grandfather, is eerily similar to that borne by Faulkner's Quentin Compson. As was the case with Walker Percy, who was equally tormented by the family's despairing past, the fact that William did not commit suicide must at some level be considered a victory in itself.[9]

"A crucial segment of the third (and in some cases fourth) generation, which was born around the turn of the century and lived through the cultural crisis of World War I, came to feel increasingly estranged from the tradition," Richard King writes.

That tradition loomed distressingly distant and overpoweringly strong, insupportable yet inescapable. This in turn raises the question which has haunted the modern world and has remained central to the culture of modernism: what does it mean to live without a tradition? Insofar as Southern writers and intellectuals were concerned with this question, they expressed a central concern of the modernist movement. The answers to the questions are various, some of which this century has seen embodied in ghastly forms. Here Hannah Arendt's work sheds light, for the loss of "the thread which safely guided us through the vast realms of the past" renders memory helpless. In the face of these difficulties "old verities which have lost all concrete relevance" may be "rehashed." Also in the absence of its traditional authorizations, present authority may degenerate into the application of violence which in turn provides counterviolence. Or finally the world may grow "fantastic." Certainly of the rehashing of old verities there was no end in the 1930s. One thinks here of the Agrarians or of William Alexander Percy. Calling upon the past to aid the present, they attempted to revitalize the tradition by turning it into a conservative, even reactionary ideology. Some, like Percy, realized that the tradition could not be revitalized in any binding, collective way and that it had become "merely" a personal code by which they could at least live. (15–16)

Percy's "reactionary ideology" was hardly uniform; as will be shown later, his personal relationships with blacks were more often than not significantly more enlightened than those of his white social peers. But his reliance on images of the past affected both his life and his writing. His grandfather was the "Gray Eagle," Col. William Alexander Percy, a Princeton graduate and Civil War hero who ruled a small kingdom in the Delta from his law office in Greenville, served as Mississippi's Speaker of the House, and retired from politics in 1878 only after helping overthrow the "Black Republicans." Percy's father, Leroy, a Sewanee graduate, evolved into a powerful landowner, corporate conservative, and influential politician in his own right. After the sudden death of U.S. senator Anselm J. McLaurin before Christmas in 1909, Leroy was awarded the vacant senate seat by an 87–82 vote in a state Democratic caucus. His campaign for re-election, against the notorious white supremacist James K. Vardaman,[10] was marked by vitriol that would leave a lasting mark on William.

William was born May 15, 1885, just seven months after his parents married; his early birth proved somewhat of an embarrassment to them and seemed to set a tone for his emotional development. We read at length about his black nurse and playmates but almost nothing about the day-to-day relationship he had with his father, who, by all accounts, was a highly energetic and intimidating presence, especially to a sensitive, aesthetic child who soon made every effort to "prove himself to be unusually quick and very, very good, as if compliance in all things would bring him greater acceptance." William wrote that, perhaps as rebellion, early on he showed "an artistic and literary aptitude quite mistrusted in the agrarian, conservative part of the South. Once, when father caught him listening to his aunt reading another sentimental novel, he snatched it away and replaced it with *Ivanhoe*, which he read himself once a year" (Wyatt-Brown, 194–95).[11] It was hard "having such a dazzling father," Percy writes. "No wonder I longed to be a hermit" (*Lanterns*, 57–58). On the very few occasions when Percy mentions his mother, it is only to reveal her scorn for her eccentric son. "I had decided to become a priest. I had anticipated dismay but not indignation. Mother rose from the flowerbed to her full height, the height, say, of Lady Macbeth or Clytemnestra; too late under the solemn fillet I saw the scorn. But her only observation was that there was no excuse for talking like a fool at my age. I must have been an unbearable little prig. I do hope I've outgrown it. If not, it wasn't Mother's fault" (78–79).

Stretching this notion further, parental absence for Percy is also symbolic of a larger cultural yearning for mythical forebears, who are equally absent and equally revered. Percy's emotional struggles with his father mirrored the struggles of the white South's own grappling with a mythic and burdening past. In a passage describing the twilight of his grandparents' lives, Percy's language becomes melancholic not just for his family but for his entire generation. "My generation, inured to doom, wears extinction with a certain wry bravado, but it is just as well the older ones we loved are gone," he writes.

> They had lived, for the most part, through tragedy into poverty, which can be and usually is accomplished with dignity and a certain fine disdain. But when the last act is vulgarity, it is as hateful and confused a show as *Troilus and Cressida*.
>
> During their last years Mere and Pere lived with us most of the time. Pere was ill a long while, but no one was very much interested. He had to sit in a dark room days on end, and there were no radios then or phonographs, and no one read to him. He rarely complained and seemed to know that those he loved were vital and busy with their living. I hope he remembered pleasant things most as he sat in the dark and awaited the end. Nor was Mere spared. I suppose her strength was a temptation to death. No wonder we hate him so unforgivingly: his ways are humiliating and his approaches brutal. His indignities we fear, not him. (63)

There is something despairing in the image of an old Civil War hero sitting alone in the dark, ignored by his family, waiting to die. Moreover, the way Percy juxtaposes the pronoun "him," referring to death, and "he" referring to his grandfather, complicates the issue. We know how ambivalent Percy felt about his heroic but neglectful father; when he writes "no wonder we hate him so unforgivingly; his ways are humiliating and his approaches brutal," the conflation with his male forebears seems perfectly apt. Not only was Percy's father humiliating and brutal, but so is the masculine Southern legacy broadly construed that Will felt compelled to shoulder. The link between death and an unyielding sense of historical imperative seems intrinsically Southern; surely it was central to Faulkner's *The Sound and the Fury* and *Absalom, Absalom!* The fascination with physical decline, and the creation of cultural mythology in its place, King writes, is evidence of a culture that "denies death and the workings of time on one level only to be obsessed by death at a deeper level. The monumental or reactionary form of historical consciousness is not necessarily wrong in a moral or substantive sense, since there are traditions which one might wish revitalized. Rather it is 'wrong' insofar as it desires the impossible—repetition—rather than the necessary working through of the past" (17).

Compared to the paralyzing alienation he felt from his parents, Percy's earliest years were marked by significant attachments to his black maid, Nain. "I was born and in May and on Ascension Day, and I have picked up the information that the incident overjoyed no one, because Father and Mother were young and good-looking, poor and well-born, in love with each other and with life, and they would have considered the blessed event more blessed if it had been postponed a year or two," he writes. "No matter how unfavorably I impressed them at the time, they impressed me not at all, and for a much longer period afterwards. I have no single memory of them dating from the first four years of my life. The only persons whose activities were important enough to dent the fairly undentable tablets of my memory were Nain, my colored nurse, and Mur, my grandmother. Nain possibly comes back to me more as an emanation or aura than a person. But make no mistake, Mur was a person" (27).

Right from the start, then, we have a glimpse at a host of components of Percy's psychology and rhetoric that recur throughout the book. He felt profoundly disregarded by his parents, even abandoned. He remembers most of his nurturing coming from a black woman, yet he remembers Nain not as an embodied presence but as an "aura," an apparition who brushed over his life apparently without leaving a physical mark. This, as we shall see, is a form of representation that reappears throughout Percy's work. He at once describes, often with great enthusiasm and joy, the relationships he had with black playmates and adult companions and pulls back in guilt and melancholic awareness of the reasons for his attachment to them. It is as if the brooding, alienating, and intolerant family that surrounded him left him no choice *but* to look to black friends for nurturing and love, yet when he recognizes this he feels ashamed, or guilty, or empty; his connection to the black world, for him, is evidence of a failure, or hollowness, in the white world. His ambivalent, disembodied descriptions of his black contemporaries are similar in kind to the disembodied memories of his heroic ancestors; they stand in for an utter lack of embodied, present, actively engaged family. Here again, dead men of honor are rather like the Negro: they fulfill the yearnings of a wasted white soul.

This parental absence seems closely linked to that discussed at such length in Lillian Smith's work, where fondness for a black nursemaid stands in for and masks a deep feeling of loss for biological parents. Smith's chapter "Three Ghost Stories" in *Killers of the Dream* is brilliant in its analysis of the myriad complications that arise when a white mother gives up the nurturing of her child to a black woman. Smith writes: "Sometimes [the child] found what he sought and formed a tender, passionate, deeply satisfying relation which he was always faithful to, despite cultural barriers. But always it was a relationship without honor in his own mind and region, and the source of profound anxiety which seeped through his personality. Yet the old longing persisted, the old desire for something he could not find in his white life" (128).

When Percy finally comes around to describing his father's death, he relies on the image of a black employee to help him mourn. Holt, "a hunting partner and an ex-slave," motions for William to sit in his late father's chair, then joins William in the office. "'Set there where he sot,' Holt says. 'That's where you b'long.' For some minutes [Holt] struggled silently, sitting there in what had been Father's office, then he let the tears gush unhindered from his eyes and the words from his heart: 'The roof is gone from over my head and the floor from under my feet. I am out in the dark and the cold alone. I want to go where he is.' He rose and hobbled out. Many of us felt that way" (270). Here Percy is unable to mourn his own father; he uses a black man to give voice to what must certainly have been one of William's most trying moments. His father, emblematic of all he loved and feared about his family and the romantic, masculine Southern culture in general, had passed away, leaving him alone, afraid, and free. Yet the man who had written and would continue to write published poems plainly based on sentimentalized and troubled visions of his father was unable to write a single sentence of unabashed emotion in his own autobiography; he turned instead to a black stand-in to do his mourning for him. Blacks, Percy goes on to say, perhaps in the service of rationalization, are more free with their feelings, less inhibited by social restraint; like the marchers during a New Orleans funeral procession, they are famously able to mourn.

Blackness for Percy, then, stands in for something of which he was somehow incapable, and which somehow he was forbidden from birth: warmth, love, emotional freedom. If Smith was quick to point out the "lack" that most whites attached to blacks, Percy often uses blackness to represent what he lacks in himself. Blacks for Percy are full of everything that he has been denied. The sociologist Hortense Powdermaker writes that, to Percy, "Negroes were happy Pan-like beings living only in the present, fundamentally and mysteriously different from white people," but this only captures part of it. This is not simply Percy attributing childlike joy or frivolity or even waywardness to blacks; Percy is markedly envious of their perceived capacity to turn away from a past that is not only heroic but paralyzing.

To be sure, Percy's imagining of blacks as joyful innocents speaks volumes about his own tightly wound existence. After a trip to Samoa in 1936, he wrote an essay entitled "The White Plague," which, rejected by his editor and never published as it was written, was later added to *Lanterns on the Levee* under the title "A Note on Race Relations." The essay exemplifies one way that Percy used blackness to embody the innocence he was convinced he and his culture had lost. He wrote:

> They [Samoans] are eager to take our comfortable beds, ice-boxes, radios and victrolas, our varied and devitalized foods, our bicycles and automobiles, never suspecting that taking these they must take too our weariness, our restlessness, our unhappy hearts. We are the nomads of the world, without home fires, wandering by stars not fixed, whose passion is to force the older and younger tribes of the race to join our tumultuous and futile pilgrimages. We bribe them with our gold and our gods, they arise from their hearths and their fields and join us, receiving from us things, amusing things, but leaving behind them the one thing for the lack of which we sob ourselves to sleep—sweet, sweet content. We give them the whole world and they fall down and adore us: we take from them only happiness which in our hands vanishes. (Baker, 160)

This, again, is more than the image of the happy-go-lucky Negro; this is transferred yearning. Percy looks to blacks in this passage much the same way he looks to the gauzy days of yore as embodying an optimism and joy that he has never known. "Blacks were for Will a symbol of innocence—children not yet consumed by the white man's passion for wealth or burdened by a sense of responsibility," Baker writes. "He feared, however, that the delta's blacks had lost much of their innocence through their constant contact with whites and their attempts to adopt white standards. The black man, Will wrote, 'makes at best a second-rate white man: He could have been something far more precious in the eyes of any god, a first-rate Negro'" (158–59).[12] There is undoubtedly an element of colonialist rhetoric here, portraying blacks as "precious" in ways that civilized whites can no longer be. But my sense is that Percy was not being disingenuous; his effort was not so much to characterize blacks as to characterize whites, and the best vehicle for him to do this was *through* blacks. The most available mirror of whiteness, for Percy, was blackness; again, unlike the "Other" of Jacques Lacan and Lillian Smith, blackness for Percy did not represent a lack but rather its opposite. Blackness was rich, whiteness impoverished. Here, the racial metaphor is a metaphor of soulfulness for which Percy, the alienated poet, could not find a more acceptable vessel.

Indeed, like Cash, Percy often works up a great deal of rhetorical energy to dignify the objects of his attention. Yet both writers manage most of all to show their hand for what it really is: unsure, unstable, dependent on caricature to justify their own separation from those they are describing. At the same time that Percy admires a black servant for standing inches from a blazing fireplace in order to shield his elderly grandmother from its heat—becoming "the more dignified" the more pain he withstands—he constantly draws parallels between his servants' alienated state and his own:

> Dinner parties were rare at our house and I disapproved of them because they meant my forced withdrawal from the dining room. But nearly always there were extra and often unexpected guests for meals. Once the ice-cream gave out just before my turn came. This was my first experience of the injustice of things. One is not born a Stoic. I took the event lying down, under the table, loud with woe, and was hustled out, conspicuous in misery. Generally, however, mealtime was a nice time and everybody talked a lot. The best thing about it was watching Willis, Mur's very black waiter. When the dining room was frigid Willis piled the coals high in the fireplace. When he piled them too high it was too hot on Mur's back and she made him stand between her and the fireplace, almost in the fire, an elegant human fire-screen. It was agreeable to watch him break out into a profuse sweat without any loss of dignity— indeed, with increased mobility and self-importance. He must have got dreadfully hot behind. His was a lofty character. (30)[13]

Here again Percy relies on an image of black suffering to exhibit the experience of his own. Little William first learns about "injustice" not when he sees Willis subjected to the fireplace flames but when he is denied ice cream; by linking the two moments in the same paragraph, he is linking his own sense of deprivation, however trivial, with that of the black servant. And this, to a sensitive young boy, was troubling. As William Andrews has written about Southern autobiographers in general,

METAPHORS OF RACE AND CULTURAL DECLINE

Mississippi recognized selfhood not as a function of the subject but of the object, namely the racial other, whose looming presence dictated the need for self-differentiation according to the strictures of law and custom rather than in creative opposition to them. What happens, however, when the southern youth discovers that the law is not a single but a double standard? This introduces the problem, among black southerners especially, of how to identify with half a society without feeling oneself to be but half a person. Among modern white southern autobiographers, the problem of identity is similarly one of incompleteness, symbolized by a sense of unresolved conflict within the self over one's attitude toward blacks. (50)

Ambivalence about the law, then, becomes ambivalence about the self, and both grow directly from the child's acknowledgment of race and race prejudice. Percy's family treated blacks as servants at best; as a child, Percy was trained to condescend to the people upon whom he most depended. In this regard Percy is similar to Cash, who once wrote to H. L. Mencken that white children often had "only" black playmates:

And in this society in which the infant son of the planter was commonly suckled by a black mammy, in which gray old black men were his most loved story-tellers, in which black stalwarts were among the chiefest heroes and mentors of his boyhood, and in which his usual, often practically his only, companions until he was past the age of puberty were the black boys (and girls) of the plantation—in this society in which by far the greater number of white boys of whatever degree were more or less shaped by such companionship, and in which nearly the whole body of whites, young and old, had constantly in their ears the accent of the Negro, the relationship between the two groups was, by the second generation at least, nothing less than organic. Negro entered into white man as profoundly as white man entered into Negro—subtly influencing every gesture, every word, every emotion and idea, every attitude. (*Mind*, 51)[14]

Raised and befriended by blacks, white boys could not have but been bewildered as children by this emotional discrepancy. Early on in *Lanterns*, Percy describes a crawfishing expedition he took with "Skillet," a black playmate who, "as a conversationalist . . . outdistanced any white child in inventiveness, absurdity, and geniality." Drifting on a pond on a hot summer day, the two boys looked up and watched as "buzzards circled dreamily, their black wings motionless, tilting, banking, coasting in wide arcs, somnambulistic symbols of the drowse and delight of deep summer. Watching them, Skillet observed in a singsong: 'If they was to ever light, the world would burn up.' As the birds seemed fixed at their vast altitude, this was a safe prophesy. But I was skeptical, as could have been expected of any horrid little white realist. Skillet, though, was so eloquent in citing reasons and authorities that my disbelief weakened and by degrees I was convinced, for the excellent old reason that I wanted to be" (48).[15]

Here is the future poet, a "horrid little white realist," learning from a black boy the musical play of language, which for him would become his dearest talent and a significant part of his creative identity. His sentiments recall the words of W. E. B. Du Bois, who in his 1903 book *The Souls of Black Folk*, which Percy surely knew, wrote,

We the darker ones come even now not altogether empty-handed: there are to-day no truer exponents of the pure human spirit of the Declaration of Independence than the American Negroes; there is no truer American music but the wild sweet melodies of the Negro Slave; the American fairy tales and folklore are Indian and African; and in all, we black men seem the sole oasis of faith and reverence in a dusty desert of dollars and smartness. Will America be poorer if she replace her brutal dyspeptic blundering with lighthearted but determined Negro humility? or her coarse and cruel wit with the loving jovial good humor? or her vulgar music with the soul of the Sorrow Songs? (12)

Later, Percy confesses that "Friday's accent, Cora's intonation, and Ligey's grammatical uses contaminated beyond hope of purification the wells of what should have been my pure English undefiled. That was their only evil influence." These lessons in the aural qualities of language could hardly have been unwelcome in a man of letters like Percy. But beyond language, Percy writes that he learned his sense of play—and, one might infer, his sense of childhood itself—from his black playmates; white children were few and far between. Indeed, "of nastiness and bad manners they taught me nothing; older boys of my own color and caste were later to be my instructors in those subjects."

From Amelia's children I learned not only gaiety and casualness and inventiveness, but the possibility that mere living may be delightful and that natural things which we ignore unless we call them scenery are pleasant to move among and gracious to recall. Without them it probably would never have occurred to me that to climb an aspen sapling in a gale is one of those ultimate experiences, like experiencing God or love, that you need never try to remember because you can never forget. . . . Now let it lunge, and gulp the wind. It will be all over you, slapping your hair in your eyes, stinging your face with bits of bark and stick, tugging to break your hold, roaring in your open mouth like a monster seashell. The trees around you will thrash and seethe, their white undersides lashed about like surf, and sea-music racing through them. You will be beaten and bent and buffeted about and the din will be so terrific your throat will invent a song to add to the welter, pretty barbaric, full of yells and long calls. You will feel what it is to be the Lord God and ride a hurricane; you will know what it is to have leaves sprout from your toes and fingertips, with satyrs and tigers and hounds in pursuit; you will never need again to drown under the crash of a manned wave in spume and splendor and thunder, with the white stallions of the sea around you, neighing and pawing. (54–55)

This passage is brimming over with racial and sexual imagery, and its rhetorical flourishes are a dramatic departure from his later, adult ambivalences about black character. From black children Percy learns joy, playfulness, presence, even the experience of the holy. But there is more here: there is violence, and not only violence, slave-catching violence. Riding a sapling in high winds does not just batter a white body, it "lashes" white undersides, eliciting terrible, primitive cries. Riding a tree, you will know what it means to be pursued by hounds; afterward, there will never again be the need to be pursued by the "white stallions" of the surf. The imagery in this passage is so pointedly allusive it can only have come from a Southerner steeped in the historic violence of slavery and segregation. Its move toward the joyous glance back at a mixed-race childhood inevitably dredges up unconscious images of the darker realities of black-white relationships.

Just prior to this sequence, Percy describes a childhood scene when doctors misdiagnosed as fatal appendicitis what in fact was temporary poisoning from a persimmon seed. Solemnly, he writes, he approached his black playmates and

explained the grisly situation and announced my approaching demise. All accepted the news with delight and prepared for the end. I lay on the ground and my faithful retainers knelt around me, in the manner of sundry versions of the Assumption of the Virgin. I closed my eyes, and fervent prayers rose loudly. Nothing happened. Nothing ever did happen. Reviving was undignified and bitterly disappointing to all concerned. As a corpse I was a fiasco, but as mourners my colored entourage displayed genius. Racially they are the best diers in the world anyway: they put more force and enthusiasm into the scene, being seriously aware it is the climax of the show, their curtain. If Friday had swallowed my persimmon seed, he would beyond question have died outright and to perfection, although it's a role one can't rehearse. (53–54)

There is something of Mark Twain here, to be sure: the black friends hamming it up better, enjoying themselves more, playing less self-consciously, than the white protagonist. Throughout his memoir Percy is writing of nothing so much as the death throes of a culture, and here he is describing people who know how to die better than he does. Blacks are the best diers in the world because they have had so much experience dying; whites, who can't even let their ancestors die, could learn much from them.

It was not only with sentiment and yearning that Percy looked to blacks for his metaphors; it was also with a certain amount of dread. If blackness represented a convenient image through which to examine his own white identity, then it also represented real economic pressures that no one in Percy's position of economic control could escape. Greenville at the time of Percy's birth was comparatively peaceful and accommodating to its several ethnic groups. Protestants and Catholics lived, worked, and married together; Leroy's law partner was a Jew. "The Delta problem," Percy writes,

is how all these folks—aristocrats gone to seed, poor whites on the make, Negroes convinced mere living is good, aliens of all sorts that blend or curdle—can dwell together in peace if not in brotherhood and live where, first and last, the soil is the only means of livelihood. Most of our American towns, all of our cities, have their unsolved problem of assimilation. But the South's is infinitely more difficult of solution. The attempt to work out any sort of one, much less a just one, as a daily living problem, diverts the energies and abilities of our best citizenship from more productive fields. A certain patience might well be extended to the South, if not in justice then in courtesy. (24)

Blacks in Greenville were treated well largely because they provided a pool of cheap labor, which in turn created both economic and racial unrest; poor whites had to push out blacks before they could flourish. After his father's death, Percy remained quite affluent; in 1936, during the height of the Depression, he had an income of $35,314.96 from the plantation, then a considerable sum; his family's 3,000 acres—about half planted with cotton, half with hay and corn, and 50 acres for garden plots—was populated by 600 members of sharecropping and tenant families (Wyatt-Brown, 264).[16] According to a 1987 study of mid-century plantations, William was considered to be a comparatively generous plantation owner; on his Trail Lake plantation, twenty miles from Greenville, most of the 150 black sharecropping families that worked the farm received half of what they earned from cotton, as well as free housing, water, fuel, pastures for their own animals, and garden plots; the last was most unusual. Percy didn't make them depend on the plantation store for their supplies (Tolson, 95).[17] As Hodding Carter wrote in *Lower Mississippi*, Percy "had position and breeding and fame and an assured income, and his was a tradition some would call feudal and some patriarchal, and some by less scholarly names. The Negroes of his Tralake [*sic*] plantation will tell you that he got and gave away a million dollars every Saturday night, a statement not precisely accurate as to figures but otherwise revealing" (401). Decidedly patrician, he nonetheless showed considerable compassion for his many black employees, often drawing the ire of his white neighbors, who called him a "Negrophile"; "nigger lover" was reserved for the less affluent. In a news story about Percy's death in its January 22, 1942, edition, the Memphis *Commercial Appeal* reported that "Mr. Percy had halted lynchings and he had talked against them before crowds of strong men. He had led and helped thousands of negro laborers and negro farmers by maintaining his large plantations."

One of the central events in Greenville's—and Percy's—history was the great Mississippi River flood of 1927, and his account of the flood showed both his magnanimity and his unblinking condescension toward blacks. During the flood, "a torrent ten feet deep the size of Rhode Island; it was 36 hours coming and four months going" (*Lanterns*, 249), Greenville's mayor made Percy the chairman of the flood relief effort; his duties included getting supplies to help the storm's thousands of homeless victims. When supplies ran out, Percy convinced the powerful levee board to evacuate people to Vicksburg, including some 7,500 blacks camped on the levee. Percy's father disagreed with the decision, arguing on behalf of Greenville's planters that if black laborers were allowed to leave they might never come back. William argued with his father but agreed to bring the issue to a vote with the levee board once more; this time, they unanimously changed their mind and voted to keep the homeless blacks in town. Only after the death of his father did William learn that the former senator had lobbied each one and had changed their minds. "He knew that the dispersal of our labor was a longer evil to the Delta than a flood. He was a natural gambler: he bet on warm weather and tents. Knowing that I could not be dissuaded by threats or even by his own opposition, he had accomplished his end in the one way possible and had sworn the committee to secrecy. Of course, none of us was influenced by what the Negroes themselves wanted; they had no capacity to plan for their own welfare; planning for them was another of our burdens" (*Lanterns*, 258). Richard Wright, in his story "Down By the Riverside," published in 1936 in the volume *Uncle Tom's Children*, portrays the black response to a flood scene quite differently. Mann, the central character, has to steal a boat to row his pregnant wife to a hospital. In the process he kills a white man in self-defense, a crime for which he knows he will be lynched. His wife dies en route to the hospital, and moments later Mann, denied even a glass of water, is forced to go to the levee and assist in the flood relief. Despite his cries of grief and physical pain, Mann is angrily dismissed by the military command leading the relief effort. "Aw c'mon, nigger! What in the hell's wrong with you? All the rest of the niggers are out there, how come you don't want to go?" (78).

Presenting blacks as incapable of planning their own welfare, of course, is the first step in taking control of their welfare for them; the discourse of "lazy" blacks was well-known to Percy, and he used it as freely as any patrician. Percy "took an almost anthropological interest in black folklore and habit," Wyatt-Brown writes. "He did so, however, only to demonstrate how apart the race was from white society. Differences in black and white social values, Percy thought, amply justified Jim Crow segregation in custom and law" (266).[18] In the foreword to *Lanterns on the Levee*, Percy's mourning for a time gone by reveals anxieties that go beyond family melancholy straight to the heart of economic fears. "The desire to reminisce arises not so much I think from the number of years you may happen to have accumulated as from the number of those who meant most to you in life, who have gone the long journey," he wrote. "They were the bulwarks, the bright spires, the strong places. When they have gone, you are a little tired, you rest on your oars, you say to yourself: 'There are no witnesses to my fine little fury, my minute heroic efforts. It is better to remember, to be sure of the good that was, rather than of the evil that is, to watch the spread and pattern of the game that is past rather than engage feebly in the present play. It was a stout world thus far, peopled with all manner of gracious and kindly and noble personages—these seem rather a pygmy tribe.' "

A devoted son of both his father and his culture, Percy wrote eloquently about his fears of the coming collapse of the world he had known so well, and as the "pygmy tribe" passage makes clear, he had no better vehicle for expressing this dread than the rhetoric of race, and, as we shall see, class. To be sure, the collapse of the South, as he observed it, was in large part the result of an increasing black presence. "A tarnish has fallen over the bright world," he wrote; "dishonor and corruption triumph; my own strong people are turned into lotus-eaters; defeat is here again, the last, the most abhorrent." The burnished world of the landed gentry, steeped in the writings of Marcus Aurelius and the Victorians, is being blackened, tarnished, by African pygmies.

Walker Percy, in his introduction to the 1973 edition of *Lanterns*, wrote that his cousin would not have been surprised, thirty years after his death, to find

> the collapse of the old moralities, for example, the so-called sexual revolution which he would more likely define in less polite language as "alley-cat morality." I can hear him now: "Fornicating like white trash is one thing, but leave it to this age to call it the new morality." Nor would he be shocked by the cynicism and corruption, the stealing, lying, rascality ascendant in business and politics—though even he might be dismayed by the complacency with which they are received. "There have always been crooks, but we've not generally made a practice of re-electing them, let alone inviting them to dinner." All this to say nothing of the lapse of civil order and the new jungle law which rules the American city. (xiv)

The "jungle law" that Walker invokes is as rich in racial weight as Will Percy's "pygmy tribes." For a Southerner, "jungle law" not only refers to the chaos of the dreaded urban landscape, so roundly disdained by the Agrarians, it also necessarily hearkens back to Reconstruction, when Union-supported black representation rose to prominence. Here, then, is a moment when contemporary anxiety about "moral" collapse relies implicitly on both racial and historical context. In one of the many moments when Percy invokes race precisely to express this anxiety, he does so indirectly, not by blaming blacks for causing political strife but by metaphorizing their character as unburdened by history. Indeed, Percy envies blacks for what he perceives to be their ability to live outside of history altogether: "No race probably ever had less knowledge of its own past, traditions and antecedents," he writes.

What African inheritance they still retain lies in the deep wells of their being, subconscious. They know not whence they came nor what manner of life they led there. Their folklore, rich and fascinating, is American, not African. Only in their practices of voodoo, their charms, potions, and incantations, can we catch glimpses of customs practiced by them in their mysterious homeland. This failure on their part to hold and pass on their own history is due, I think, not so much to their failure to master any form of written communication as to their obliterating genius for living in the present. The American Negro is interested neither in the past nor in the future, this side of heaven. He neither remembers nor plans. The white man does little else: to him the present is the one great unreality. (23)

Blacks, Percy writes, are not compelled to shoulder their history, and this "failure on their part," for one so obsessed with history, is more than a Sin against the Fathers; given the ambivalent feelings toward the Fathers, oblivion to ancestry is also an incalculable relief. Blacks, to Percy, are unencumbered by the ominous portraits of war heroes, with all the honor and torment they imply, staring down at them from the marble balustrade. It is a particularly Victorian impulse among Southerners to bend their cultural rhetoric to serve their own economic and political positions, writes Daniel Joseph Singal.

Those who possessed culture were thought to be "civilized," those who lacked it were "savages." The latter category, rarely well-defined, was made to include an assortment of people the Victorian middle class feared or did not like—the lower classes, those whose origins were other than European, and races whose skin color was other than white. Most important of all, the barrier between civilization and savagery, between the cultured and the uncultured, was considered virtually uncrossable, except through the very gradual effects of generational mobility. This radical dichotomy pervaded everything the Victorians said and did; even when they spoke optimistically of uplift and reform it was not far from their minds. This separation between the barbaric and the civilized, the animal and the human, became in fact the very bedrock assumption of their thought. (5)

Percy's position as an alienated, fragile poet born to a family of powerful landowners, then, was matched in its ambivalence only by his position as a sensitive humanist who nonetheless inherited and had to run an exploitative plantation system. As a writer, he considered himself devoted to aesthetics outside of any encroachment by overtly political forces, and he wondered why he was so frequently criticized for appearing to stand apart from the racial fray. "Another thing that irritates me is the expectation that all artists in prose or verse should write about the poor and the illiterate and the ill-bred," he wrote in a letter to Donald Davidson. "I know nothing about the psychology of the negro nor of the poor white. But I do know something of the feelings and problems of that class which was once the slave owner class in the South. I never could see any point when you are born a gentleman in trying to act as if you were not one." To the critic John Chapman he wrote: "I am interested in contemporary problems—the conflict between capital and labor, the injustice of the present tariff, etc. etc. etc., but I am much more interested in what seems to me the eternal things of human nature—Man and God, man and love, man in the trap of fate" (Baker, 154).

This stance, as a man committed to "art" at the same time that he is deeply connected to a feudal system of economy, makes Percy's language a fascinating study in the confluence of aesthetics, race, and class. In his introduction to *Lanterns on the Levee*, Walker Percy offered what many critics consider to have been an uncharacteristically shrill defense of his cousin, and the language he uses is useful to an understanding of William Percy's determination to remain outside of politics.

Lanterns on the Levee deserves better and of course has better readers. Its author can be defended against more extreme readers, but I wonder if it's worth the effort. Abraham Lincoln was a segregationist. What of it? Will Percy was regarded in the Mississippi of his day as a nigger-lover and reviled by the sheriff's office for his charges of police brutality. What of that? Nothing much is proved except that current categories and names, liberal and conservative, are weary past all thinking of it. Ideological words have a way of wearing thin and then, having lost the meanings, being used like switchblades against the enemy of the moment. Take the words *paternalism, noblesse oblige* dirty words these days. But is it a bad thing for a man to care like a father for his servants, spend himself on the poor, the sick, the miserable, the mad who come his way? It is surely better than watching a neighbor get murdered and closing the blinds to keep from "getting involved." It might even beat welfare. (xiii)

The energy exerted by the two Percys to defend art against "weary" ideological criticism is rich in itself. Toni Morrison has written that "the habit of ignoring race is understood to be a graceful, even generous, liberal gesture." I would extend this argument to include class as well; part of the sentimentality and backward-gazing that is so central to *Lanterns on the Levee* is a willful move to avoid what were often violent clashes of race and class. "I may seem to have implied that all Delta citizens were aristocrats traveling luxuriously up and down the river or sitting on the front gallery, a mint julep in one hand and a palm-leaf fan in the other, protected from mosquitoes by the smudge burning in the front yard," Percy writes. "If so, I have misinterpreted my country" (16). The passage is rich for the rhetorical energy spent describing what the South *isn't*; Percy says he has *misinterpreted*, not misrepresented the Delta, and fifty pages later he in fact gives a recipe for a mint julep. George Tindall's noted essay on Southern mythology is useful here in its assessment of the accepted narrative of Southern gentility. The standard visions of the Old South, Tindall writes,

> are enough to trigger in the mind the whole euphoric pattern of kindly old marster with his mint julep; happy darkies singing in fields perpetually white to the harvest or, as the case may be, sadly recalling the lost days of old; coquettish belles wooed by slender gallants in gray underneath the moonlight and magnolias. It is a pattern that yields all too easily to caricature and ridicule, for in its more sophisticated versions the figure of the planter carries a heavy freight of the aristocratic virtues: courtliness, grace, hospitality, honor, *noblesse oblige*, as well as many no less charming aristocratic vices: a lordly indifference to the balance sheet, hot temper, profanity, overindulgence, a certain stubborn obstinacy. The old-time Negro, when not a figure of comedy, is the very embodiment of loyalty. And the southern belle: "Beautiful, graceful, accomplished in social charm bewitching in coquetry, yet strangely steadfast in soul," Gaines has written, "she is perhaps the most winsome figure in the whole field of our fancy." The plantation romance, Gaines says, "remains our chief social idyll of the past; of an Ar-

cadian scheme of existence, less material, less hurried, less pro-
saically equalitarian, less futile, richer in picturesqueness, festivity,
in realized pleasure that reeked not of hope or fear or unrejoicing
labor." (in Grantham, 5)[19]

Beyond ignoring race, as we have seen, Percy constantly blurs distinctions between the plight of his own family and that of the blacks
that worked for them. "No class or individual among us has ever known
riches," he writes at one point.

> Some years the crop and the price are good and we take a trip or
> sport an automobile or buy another plantation; most years the
> crop fails or the bottom drops out of the market and we put on a
> new mortgage or increase the old one. Even then no one goes
> hungry or cold or feels very sorry for himself. If we become too
> prosperous and entertain the impression we are independent and
> frightfully efficient (farmers feel that way in a good year), the levee
> breaks and the wise river terrifies his silly children back into hu-
> mility and that cozy one-family feeling of the inmates of the Ark.
> Behind us a culture lies dying, before us the forces of the un-
> known industrial world gather for catastrophe. We have fields to
> plow and the earth smells good; maybe in time someone will pay
> us more for our cotton than we spend making it. In the meantime
> the darkies make up new songs about the boll-weevil and the river,
> and the sun pours over us his great tide of warmth which is also
> light. (24)

The habit of masking economic hardship, beyond the gesture of sentimentality, is "an absolute necessity in a profit economy which needs
outsiders as a surplus people," Audre Lord writes. "As members of such
an economy, we have *all* been programmed to respond to the human differences between us with fear and loathing and to handle that difference in one of three ways: ignore it, and if that is not possible, copy it
if we think it is dominant, or destroy it if we think it is subordinate. But
we have no patterns for relating across our human differences as equals.
As a result, those differences have been misnamed and misused in the
service of separation and confusion" (qtd. in West, 63).

Economics, then, as it drives racist discourse, allows landowners to
convince themselves that it is ultimately their *race* that has provided for
their prosperity. Rich fields, singing darkies, and warm sunlight is imagery pulled wholesale from antebellum discourse; the narrative impulse

to sentimentalize, or mask, references to actual physical hardship stems from proslavery propaganda, and as much as anything perpetuated the image of "the Sunny South," the historian Catherine Clinton writes. Prewar propagandists

> tried to shift the image of slavery from "necessary evil" to "plantation school" by means of this picturesque fictional portrait. Literature celebrated the familial mingling of black and white on the plantation and the beneficence masters bestowed on slaves. Planters sentimentalized to the point of caricature the image of happy darkies singing in the fields—omitting all reference to whips, chains, braids, maiming, selling families apart, and rape, among the numerous atrocities slavery allotted to blacks only. The masters sought to legitimate their authority by emphasizing their benevolent paternalism, the alleged Christian motivation of the enslavement of blacks. (14)

This is precisely the kind of rhetorical move that Etienne Balibar calls "neo-racism" or "differentialist racism," indicative of an ideology that purports to be beyond, or above, racism but yearns for a separation of "cultures" instead. Neoracists do not say that a person's *race* marks him as inferior but that one's *culture* is different; the neoracist fears risking eroding his own cultural identity by inviting another's to join in. This way of thinking is deeply conservative, since it depends on the fixity of *all* cultures, and closes off any path toward actual, rather than rhetorical, integration or cultural mixing, Balibar writes.[20]

Beyond the emotional level, the fear of abolished cultural frontiers is surely what Percy was writing about. His reliance on the past, which he was able to polish and embroider far more easily than the present, was his vehicle for yearning for a more ordered, less chaotic, less changeable time. For it was not only his culture, it was his own identity that was at stake, and the threats to one were a threat to the other. It is here again that we can see the close connection between the reliance on gilded images of ancestors and the desire to occlude contemporary troubles: both rhetorical moves allow the writer to create an image of relative stasis in a time of pressing change. The search for cultural and historical stability is parallel to the search for a stable individual—and, we might say, racial—identity, Stuart Hall writes. "The logic of the discourse of identity assumes a stable subject, i.e., we've assumed there is something which we can call our identity which, in a rapidly shifting world, has the great advantage of staying still."

Identities are a kind of guarantee that the world isn't falling apart quite as rapidly as it seems to be. It's a kind of fixed point of thought and being, a ground of action, a still point in the turning world. That's the kind of ultimate guarantee that identity seems to provide us with. . . . Marx begins the de-centering of that stable sense of identity by reminding us that there are always *conditions* to identity which the subject cannot construct. . . . History has to be understood as a continuous dialectic or dialogic relationship between that which is already made and that which is making the future. . . . Marx reminds us that we are always lodged and implicated in the practices and structures of everybody else's life. (10–11)

Marking blacks as living "outside history" reveals more than a sentimental impulse, then; it shows Percy's determination to remain outside history himself, to remain aloof from the historical pressures of his own time, and to ignore the discomfort of his own sexuality. Beyond this, of course, is the "great unreality" of the present, which allows, even compels, Percy and his contemporaries to live outside the pressures of the moment. It is to this that Toni Morrison speaks in *Playing in the Dark*. "It has been suggested that romance is an evasion of history (and thus perhaps attractive to a people trying to evade the recent past)," she writes.

But I am more persuaded by arguments that find in it the head-on encounter with very real, pressing historical forces and the contradictions inherent in them as they came to be experienced by writers. Romance, an exploration of anxiety imported from the shadows of European culture, made possible the sometimes safe and other times risky embrace of quite specific, understandably human, fears: Americans' fear of being outcast, of failing, of powerlessness; their fear of boundarylessness, of Nature unbridled and crouched for attack; their fear of the absence of so-called civilization; their fear of loneliness, of aggression both external and internal. In short, the terror of human freedom—the thing they coveted most of all. (24)

Morrison's use of the metaphor of an inexorably creeping, slithering, spreading "Nature" is perfect here; one thinks of Cash, with his descriptions of "the jungle growth of poverty and ruin [that] is closing on the Southern white man's clearings faster than he can make them, and threatening—as time goes on, threatening with increasing force—to stultify the gains made in the political field" (*Mind*, 149). This metaphor also brings up the ubiquitous swamp imagery in Lillian Smith's writing: swamps, like "jungles," are always on the dark edge of town, always threatening to break through boundaries of "civilization" and through known culture into chaos. Behind these anxieties were more than just issues of race, although Percy continued to use race as a metaphorical structure to describe them. What drove the South's fears of chaos was also the growing reality of hardscrabble economics.

As an endnote, and as a point of connection with Cash, it is important to acknowledge that it was not only to blacks that Percy condescended, just as it was not only blacks who threatened the Percy economic stronghold. Poor whites, and the ideologues that led them, were far more openly and unambiguously reviled in his memoir, and their racial and class positions are central to an understanding of Percy's work. The fight against the Ku Klux Klan, which Percy and his father undertook throughout their lives, came to represent an economic battle as much as a racial or ideological battle, and Percy's empathy for and protection of black workers can be read as an effort both to preserve a healthy workforce and to antagonize political enemies. The senator warned that although the Klan claimed not to injure Negroes unless they misbehaved, the black people in the Delta "don't know whether they are going to behave so as to suit those 1,000,000 Klansmen or not. Can't you see Sheriff Nicholson, if he wanted to arrest a Negro for robbing a henroost, writing to Nashville for a posse of klansmen and going down the road with a gang of white-robed men behind him to arrest the Negro? You would have to advertise to find the negro after that parade" (Wyatt-Brown, 230).

Unlike other times and other places in Southern history, the Mississippi Delta in the 1930s and 1940s did not witness whites of disparate classes joining against a common black enemy; here, the push of poor whites looking for work—and using racial violence to get it—became the central political issue of the day. "In the cotton counties along the river in Mississippi, where there are three black skins for every white one, the gentlemen are afraid. But not of the Negroes," Jonathan Daniels, a Percy contemporary, wrote in *A Southerner Discovers the South*. "The gentlemen and the Negroes are afraid together. They are afraid of the rednecks, the peckerwoods, who in politics and in person are pressing down upon the rich, flat Delta from the hard, eroded hills. They may lynch a Negro; they may destroy the last of a civilization which has great vices and great virtues, beauty and strength, responsibility beside arrogance, and a preserving honesty beside a destructive self-indulgence"

(172). As poor whites gathered political influence, they sought to over-throw not only blacks of a similar class but wealthy white landowners as well, and the Ku Klux Klan, which had enjoyed a significant rise in membership in 1916 after the publication of D. W. Griffith's *Birth of a Nation*, saw its ranks swell to four million by 1924.

Recent scholarship about the Klan, Wyatt-Brown writes, has played down religious and racial bigotries and stressed the quarrel with big-business capitalism, concern for community morality, and resentment of business elites. The Klansmen's first agenda was not to bring down Wall Street but to restore a Protestant moral order, but their resentment of high-toned traditional leaders like the Percys and their alien friends—Catholics, Jews, and dependent blacks—had its origins in economic dis-content and the widespread suspicion that people like the Percys had no respect for the lower orders. "Much more was involved than a simple righteous stand against intolerance," Wyatt-Brown writes.

The ascendancy of the Percys in the Delta was at risk. By no means were all anti-Klan stalwarts under Percy influence, but without the efforts of the Percys the Klan would have assumed complete con-trol of the county offices with ugly results not only for the blacks but for also the substantial number of Catholics, Jews, and mem-bers of other ethnic minorities in Greenville. The Percys were well aware that a victory for the Klan would have meant the end of their dynastic leverage in local affairs. Moreover, the anti-Catholic character of the Klan affected the family personally, since Camille Percy and her kin belonged to that much suspected faith. In addi-tion, the anti-Negro aspects of the hooded order threatened the stability of the Delta labor supply in general and the Percy's eco-nomic interests in particular. (230, 227–28)[21]

William and Leroy Percy stood up to the Klan, as the Grey Eagle had stood up to the carpetbaggers before them, in large part not because of racial enlightenment but because the Klan threatened their own political and economic base. As it is in Cash's work, Percy's racial rhetoric is full of class and sectional resonances, and getting at the conflation of race and class, particularly as it is articulated by a writer who thought himself unsullied by either, is vital to understanding the uses of racial and class-based rhetoric.

Unlike his literary contemporaries of the 1930s, notably James Agee,

Faulkner, and the Agrarians, Percy had little time for engaging with poor whites in his writing or his life. After nearly two decades of social realism in American fiction, Percy's highbrowed jabs at poor whites seem especially sharp. His language shows both disdain and aloofness, as if he has only *heard* about the existence of poor whites and never rubbed shoulders with them; for someone whose livelihood depended on the labor of hundreds of farm workers, this could hardly have been the case. Cash marked this disjuncture in his own work. "Once more," he wrote,

> this glorification had a marked influence, I think, on the fact that, at the same time when Southerners were being continually bound closer together in the broad social sense, and public haughtiness was in recession, the narrow, private pride of the old ruling class was not weakened but even distinctly enhanced. The enlarged idea of the heritage, the fact that it was bound to the past, and that therefore the charmed circle existed as a sort of closed corporation to which those who had not belonged before could not fully ever penetrate now—all this tended to widen the gulf, to erase the memory of ultimate kinship with the common whites. (*Mind*, 129)

Brought up to give the highest social value to a family's—and a race's—lineage, Percy dismisses poor whites as being of undistinguished heritage. "The poor whites of the South: a nice study in heredity and environment," he writes. "Who can trace their origin, estimate their qualities, do them justice? Not I."

Some say their forefathers served terms in English prisons for debt and were released on condition that they migrate from the mother country to the colonies. The story continues that they congregated in Georgia. The story may or may not be true; it is unpopular, needless to say. This much, however, it is safe to assert: they were not blest with worldly goods or mental attainments. The richer coast and tidewater country was not for them; their efforts at tilling the soil had to be among the unfertile hills. Farther and farther west they were pushed by an unequal competition until they lodged in the mountains of North Carolina, Tennessee, and Kentucky and in the clay hills of Alabama and Mississippi. Pure English stock. If it was ever good, the virus of poverty, malnutrition, and interbreeding has done its degenerative work: the present breed is probably the most unprepossessing on the broad face of the ill-populated earth. I know they are responsible for the only American ballads, for camp meetings, for a whole new and excellent school of Southern literature. I can forgive them as the Lord God forgives, but admire them, trust them, love them—never. Intellectually and spiritually they are inferior to the Negro, whom they hate. Suspecting secretly they are inferior to him, they must do something to him to prove to themselves their superiority. At their door must be laid the disgraceful riots and lynchings gloated over and exaggerated by Negrophiles the world over. (20)

Percy's determination to blame poor whites for race hatred is a common move that we also see prominently in Cash; plantation owners, like Percy, were enough removed from the ground-level economic hardship imposed on their workers, white and black, that they could convince themselves that they were above the fray. He begins by dismissing poor whites as coming from untraceable stock, perhaps the worst sin a man can commit. "A nice study in heredity and environment" emphasizes the doom to which poor whites are destined from birth; if Percy, like Faulkner, is attached to an image of a collapse that includes all classes and races of men, his vitriol here seems out of place. The rich may be in steep decline, but theirs is a heroic demise; the poor had it coming to them.

CHAPTER FOUR

I Know the Fears by Heart

Segregation as Metaphor in the
Work of Lillian Smith

Segregation . . . a word full of meaning for every person on earth. A word that is both symbol and symptom of our modern, fragmented world. We, the earth people, have shattered our dreams, yes; we have shattered our own lives, too, and our world.

LILLIAN SMITH, *Killers of the Dream*

During one of the many nights she slept in a separate part of the house from her husband, Alma Deen, mother of the protagonist in Lillian Smith's 1944 novel *Strange Fruit*, discovers a male pelvis that her daughter had made out of clay. "She found it in Laura's drawer, wrapped in a wet cloth. Uncovered, it lay in her hand, urgent, damp, like something in gestation. A lump of wet dirt. She was not able to take her eyes from it. And as she stood, unmoving, a bright red spot appeared in each cheek, her clamped jaws squared, shuttling her face into fresh planes, destroying the glaze which gave Alma Deen what her friends ardently called her 'spiritual look.' She held the little figure, stared at each detail as if she saw nakedness for the first time. As if all she had feared had come to life in that lump of dirt" (67).

Mrs. Deen is traumatized by the figure. "A pelvis . . . what had she been thinking of that would make her want to make a pelvis? A man, a boy—you could understand men being dirty like that—men seemed made that way. But your own daughter . . . spending her time making naked things. . . . What did she do it for?" Mrs. Deen throughout the novel is cast as a cold, utterly desexed woman; the "spiritual look" that she presents to the world, and to her family, is treated as one of disembodied moralizing. Sexuality, for Mrs. Deen, is something to be avoided at all cost. It is dirty, degraded, something to be indulged in only by men, in their weaker moments—and, of course, by blacks. As Mrs. Deen is contemplating the clay, something else is revealed to be bubbling under the surface of her mind: a memory of the time when she found her son Tracy and his black playmate Henry "playing Africa" without any clothes on.

> Naked, unmindful of the broiling sun, they were crouched before an upturned washpot, beating upon it. Sweat poured from their grave faces, down their bodies.
>
> "We're playing savages," Tracy declared stoutly, deserted by Henry, who upon her appearance had shot like greased lightning into his mama's cabin.
>
> "Savages?"
>
> "Yes'm. We're playing Africa." Six-year-old blue eyes looked into hers unwaveringly.
>
> "Why did you take your clothes off, Tracy?"
>
> "To play Africa."
>
> "Couldn't you play Africa with your clothes on?"
>
> "No mam."
>
> "Why?"
>
> "Cause Africa is nothing on." (69)

The homoeroticism of the scene is also not lost on Tracy's mother; she demands to know whether the two boys have been "doing anything else." But what is remarkable is the psychological move Mrs. Deen makes from horror at imagining her daughter's active sexuality to the memory of a homoerotic scene involving her son and a black playmate. In this, the scene is emblematic of Smith's work as a whole: the close scrutiny of the way the white Southern mind masks a deep sexual repression—at all levels—behind a screen of racialized discourse. Mrs. Deen's dread of her daughter's sexuality—and her own—moves lightning quick to find an outlet, and it is in a venting of anger and disgust at homosexuality and black sexuality that she finds it.

Throughout her work, Smith examines the psychosexual damage the discourse of racism does to whites, and white women particularly. As she wrote in a letter to Frank Taylor, the publisher of *Strange Fruit*, "I think it is first a love story of special tenderness, but I think it is also a racial fable that applies not only to the South but to the white race in its relationships the world over: the ambivalences, the conflicts, the love, the hate, the anger, the frustration, the terrible humiliations of the dark man's spirit . . . the gradual wearing away of the white man's civilized and humane feelings" (Gladney, 72).

Smith regularly conflated the legacies of racial segregation and Victorian sexual repression, both heterosexual and homosexual. In *Killers of the Dream*, she often used the word "segregation" to denote parts of the body that were "off limits," just as parts of a town—lunch counter, bus station, playgrounds—were off limits to blacks.

> Now, parts of your body are segregated areas which you must stay away from and keep others away from. These areas you touch only when necessary. In other words, you cannot associate freely with them any more than you can associate freely with colored children. . . . Now, on the other hand, though your body is a thing of shame and mystery, and curiosity about it is not good, your skin is your glory and the source of your strength and pride. It is white. And, as you have heard, whiteness is a symbol of purity and excellence. Remember this: Your white skin proves that you are better than all other people on this earth. Yes, it does that. And does it simply because it is white—which, in a way, is a kind of miracle. (87)

To Southern Victorians, Daniel Singal has written, "the world was filled with what one writer called 'furious provocatives to unbridled sensuality and riotous animalism,' any of which might undermine their elaborate efforts at self-mastery. One must accordingly drape the legs of chairs and pianos and in some instances carefully separate the works of male and female authors on library shelves to block out dangerous stimuli. . . . The true purpose of marriage, warned a minister, 'can be fulfilled only when the two parties in the relation are agreed to *make no provision for the flesh* in thought, desire, or practice'" (28). Like McCullers, Smith was well aware of the manner in which white Southern discourse propped up its mythical notions of sexual innocence by demonizing those who did not play by the same rules. For not only was she a racial liberal in the conservative South, she was a lesbian in a culture obsessed with maintaining traditional images of sexual conduct. She lived for many years with Paula Snelling, a writer and editor who helped publish her magazines. Although she was reticent about her own sexuality, her published writings about sex were, in Morton Sosna's words, "to say the least, avant garde. She would deal frequently with the need to encourage children to feel proud rather than guilty about their sexuality, with

the feminine side of nature, with the potential healthiness of masturbation and homosexuality, and with Protestantism's failure to appreciate a
'mature genitality'" (179).

Smith considered Dorothy Baker's book *Cassandra at the Wedding* to be
"the most candid and perceptive account ever printed of girls and
women and their feelings for each other and themselves" and "an astute
revelation of female homosexuality" (Loveland, 183). In a letter to
Rochelle Gibson, the book editor at *Saturday Review*, she wrote that a
book she had recently read was "highly contemporary; its homosexual
overtones are fresh and muted tastefully but intertwined with the sym-
biotic relationship: an astute revelation of female homosexuality which
is, in my opinion, as different as day from night from male homosexuality. There is no such thing as 'the homosexual' anyway" (Gladney, 295).

A novel Smith wrote about China, later destroyed in a fire, contained
"a good bit of homosexuality" based on the relationships she had observed between the female missionaries and students she had met while
working there. In a letter written to Jerome Bick, a film agent, she wrote
that it was the "across-the-barrier relationships" in *Strange Fruit*, not only
black-white but homosexual, that she considered "the real story." In the
novel, Tracy's mother, Alma Deen, worries about her daughter's attachment to Jane Hardy, an older woman who teaches school in Maxwell and
encourages her artistic skills: "'There're—women, Laura, who aren't
safe for young girls to be with. . . . There're women who are—unnatural.
They're like vultures—women like that. They do terrible things to
young girls. . . . I don't believe a woman is the right kind of woman who
talks about the naked body as Jane does" (243). Laura responds: "You
knew you could talk to Jane, you could tell her about your sculpture and
your verses, about your fears and your feelings. . . . And you loved her.
Yes, you loved her and wanted to be with her. And now Mother was la-
beling it with those names that the dean of women at college had
warned you about. . . . [I]f Mother made an issue, if she labeled this
feeling for Jane with those names, there'd be no more feeling. . . . You
wouldn't want it. You wouldn't want your relationship with Jane when
Mother finished with it. You wouldn't want—anything" (246).

The novel *One Hour* is even more explicit in its treatment of lesbian-
ism. In that novel, Smith writes of the seduction of fifteen-year-old
Grace Channing by "the Woman," whom she had met at a camp and
who awakened her intellectually and aesthetically as well as sexually:
"And then the camp closed and Grace went back to school and a doctor came and told the girls about the facts of life. And she learned dur-

ing that lecture on 'normal love' that this amazing creature who had seemed to come out of a myth, who did not quite belong in the ordinary world, was nothing but a homosexual. I struggled to hold on to my image of her, to cling to the validity of what I had experienced, but I couldn't. I fought the word the doctor had used, but it whipped me after two or three weeks" (353).

Smith's sense of alienation as a lesbian certainly contributed to her understanding of the damage done by discourses of power and intolerance. In *Killers of the Dream*, she despaired of her girlhood exposure to

the edgy blackness and whiteness of things . . . the breathing symbols we made of the blackness and the whiteness . . . the metaphors we created and watched ourselves turning into . . . the shaky myths we leaned on even as we changed them into weapons to defend us against external events. Now, suddenly, shoving our pleasures and games and stinging questions come the TERRORS: the Ku Klux Klan and the lynchings I did not see but recreated from whispers of grownups . . . the gentle back-door cruelties of "nice people" which scared me more than the cross burnings . . . and the singsong voices of politicians who preached their demonic suggestions to us as if elected by Satan to do so: telling us lies about skin color and a culture they were callously ignorant of—lies made of their own fantasies, of their secret deviations—forcing decayed pieces of theirs and the region's obscenities into the minds of the young and leaving them there to fester. (12–13)

The ambient white voices that took images of race, twisted them to fit their own "secret deviations," and then fed them to the South's children not only fired Smith's imagination but led her to draw heavily on her own experiences in her writing. She wrote that *Strange Fruit* reflected the "splits and estrangements" in her own life, that "every tension was an echo of a tension in my own life" (Loveland, 64). In *Killers of the Dream*, she writes of the anguish felt by children upon learning that compassion and generosity are to be extended to others only as their skin color merits. "The mother who taught me what I know of tenderness and love and compassion taught me also the bleak rituals of keeping the Negroes in their 'place.' The father who rebuked me for an air of superiority toward schoolmates from the mill and rounded out his rebuke by gravely reminding me that 'all men are brothers,' trained me in the steel-rigid decorums that I must demand of every colored male. They who so gravely taught me to split my body from my mind and both from my 'soul,' taught me also to split my conscience from my acts and Christianity from southern tradition" (27).

It is the "being kept in place," the boxing in of the spirit, that Smith wrote about with such fervor. Her own segregation as a lesbian nurtured a deep anger over another, far more visible brand of racial segregation, but the two worked hand in hand to form her imaginative powers. When she writes of the Southerners who taught her to "split my body from my mind," she is conflating racial and sexual repressions in a way that allowed her unique insight into the Southern mind.

In April 1939, Billie Holiday recorded a song about lynching. Written by Lewis Allen, the song was vivid, visceral, violent; some club owners and radio executives feared that its graphic lyrics—"Black bodies swinging in the Southern breeze"—would offend listeners, particularly in the South, where lynching continued to be the most graphic emblem of a generation's struggle and obsession with race.[1] The lyrics of the song were haunting:

> Southern trees bear a strange fruit
> Blood on the leaves, and blood at the root
> Black bodies swinging in the Southern breeze
> Strange fruit hanging from the poplar trees
>
> Pastoral scene of the gallant South
> The bulging eyes and the twisted mouth,
> Scent of magnolias, sweet and fresh,
> Then the sudden smell of burning flesh.
>
> Here is a fruit for the crows to pluck
> For the rain to gather, and the wind to suck
> For the sun to rot and the trees to drop
> Here is a strange and bitter crop.

The song had a particular resonance for Holiday, whose father, two years previously, had died of pneumonia after being denied admission to numerous segregated Dallas hospitals. "It wasn't the pneumonia that killed him, it was Dallas, Texas," she said. The jazz critic Rudi Blesh wrote that Holiday made the song her own so that no one else would dare try it: "She had been there. Lynching, to Billie Holiday, meant *all* the cruelties, *all* the deaths, from the quick snap of the neck to the slow dying from *all* kinds of starvation."[2]

As shocking as the lyrics are, they are also captivating in their perception of a central irony of Southern life, of the violence that lies just beneath the veneer of sentiment and romance. The word "strange" in particular conjures up the physical deformity and grotesquerie that abounds in the writing of Erskine Caldwell, Flannery O'Connor, and Carson McCullers. "Strange," too, as in the other writers' work, stands for disfigurement encountered unexpectedly. Magnolia trees, "sweet and fresh," are an iconographic image of the "gallant South," but a closer look, a keener smell, reveals the brutal irony that lay beneath the sentiment, naming as myth a romance built upon the mutilation of black bodies. This abrupt, deep irony is very much in line with the images found in Cash, as we have seen; blacks are tortured, burned, or hung to manifest physically the white craving for rhetorical and political superiority.

Five years after the recording of "Strange Fruit," Smith published a novel by the same name that revolved around a small Georgia town and a forbidden love affair between a wealthy white boy and a college-educated black maid. As central and controversial as the song was to the career of Holiday and to the heart of a culture in turmoil, so too was the novel. *Strange Fruit* was banned by booksellers—for lewdness, ironically, not for violence or racial provocation—in Boston and Detroit, and by the U.S. Postal Service; it took an intervention by President Roosevelt, acting on a request from his wife, Eleanor, to have the ban lifted (Loveland, 71).[3] In part due to this controversy, the book sold 140,000 copies in its first two months and took over the top spot on the best-seller list of the *New York Times Book Review*, where it was favorably reviewed by W. E. B. Du Bois. He praised "its explicit depiction of the tragedy of the South. . . . On each page the reader sees how both elements (white and black) in Maxwell are caught in a skein (economic, ethnic, emotional) that only evolution can untangle or revolution break."[4]

Diana Trilling wrote that *Strange Fruit* "is so wide in its human understanding that its Negro tragedy becomes the tragedy of anyone who lives in a world in which minorities suffer; when it ends in a lynching, we are as sorry and frightened for the lynchers as for the victim. Indeed, we are terrified, for ourselves, at the realization that this is what we have made of our human possibility." In the South, the reaction was mixed. The most vitriolic attack appeared in the *Hapeville (Ga.) Statesman*, whose associate editor was Eugene Talmadge, the former segregationist governor. A front-page story in the newspaper charged that the book portrayed "a romantic love affair between a white Georgia boy and a negro girl . . . in such glamour that will make courtships between negroes and whites appear atractive [*sic*]." A few Southern reviewers contended that the picture *Strange Fruit* drew of race relations in the South was outdated and distorted, that the events of the book took place immediately after World War I, but the South had changed greatly in the twenty-five years since then. Indeed, a reviewer in *Social Forces*, published by Howard Odum's institute in Chapel Hill, thought Smith should have omitted the lynching, arguing that "the decreasing rate of lynchings (in the South) has made this climax a little stale as literature and reality" (Loveland, 69–71).[5]

But although the novel *Strange Fruit* moves inevitably toward a lynching, Smith's use of the title referred to something subtly, and provocatively, different. She had originally used the term in a column entitled "Two Men and a Bargain," written for the magazine *South Today* that she published along with Paula Snelling. The column, which she later expanded into a chapter for her 1949 book *Killers of the Dream*, was a parable about the relationship between rich and poor whites and the specter of an emerging black workforce. "Mr. Rich White," lamenting the breakdown of his bargain with "Mr. Poor White," dreads the time when the latter will begin "filling his unions with niggers, keep right on filling them, making them bigger and stronger, and first thing you know he may not even *care* whether he's better than niggers."

> Something whispers not to worry. "Long as you have segregation none of these things can happen!" it says. "Just keep saying *nothing can change it. Nothing!*" When Mr. Rich White complains that everybody's against him, Something reassures him. "I'm for you, I'm for the guy who wants to be first, I'm for the guy who loves his own image, I'm for the guy who rides the front seat, always the front seat and won't let others ride with him." "Who are you?" asks Mr. Rich White. "You know me," Something replies. "Every man from the womb knows me until death stops the knowledge. But some won't make me a bargain. You did. . . . Who am I? Listen, I'll tell you. I'm that which splits a mind from its reason, a soul from its conscience, a heart from its loving, a people from humanity. I'm the seed of hate and fear and guilt. You are its strange fruit which I feed on." (Loveland, 66–67)[6]

In a weekly column for the *Chicago Defender*, which she wrote for forty-three weeks in 1948–49 alongside columns by Walter White, Langston Hughes, and Mary McLeod Bethune, Smith wrote that the "strange fruit" she conceived of was not lynching or miscegenation (a word I hate) but the white man himself and his children and his Tobacco Roads and his own wasted life; the "strange fruit" was man dehumanized by a culture that is not good for the growth of either white or colored children. I do not believe it is possible to understand the white man in America and his strange paranoid notions about his "superiority" without considering his equally strange childhood and the training he received before he was six years old, the heavy guilt laid on heart and body while both were so young and weak, and finally the strange fruit which this has borne, not only of White Supremacy but of mental illness, alcoholism, child delinquency, exploitation, and war-making. (Blackwell and Clay, 41–42)

In Smith's hands, then, "strange fruit" refers not to black bodies swaying in the summer breeze, although that image adds an acute dramatic weight, but to the damaged, "split," primarily *white* people raised in a culture of deep racial, sexual, and class-based taboos and conflict. Much of this thinking grew out of the experiences she had had growing up in, and then reporting on the events of, the midcentury South.

She was born Lillian Eugenia on December 12, 1897, in Jasper, Florida, just south of the Georgia border and just southwest of the Okefenokee Swamp; she was the seventh child among four girls and five boys. The family lived in a nice part of town across from the Methodist church. Her father, Calvin Warren Smith, made a good living, employing hundreds of whites and blacks in his wholesale lumber and retail stores. Both of Lillian's parents came from slaveowning families in Georgia; her father's people were Scotch-Irish farmers who had migrated from North Carolina to settle in Ware County, Georgia; her maternal grandfather had been born in New York City. Educated in a Canadian monastery to be a Jesuit priest, he had rebelled and, before taking his final vows, escaped to the South, where he married the young and beautiful daughter of a prosperous Georgia planter. When the Civil War came, he fought with the Confederates, "not for slavery but for States Rights and for his bride."

Lillian graduated from high school in Jasper in 1915. That same year, her family moved to Rabun County, Georgia, a mountainous region tucked into a triangle formed by North and South Carolina. After her father's business failed, the family transformed their summer home into a small inn, the Laurel Falls Hotel, on Old Screamer Mountain. In 1920, Calvin Smith turned the inn into a private camp for girls. A talented pianist, Lillian went to the Peabody Conservatory in Baltimore in 1917, then spent three years in Huchow, Chekiang Province, China, as head of the music department of the Virginia School, a Christian Missionary School for wealthy Chinese girls. It was in China that she first read Gandhi and where she first responded to dramatic disparities in wealth and privilege. "The young woman who had shocked Clayton [Georgia] by being the first to bob her hair and wear short skirts was completely unprepared for the cultural and intellectual shock of China," writes her biographer, Anne Loveland. "It was a land of sharp contrasts, of enchanting beauty and cultural richness alongside 'dreadful disease and dirt and poverty and ignorance'" (11–12).[7]

Seeing the white colonials do "so many ugly things" in China disturbed Lillian and raised questions about segregation in the South. "'Seeing it happen in China made me know how ugly the same thing is in Dixie,' she recalled. 'For the first time in my life I was ashamed of my white skin. I began almost to believe that "whiteness" cast an evil spell over all that it came into contact with'" (Loveland, 40). Returning from China, and with her parents in failing health, Lillian took over the direction of Laurel Falls camp and remained there, running the camp, editing magazines, and writing, for the remainder of her life. The camp was to remain a touchstone for Smith's thinking and writing; when she took over the camp after her father's death, she added cultural and literary studies and held weekly talks with campers and counselors that would provide ideas for much of her later writing. Her efforts to integrate her camp met with angry reactions from both the parents of her white students and the people near Clayton, who viewed her with great suspicion. In 1955, eleven years after a house fire consumed hundreds of her letters, a much larger fire, this one destroying an enormous body of her unpublished work, was found to have been set by two local white boys; although there was no publicity and no trial, the two boys were "whisked out of town" to another state. Smith tried to believe it was just the work of juvenile delinquents but feared it might have been because she'd had white and black children to gatherings at the camp (Loveland, 130).

Her literary influences were broad. She read Hemingway, Proust, Joyce, and Woolf, whom she liked "only temperately." She disliked Faulkner and would come to spar with him over the speed with which the South was becoming integrated.[8] She largely objected to the writers of her own day, considering the French brand of existentialism particularly too self-involved and removed from the political tumult of their time. "What has Albee given us? Alice? Genet? Sartre? Mailer? Most cannot tear their eyes from their own small depravities. So: they are giving us fragmented sketches of sick people; they hold before us in play and story a never-ending bleak view of miserable, lost, lonely schizophrenics" (Cliff, 162). If her criticism of these writers seems naive, her exasperation is with these writer's unmistakable narcissism; her own brand of political journalism and fiction pointed distinctly outward, away from her own life, rather than inward, a style that undoubtedly rendered her nonfiction more effective than her fiction.

Smith was also a devoted reader of psychoanalytic texts; she studied Freud, Sandor Ferenczi, Otto Rank, Carl Jung, Alfred Adler, and Karl Menninger, whose *Love against Hate* was published in 1942, two years before *Strange Fruit*. It was her investment in psychology that led her to her most dramatic claims about racism's legacy of broad spiritual damage. She also read a large body of black writing, including the literature and sociology of W. E. B. Du Bois, E. Franklin Frazier's *The Negro Family in the United States*, and Horace Mann Bond's *Negro Education in Alabama*. She praised the work of white writers, like John Dollard's *Caste and Class in a Southern Town* and Howard Odum's *Southern Regions of the United States*, but was skeptical of the unending white fascination with the Civil War. "What Negro," she wrote, "can ever forget that one decade of this era of good feeling which produces [historian Paul Buck's] lyricism also produced 1,035 lynchings of black men?" (Loveland, 176, 27).

Smith was a remarkably prolific writer. In 1943, as her magazine writing was peaking but before her first book was published, she was honored by the Schomburg Collection of the New York Public Library as one of six whites, along with Franz Boaz and Wendell Wilkie, on its Honor Roll of Race Relations; the Schomburg cited Smith for maintaining "a consistent liberalism in a land where it takes courage to be a liberal." In addition to *Strange Fruit* and *Killers of the Dream*, the primary texts to be examined here, she published the novel *One Hour* (1959) and several books of nonfiction, *The Journey* (1954); *Now Is the Time* (1955); and *Our Faces, Our Words* (1964). She also lost a massive body of writing to a house fire in 1944: three manuscripts, including novels about China (*And the Water Flows On*) and the South (*Tom Harris and Family*); and a novella (*Every Branch in Me*); some 13,000 letters; sketches for future books; and all her notes from a recent six-month trip to India.

The magazine she edited with Paula Snelling, known at its founding in 1936 as *Pseudopodia*, then as the *North Georgia Review*, and finally as *South Today*, was brazen in its antisegregationist rhetoric; W. E. B. Du Bois called the magazine "stunning and courageous." J. Waties Waring, the

South Carolina federal judge who had ruled against his state's effort to maintain the white primary, referred to Smith's denunciations of racism as among the most penetrating analyses of the South he had ever read. "If people of this country and of the world can only see and understand the disease which has long lingered under a scab of romance wrapped in the Confederate flag," he wrote, "they can and will find a way to restore to health our poor pitiful people whom you and I love and weep for." Smith's editorial voice represented the magazine's high-water mark; in it, she developed both her literary ear and her sharp political voice. Much of her rhetorical anger she reserved for matters of race; her commentary so infuriated her detractors that she began receiving threats not only from local and state bureaucrats, who threatened to prevent her from mailing her magazine, but from the Ku Klux Klan. In a searingly sarcastic column arguing against U.S. involvement in World War II in the spring of 1939, Smith mocked a culture that exerted so much energy keeping blacks down yet would send them abroad to fight racial hatred. Negroes, she wrote, could be sent overseas as shock troops, "since they have the longest and most persistent record of being splotches."

They could go, calling out in their deep mellow voices "But we live in God's country and that's a fact, en it's a fine place to live in ef yo knows yo place, and we knows our place, yeah Lawd! Now we'se come to lay down our lives for those Jews Mister Hitler's been pickin' on. We hear tell he takes their property and their money and kicks them about and spits on 'em and burns their books. An' all that makes our democratic blood about boil over. Yas suh! For hit sho must be terrible to live in a country whar yo has yo money tuk (our ways a lot better cause we has no money to be tuk—just a little furnish which is et up and gone fo yo can say scat) and it sho must be a awful sight to have yo books burned—hit's a lot better never to learn how to read and write like us, we'se tellin you. And to be spit at in the face! That just shows the awful wickedness of that facism business. Now in our country things are worked out mighty well, a sight better'n that. Theah's plenty of back streets to walk on in every town and back doors what you can go in and out of. And theah's always the Quarters. You don need to scrounge up close to folks, close enough for 'em to spit at you! You can always step off the sidewalk. And if worse comes to worst you kin run yo tail off and make it to the Swamp. Yeah Lawd . . . there ain't nothin so plumb democratic as a good cypress swamp. . . . Ef them Jews hada jes ad a coupla cypress swamps it'd sho helped them get rid of fascism. Yeah, man." (Loveland, 193–95)

As awkward as the caricature sounds today, its bitter use of a black voice to upbraid a racist brand of governance shows some of the impulses Smith would refine and use more effectively in her books. Her journalism, if rough-edged, was nonetheless influential; her magazines were considered among the most important liberal voices of the decade. Moreover, her writing allowed her the chance to explore the far reaches of the South, both white and black; during two years of travel in 1939 and 1940, on a grant from the Rosenwald Fund, Smith and Snelling attended sharecroppers' and miners' union meetings, visited black and white schools and universities, mental hospitals, orphanages, homes for delinquent children, and the federal penitentiary in Atlanta. They talked with planters and industrialists, with social workers and judges, with New Dealers working for the Farm Security Administration. They spent a month at the University of North Carolina at Chapel Hill, where they talked with English and history professors, attended several of Howard Odum's seminars, and renewed their friendship with William Couch of the University of North Carolina Press. She said that during her travels as a Rosenwald Fellow, "I broke every barrier I could in the South to try to 'see things as they are'" (Loveland, 29). As an early and ardent supporter of the 1954 *Brown v. Board of Education* decision, a member of the board of the Congress of Racial Equality, and an admirer and associate of Martin Luther King Jr.,[9] Smith was "a standing rebuke to more timid Southern liberals and moderates. In refusing to become influential in conventional ways, she acquired a moral authority that far outweighed her institutional connections" (King, 176). Her battles with Ralph McGill, the editor of the *Atlanta Constitution* and the self-styled voice of Southern racial liberalism, were public and occasionally vicious. In his review of *Killers*, McGill wrote, "Miss Smith is a prisoner in the monastery of her own mind. But rarely does she come out of its gates, and then, apparently, seeing only wicked things to send her back to her hair shirt and the pouring of ashes on her head and salt in her own psychiatric wounds" (Loveland, 104). To Richard King, McGill's rage was so acute because "hell hath no fury like a Southern moderate whose hand has been called," and this Smith surely considered one of her primary functions. She was a clear-eyed, politically marginal but rhetorically forceful voice pushing the South to examine its obsession with race for what it was: dark, inextricable, spiritually damaging in the extreme.

Smith's reporting instincts, and even her language, seemed at times remarkably like those of Gunnar Myrdal, whose *American Dilemma* was published in the same year as *Strange Fruit*. In a letter she wrote to the Southern Regional Council in June 1944, later reprinted in the *New Republic*, she wrote:

Racial segregation, political and economic isolationism cannot be considered apart from man's whole personality, his culture, his needs. Neither can man's needs be considered apart from the destroying effects of segregation. Nor can the South's major problems be solved by trying to put a loaf of bread, a book and a ballot in everyone's hand. For man is not an economic or political unit. To believe that he is, is to ignore personality and cheapen the human spirit. And by ignoring personality, we oversimplify a complex, subtle, tragically profound problem. It helps us sometimes to see this in perspective if we will look at the restricting name of segregation in terms of the needs of children. A child's personality cannot grow and mature without self-esteem, without feelings of security, without faith in the world's willingness to make room for him to live as a human being. . . . No colored child in our South is being given today what his personality needs in order to grow and mature richly and fully. No white child, under the segregation pattern, can be free of arrogance and hardness of heart, and blindness to human need—and hence no white child can grow freely and creatively under the crippling frame of segregation. . . .

We simply cannot turn away and refuse to look at what segregation is doing to the personality of every child, every grown-up, white and colored, in the South today. Segregation is spiritual lynching. The lynched and the lynchers are our own people, our own selves. (Gladney, 86–87)

Within this passage are all of the elements of Smith's literary work: the link between racial segregation and psychological splitting; the fragility, indeed the illusoriness, of racial identity; and the wake of broad spiritual damage left by racist ideologues. In a passage from the 1961 foreword to *Killers of the Dream*, the word "segregation" stands in for all that is fractured in Smith's cultural moment.

Segregation . . . a word full of meaning for every person on earth. A word that is both symbol and symptom of our modern, fragmented world. We, the earth people, have shattered our dreams, yes; we have shattered our own lives, too, and our world. Our big problem is not civil rights nor even a free Africa—urgent as these are—but how to make into a related whole the split pieces of the human experience, how to bridge mythic and rational mind, how to connect our childhood with the present and the past with the future, how to relate the differing realities of science and religion and politics and art to each other and to ourselves. Man is a broken creature, yes; it is his nature as a human being to be so; but it is also his nature to create relationships that can span the brokenness. This is his first responsibility; when he fails, he is inevitably destroyed. (21)[10]

In this passage Smith is fully engaged with notions that are now considered staples of postmodern racial thought, that constructions of "Otherness"—embodiments of the subject's opposite or antithesis—are not only *not* apart from the subject but are located specifically *within* the subject, are indeed something on which the subject depends for its very existence. Jacques Lacan, Juliet Mitchell, and Jacqueline Rose have defined the objective of psychoanalysis as the effort to break "the confusion behind this mystification . . . whose conflation he saw as the elevation of fantasy into the order of truth." Woman (or black, in our case) is constructed as an "absolute category" that serves to guarantee the unified identity of the man (or white). Whites define themselves not by what they are but by what they are *not*, that is, black; black is thus construed both as a "lack," an inadequacy, "what (white) is not," and a "loss," something that is at once loathed and yearned for, reviled and mourned. Black, then, is ultimately nothing more than a "fantasmatic place" onto which whites can build structures of racial and political discourse. Lacan defined the objective of psychoanalysis as the effort to break "the confusion behind this mystification . . . whose conflation he saw as the elevation of fantasy into the order of truth" (Mitchell and Rose, 47–48, 50).

In his autobiography *A Man Called White*, Walter White writes of the more sinister side of this identity equation: how blacks learn their identity precisely as a result of white racism. Recounting the Atlanta race riots of 1906, in which his father stood in the family's doorway protecting his family with a rifle, White writes:

In the flickering light the mob swayed, paused, and began to flow toward us. In that instant there opened up within me a great awareness; I knew then who I was. I was a Negro, a human being with an invisible pigmentation which marked me a person to be hunted, hanged, abused, discriminated against, kept in poverty and ignorance, in order that those whose skin was white would have readily at hand a proof of their superiority, a proof patent and inclusive, accessible to the moron and the idiot as well as the to the wise man and the genius. No matter how low a white man fell, he could always hold fast to the smug conviction that he was superior to two-thirds of the world's population, for those two-thirds were not white. (11)

Similarly, Smith hoped to cut away the cultural logic that hierarchized men and women, heterosexuals and homosexuals, whites and blacks, to pressure notions of gender and racial authority, to see how the discourse of racism damaged both races by binding them together in destructive rhetorical manacles. Breaking down the confusion behind racial mystification was Smith's both political and literary objective. She wrote *Strange Fruit*, she said, "because I had to find out what life in a segregated culture had done to me, one person; I had to put down on paper these experiences so that I could see their meaning for me. I was in dialogue with myself as I wrote, as well as with my hometown and my childhood and history and vertical exploration. It has to true itself with facts but also with feelings and symbols, and memories that are never quite facts but sometimes closer to the truth than is any fact" (*Killers of the Dream*, 13).

In *Strange Fruit*, then, Smith examines both the fissures in her own psychology, largely rooted in her sexual isolation, and the cultural scars that were for her the twin legacies of race in the South; for her, the personal and the political were always linked, always cross-pollinating. The novel revolves around a love affair between Tracy Deen, the white son of a prominent Southern family, and Nonnie Anderson, a black college graduate returned home to the town of Maxwell, Georgia. Their romance is tormented by social restrictions on racial mixing. Tracy, in a flurry of self-destructiveness, converts to be a Southern Baptist, beats up Nonnie, and agrees to marry the white daughter of another well-to-do local family. Soon afterward, Tracy is found dead, and the town burns with rumors about the identity of his murderer. His killer, it turns out, is Nonnie's brother Ed, but it is Henry McIntosh, a black companion of Tracy's since birth, who finds himself in the wrong place at the wrong time and is blamed.

The opening sentence of the novel begins with a raceless, nameless woman, ominously looking over a small town: "She stood at the gate, waiting; behind her the swamp, in front of her Colored Town, beyond it, all Maxwell. Tall and slim and white in the dusk, the girl stood there, hands on the picket fence" (1).[11] From the first sentence we are presented with a subject who is at once proscribed, ambiguous, and threatening. The unnamed "She" is a creature emerging from a swamp, "waiting," eyeing not only Colored Town but "all Maxwell." Yet when race is invoked in the second sentence, it is not blackness that is evoked but whiteness; color does not describe here, it misleads. "She" is "tall and slim and white in the dusk . . . hands on a picket fence," an image of Southern femininity; racial misrecognition is invoked from the very beginning. Here is a creature that is both white and dark, gentle and threatening; an image, indeed a body, to be interpreted in any way an observer chooses. The way this image is made into a metaphor is precisely what interests Smith, and it is just this—the instability of racial identity and the ways one race uses the other to define itself—that I would like to examine.

As the novel develops, word of the murder begins to spread through the switchboard of Miss Sadie, the town's operator, through whom all local gossip travels first. "Miss Sadie looked out of the west window across the ballground to the swamp. Black clouds had massed up over the tree line, throwing deep shadows over the town, and by some trickery of the hidden sun clumps of palmettos stood out in startling greenness. The light, dark as the afternoon was, was so intense that she could see moss hanging from the cypress back of the Negro Lodge, something she couldn't remember being able to see before. A low roll of thunder came from the northwest" (276).

The colors of the storm imagery are plain: the clouds massing menacingly over the tree line are black; they throw deep shadows over the town. To Miss Sadie, to white Maxwell, the death of a white son at the hands of what they assume to have been a black man is apocalypse foretold; it is the manifestation of their worst racial fears, blackness spreading over their town like a biblical plague. The darkness visible that Miss Sadie fears is the same one Thomas Dixon fears; the low roll of thunder that follows it is a portent of a culture in danger, in the throes of collapse. This is Smith playing on the fears she sees manifest in her fellow whites, and she points to the same polarity that Ralph Ellison acknowledged as the mythical discourse of identity. In *Shadow and Act* Ellison writes:

Being "highly pigmented," as the sociologists say, it was our Negro "misfortune" to be caught up associatively in the negative side of this basic dualism of the white folk mind, and to be shackled to almost everything it would repress from conscience to consciousness. The physical hardships and indignities of slavery were benign compared with this continuing debasement of our image. Because these things are bound up with their notion of chaos, it is almost impossible for many whites to consider questions of sex, women, economic opportunity, the national identity, historic change, social justice—even the "criminality" implicit in the broadening of freedom itself—without summoning malignant images of black men into consciousness. (63)

For whites, Ellison writes, blackness signifies "chaos," a malignancy; in Smith's passage, black storm clouds signify an occlusion of lightness, a haunting, an overpowering. Black is Other, dangerous, perilous, and the more complex for the juxtaposition of the words "light, dark": "'The light, dark as the afternoon was, was so intense that she could see moss hanging from the cypress back of the Negro Lodge, something she couldn't remember being able to see before." Light is not separate, or set off, from dark, or defined by dark, it *is* dark; indeed, the "dark light" is so intense that Miss Sadie is "able to see things she has never seen before." Darkness is not Other, it is inherent in the light; otherness is tied up inextricably with subjectivity, blackness with whiteness. One does not exist without the other.

The third color in the above passage—the "startling greenness"— is equally interesting, particularly as it stands against light and black. Several chapters after this moment we find the word "green" again, as Sam Perry, a black friend of the innocent Henry McIntosh, is in the law office of Tom Harris, trying to convince him that Henry will be lynched unless Harris comes to his aid. As Sam presses his case, Harris repeatedly tries to convince him that Henry is safe, hidden in the one place a mob would never think to look, the county jail. Sam will have none of it:

"Mr. Harris," Sam's voice was quiet, "first time in my life I interrupted a white man. I've lost control,—yes. Got to say it. All my life I've bowed and scraped, for the sake of the others beneath me, I thought, who needed help. I'd do it the white way, I'd say. It's worth licking a few hands for, I'd say—God!" he breathed, "God."

You could hardly hear him now. He looked across the room as if he had stopped, had long ago forgot to go on.

"It's more than starving . . . low wages . . ." the voice picked up

words again, "more than Jim Crow—it's you white men . . . sucked
as dry as your land . . . taking our women . . . yes, taking them as . . .
manure, that's all they are to you . . . dung . . . to make something
grow green in your life. That's all they mean to you . . . My sister . . ."
voice like wind beating palmetto ". . . my own mother . . . that's all
. . . the woman I love . . . white man took her . . . used her . . . threw
her aside like . . . something filthy and stinking . . . Why can't you
leave them alone? God Jesus, why does the Negro have to bear
this!" His voice grew suddenly quiet. "I know I can't drag God in.
What would a decent God have to do with a thing like—"
    Tom Harris stood, struck the table hard with his hand, "Hush,
you fool! You black damned son of a—" stopped as if a hand had
caught his arm . . . Began again, "You've forgot, Sam," he said
slowly, "there're things no nigger on earth can say to a white man!"
(341)

Blackness, here, is construed as both excrement and vital to growth,
both poison and nutrient, both buried to be hidden and buried to fertil-
ize. Whiteness is cotton, a particularly destructive plant sucking nutri-
ents from and destroying the land—the black earth—upon which it
feeds. Toni Morrison has written in *Playing in the Dark* that metaphors of
blackness are frequently required to carry the weight of doubleness, and
her argument fits well with the passage above. She writes, "If we follow
through on the self-reflexive nature of these encounters with African-
ism, it falls clear: images of blackness can be evil *and* protective, rebel-
lious *and* forgiving, fearful *and* desirable,—all of the self-contradictory
features of the self. Whiteness, alone, is mute, meaningless, unfathomable, pointless, frozen, veiled, curtained, dreaded, senseless, implaca-
ble. Or so our writers seem to say" (59). Morrison's comment, mirroring
the thoughts of Lacan and Rose, makes clear the double-edged blade
that cuts both races to the quick: not only do metaphors of virility and
desire and danger demonize blacks, the Other, they eviscerate the souls
of whites, who are ironically denied access to the very life forces they
have demonized blacks for embodying. This, for Smith, was a system of
inquiry that found effective articulation throughout her work, but it is to
one particular field of vision, her treatment of women and children, that
I will now turn. Her writing brims with descriptions of children who are
spiritually damaged before they can even define what race is, and with
white women who have become utterly detached from their own physical and spiritual presences. They float through her work like disembod-

ied ghosts, pale, shriveled, human voids. The Southern offer of a detached, ambient, pervasive "glory" in exchange for sexual and spiritual neglect, it becomes clear, was a high price for women both black and white.

In *Killers of the Dream*, the chapter "Three Ghost Stories" plunges us into one of the South's most enduring racial and sexual images: that of a white slave master raping a black slave. Perhaps taking a cue from Faulkner's engagement with this subject in *Absalom, Absalom!*, Smith writes of the debilitating consequences of such an encounter for all relationships involved—male/female as well as white/black. The first "ghost" that emerges from this bleak alliance is the ghost of miscegenation itself, with all it implies about "broken taboos and guilt too terrible to say aloud." White women have become so "pure," so desexed, that white men turn to black women for sexual release. White women become disembodied and physically neglected, black women become troped as erotic and dangerous, and both are degraded. The second ghost represents the South's "rejected children," born of a white father and a black mother and rejected by both. Children are the living testament of both the broken link between white man and white woman and of the exploitative alliance between white man and black woman. The third ghost is the relationship between white children and their black nurses, a bond that not only exploits the black woman but supplants the white mother–white child connection, damaging all three members of that triangle. White mothers are removed from the mothering process and are thus alienated further from their own bodies and their own families; white children are raised by black women, with whom they form a deeper bond than they do with their own mothers, but at some point are told that, by dint of race, these same women—and their black children—are not worthy of respect or love.

In each of these connections, Smith writes, women and children, white and black, suffer immeasurable and unknowable spiritual damage, and it is this damage that drives much of her work. In *Strange Fruit*, Smith describes Tracy's mental image of his white fiancée, Dottie Pusey, as she undresses; although Tracy has had a long and rich sexual relationship with his black girlfriend, Nonnie, he "had never seen Dottie undress and had no desire to" (42–43).[12] The scene continues: "Now the light was off. Dottie was saying her prayers. In a moment she would lie in her bed, cool, clean, composed, all of her life completely contained in the rigid little box which shut the right way to do things away from the wrong. Dottie praying . . . What would she pray about? Sins? Tracy liked the thought of Dottie sinning. He laughed, lit his cigarette again, enjoyed smoking it. What would Dottie's sins be? In a life so neat, so orderly, like a folded handkerchief carried around all day and never crumpled— where would there be room for a life-sized sin?"

Dottie is the embodiment of what Hazel Carby has called the "cult of true womanhood"; she is serene, fragile, pious, utterly desexualized. More than that, however, her containment "in a rigid little box" points to the spiritual wounds inflicted on white women directly because of their disembodiment. Tracy bitterly envisions Dottie (and his mother, who sleeps in her daughter's bed to "escape her husband Tut's masculinity") as "white goddesses, pure as snow—dole out a little of their body to you—just a little—see—it's poison—you can't take but a few drops—don't be too greedy—do as I tell you—do as I tell you now— be good boy—do as I tell you—just a little now—Tracy!—That's not nice—that's not nice—" (195). Dottie and Tracy's mother are "pure" and cold as snow, goddesses untainted by physical presence, or sexual appetite. Sex is "poison" among white women; a few drops are all one is allowed. The image of a "few drops" also carries with it a faint echo of the fear of miscegenation; a "few drops of ink" was all that was required to contaminate a "pure" glass of water. Sex is troped as black, alluring, deadly.

Catherine Clinton has written that the discursive vines constricting white women find their roots far back in the antebellum South. "Men were virtually obsessed with female innocence," she writes.

> The notion of white women as virginal precipitated a whole series of associations: delicate as lilies, spotless as doves, polished as alabaster, fragile as porcelain—but above all, pure as the driven snow (with its inherent connotation of coldness). Without the oppression of all women, the planter class could not be assured of absolute authority. In a biracial slave society where "racial purity" was a defining characteristic of the master class, total control of the reproductive females was of paramount concern for elite males. Patriarchy was the bedrock upon which the slave society was founded, and slavery exaggerated the pattern of subjugation that patriarchy had established. (6, 88)

Smith picks up on this legacy of discursive imprisonment throughout her writing; her awareness of the intricacies of sexual discourse are always tied inextricably to her awareness of racial discourse. Her chapter in *Killers of the Dream* entitled "The Women" marks the damage done to black and white women at the hands of an unyielding structure of white male domination. She quotes at length "one of Mississippi's politicians" whose language in 1948 is emblematically steeped in racial and sexual mythology:

> Now what of the ladies? When God made the Southern woman he summoned His angel messengers and he commanded them to go through all the star-strewn vicissitudes of space and gather all there was of beauty, of brightness and sweetness, of enchantment and glamour, and when they returned and laid the golden harvest at His feet he began in their wondering presence the work of fashioning the Southern girl. He wrought with the golden gleam of the stars, with the changing colors of the rainbow's hues and the pallid silver of the moon. He wrought with the crimson that swooned in the rose's ruby heart, and the snow that gleams on the lily's petal; then, glancing down deep into His own bosom, he took of the love that gleamed there like pearls beneath the sun-kissed waves of a summer sea, and thrilling this love into the form He had fashioned, all heaven veiled its face, for lo, He had wrought the Southern girl. ... (170)[13]

As much as anything, the reliance on natural images in this passage mocks the Southern reliance on fantasy, especially given the work of Smith's contemporary regional writers like Erskine Caldwell and James Agee. "Star-strewn vicissitudes," "golden harvests," and "summer seas," particularly, comprise the rhetoric of romance, not of the hardscrabble reality of the Southern landscape. Moreover, the images of fragility and purity imply more than just innocence; like all metaphors, they are as rich for what they reject as for what they enhance. Here, "pallid silver" and lily petals imply not only sensitivity and grace but a disengagement from manual labor and sexual appetite. These images are, in turn, distorted, caricatured, and draped over bodies discursively unable to shed them: black women. Carby writes that when assessing this image of "true womanhood" it is

> important to consider two aspects of its cultural effect: it was dominant, in the sense of being the most subscribed to convention governing female behavior, but it was also clearly recognizable as a dominating image, describing the parameters within which women

were measured and declared to be, or not to be, women. The sexual ideology of the period thus confirmed the differing material circumstances of these two groups of women and resolved the contradiction between the two reproductive positions by balancing opposing definitions of womanhood and motherhood, each dependent on the other for existence. (23)

W. J. Cash, in his own complicated way, also explored the troubled relationship between Southern white women and their bodies. Typically, Cash's tone reflects precisely that which he is ostensibly critiquing. The following paragraph from *The Mind of the South* is representative of a writer embodying, more than distancing himself from, a tradition steeped in the mythologic treatment of women and sexuality.

The upshot, in this land of spreading notions of chivalry, was downright gyneolatry. She was the South's Palladium, this Southern woman—the shield-bearing Athena, gleaming whitely in the clouds, the standard for its rallying, the mystic symbol of its nationality in face of the foe. She was the lily-pure maid of Astolat and the hunting goddess of the Boeotian hill. And—she was the pitiful Mother of God. Merely to mention her was to send strong men into tears—or shouts. There was hardly a sermon that did not begin and end with tributes in her honor, hardly a brave speech that did not open and close with the clashing of shields and the flourishing of swords for her glory. At the last, I verily believe, the ranks of the Confederacy went rolling into battle in the misty conviction that it was wholly for her that they fought.

"Woman!!! The center and circumference, diameter and periphery, sine, tangent and secant of all our affections!" Such was the toast which brought twenty great cheers from the audience at the celebration of Georgia's one-hundredth anniversary in the 1830s. (89)

As is typical of Cash, this passage offers a critique of Southern mores, but it is also plainly enamored with the image it describes. Cash spent much of his own life both yearning for female sexual innocence and battling chronic impotence; sexual purity, for him, stands in rhetorically for sexual anxiety. Women are only idealized as "pure" if their "impurity" is threatening to the men describing them.

The image of the untouchable, and untouched, woman of society is also reminiscent of a moment in Percy's *Lanterns on the Levee* in which he describes his Aunt Fannie, who was "in looks all that the Surry of

Eagle's Nest and Marse Chan school of writers would have you believe elderly Southern gentlewomen invariably were."

> She had exquisite slender white hands, usually folded in idleness on her lap; upon her neat curly white hair, parted in the middle, reposed a tiny white thing of frills and lace which may have been a cap but which looked more like a doily; her face was small and white, with truly a faded-flower look; her dress was black and fitted well and with a sort of chic her still slender figure; she smelled faintly of orris-root, a bit of which she usually chewed with no observable cud-motion. (I don't know why old ladies abandoned orris-root—it's the right smell for them. But, after all, there are no more old ladies now.) It was not these things, however, but certain little personal eccentricities of Aunt Fannie's that endeared her to me as a child. She would suddenly drop into a little nap, sitting bolt upright in her chair and with the animated company around her pretending not to notice it. Or, equally inexplicably and with equal disregard of surroundings, she would sob gently and delicately and wipe real tears from her eyes with her diminutive orris-scented handkerchief. I attributed this phenomenon to some old and overwhelming sorrow which she carried in her heart and was too proud and ladylike to reveal. Only years and years later I learned that these engaging little habits of hers arose from another little habit: Aunt Fannie took her grain of morphine every day. Being the only wicked thing she ever did, it must have been doubly consoling. (8)

There is soft irony here, but Percy nonetheless held an overpowering nostalgic reverence for such images of effete elegance. What is striking in Percy's work is his refusal to explore the pain behind the "engaging little habits" of his grandmother, or of himself. Tears, here, are only to be "gently and delicately" wiped away, as if the important thing about grief is to bear it elegantly, not to understand or discuss a pain that requires a morphine addiction to survive. For Smith, such passages were emblematic of the suffering inflicted on women by such oppressive social mores. The repeated adjectives "tiny" and "small" and "little" and "gentle" and "delicate" marked an image of woman as uncalloused by manual work, even domestic work, as she was unsullied by any thoughts of a sexual life. While fragility was valorized as the ideal state of white womanhood, heavy labor, requiring other physical attributes, was associated only with poor whites and blacks. "Strength and the ability to bear fatigue, argued to be so distasteful a presence in a white woman, were positive features to be emphasized in the promotion and selling of a black female field hand at a slave auction," Carby writes. "It is worth considering that a delicate constitution was an indicator of class as well as racial position; woman as ornament was a social sign of achieved wealth, while physical strength was necessary for the survival of women in the cotton fields, in the factories, or on the frontier" (25).

Moreover, the perfectly disembodied vision of Aunt Fannie "chewing with no observable cud-motion" is as desexed as Smith's writing is sexed. And the image of an elderly woman sobbing quietly to herself, full of a sorrow she was "too ladylike to reveal," is exactly the social tradition Smith was writing against. (Percy, as we have seen, described his heroic grandfather being shunted off into a dark room to do *his* aging.) The point is, all emotion, all physicality, all sexuality, was, for white women, to be denied, rejected, shut down. "In order to qualify as a paragon of virtue it was necessary to repress all overt sexuality," Barbara Berg has written. "The cult of purity denied that [white] women had natural sex drives," for the dominant view was that "the best mothers, wives, and managers of households know little or nothing of sexual indulgence. Love of home, children, and domestic duties are the only passions they feel" (84).

Smith is far more explicit about this connection in *Killers of the Dream*. "The majority of southern women convinced themselves that God had ordained that they be deprived of pleasure and meekly stuffed their hollowness with piety, trying to believe the tightness they felt was hunger satisfied," she writes. "Culturally stunted by a region that still pays nice rewards to simple-mindedness in females, they listened to the round words of men's tributes to Sacred Womanhood and believed, thinking no doubt that if they were not sacred then what under God's heaven *was* the matter with them! Once hoisted up by the old colonel's oratory, they stayed on lonely pedestals and rigidly played 'statue' while their men went about more important affairs elsewhere" (141).

More important affairs, of course, frequently meant visits to Colored Town to find the sexual fulfillment the men had successfully shut off from their white women. Late in *Strange Fruit*, when Tracy visits Preacher Dunwoodie to ask about joining the church, he hears a fevered speech about the temptations of black flesh. Throughout her work Smith saved her most vicious attacks for religious rhetoric, and nowhere in *Strange Fruit* is it as florid as in the following passage. The conversation takes place both in Tracy's car and, later, under the same oak tree where Tracy and Nonnie first made love.

"Now there's another sin. Lot of men, when they're young, sneak off into Colored Town. Let their passions run clean away with them. Get to lusting—burning up! And they get to thinking . . . they'd rather have that kind of thing than marriage. A lot rather! Scared of white girls. Scared nice white girls can't satisfy them. And they're right! Of course no decent fine white woman can satisfy you when you let your mind out like you let out a team of wild mules racing straight to . . ."

Preacher Dunwoodie's voice had risen shrilly. Suddenly he stopped. Spoke more quietly. "Well, that's youth," he said and wiped his face with his big handkerchief. "This world's full of young folks wanting—strange things. That's youth and the devil," he added softly, "and sooner or later you have to face it. Funny thing," he said, "once you make up your mind to leave colored women alone and stick to your own kind, you soon get weaned." He laughed shortly. "You don't think you can. But you do. I know . . ." he sighed. "As for the colored women, they manage all right. Always have, haven't they! Most of them sooner or later get a man their color, maybe marry him. Live a fairly decent, respectable life—that is, if a nigger woman can live a decent respectable life." Voice suddenly bitter.

Someone's been talking to him. He's too smooth—knows too much.

"You see, Deen, you have to keep pushing them back across the nigger line. Keep pushing! That's right. Kind of like it is with a dog. You have a dog, seems right human. More sense than most men. And you a lot rather be around that dog than anybody you ever knew. But he's still a dog. You don't forget that." (87–88)

Here, then, Smith is conflating the three steps of "sin and segregation," one of her favorite themes. Preacher Dunwoodie, no stranger to lust or to interracial longing, wipes his face and at once mocks white female sexuality and equates black female sexuality with "strange things," "the devil," and "a dog." He at once acknowledges that white men can and must be "weaned" from black women, suggesting not only sexual desire but their reliance on black mothering, and raises himself to a pitch of overtly racist language beyond any yet encountered in the novel. He moves quickly from a discussion of black enticement to a diatribe about divinely ordained white supremacy, a move Smith recognized as all too common among Southern white men. Yet his descriptions of this supremacy are labored; the reliance on a trio of adjectives to say that no "decent fine white woman" could satisfy adolescent passions seems to reveal a mind trying to convince itself more than its youthful audience. Here again the myth of the cult of white womanhood is revealed; white women are so beyond sexuality that they "scare" men. Black bodies come to stand in for this lack of sexuality and become troped, logically enough, as insatiable.

"Overt sexuality," Carby writes,

> emerged in images of the black woman, where "charm" revealed its relation to the dark forces of evil and magic. The effect of black female sexuality on the white male was represented in an entirely different form from that of the figurative power of white female sexuality.
>
> Confronted by the black woman, the white man behaved in a manner that was considered to be entirely untempered by any virtuous qualities; the white male, in fact, was represented as being merely prey to the rampant sexuality of his female slaves. A basic assumption of the principles underlying the cult of true womanhood was the necessity for the white female to "civilize" the baser instincts of man. But in the face of what was constructed as overt sexuality of the black female, excluded as she was from the parameters of virtuous possibilities, these baser male instincts were entirely uncontrolled. Thus, the white slave master was not regarded as being responsible for his actions toward his black female slaves. On the contrary, it was the female slave who was held responsible for being a potential, and direct, threat to the conjugal sanctity of the white mistress. (27)

One outgrowth of the cult of true womanhood, then, was a long-standing and largely overlooked tradition of white men finding their sexual outlet in the bodies of black women. It is Smith's descriptions of black women's bodies—far more erotically engaged than her depiction of white women—that reveal her awareness of these racial and sexual legacies. At one point in *Strange Fruit*, Ed encounters a group of young black girls, including one "like a jack-rabbit, a little somebody in a bright pink waist and black skirt" who "collided with him, stopped with a stumble of high-heel pumps and a twist of her torso." The girl is described as having "a perfect face the color of pine cone laughing into his. He saw a full mouth, slender neck, tipped-up breasts. He saw big laughing eyes that looked as if they would grow solemn any minute, under a hat with three red roses flopping on it, perched on the side of her head." Ed laughs "as she switched her little tail in answer and ran toward the titillated cluster of girls. Nice little rumps, hard from chopping cotton, light, bouncy, India rubber" (12). Earlier, "white boys, whistled softly when [Nonnie] walked down the street, and said low words and rubbed the back of their hands across their mouths, for Nonnie Anderson was something to look at twice, with her soft black hair blowing off her face, and black eyes set in a face that God knows by right should have belonged to a white girl. And old Cap'n Rushton, sitting out in front of Brown's Hardware Store as he liked to do when in from the turpentine farm, would rub his thick red hand over his chin slowly as he watched her wheel drooling, lop-headed Boysie Brown in to see his papa" (2).

The overtly erotic language in this passage, combined with the plain white gaze at a black body, set it off in stiff irony not only to the way white women are described but in relation to the manner in which the novel later turns: white men, having forsaken their soul-less white wives, are free to leer at black women, but black men are forbidden from so much as speaking to white women. Here, a white man rubs his "thick, red" hand over his chin as a black woman walks by; the notion that Nonnie's sexuality "by right should have belonged to a white girl" reveals Smith's conception that "sexing" blackness does a double disservice: attributing eroticism to blackness not only objectifies blackness, it inherently desexualizes whiteness. Not only does it imply that white girls do not have Nonnie's sexuality, it implies that Nonnie must have *stolen* their sexuality. Indeed, by virtue of the town's sexualized discourse, she has. Nonnie carries the weight not only of white male sexual fantasy but of white female sexual repression; she is lusted after by white men and hated by white women, who are in turn rejected by their white boyfriends and husbands. "By the historical 'accident' of slavery, our slave holding puritan ancestors were juxtaposed to a dark people, natural, vigorous, unashamed, full of laughter and song and dance, who, without awareness that sex is 'sin,' had reached genital maturity," Smith writes in *Killers*. "From all that we know of them they seemed to have had, even as some have now, a marvelous love of life and play, a physical grace and rhythm and a psychosexual vigor that must have made the white race by contrast seem washed out and drained of much that is good and life-giving. It was natural that the white man was drawn to them. Laughter, song, rhythm, spontaneity were like a campfire in a dark, tangled forest full of sins and boredom and fears" (117).

The attachment of "genital maturity" to black sexuality was as revealing for Percy as it was for Smith; in both cases, blackness represented both a freedom from repression and an embodiment of the forbidden that resonated with their own sexuality. Taken one way, of course, the attachment of sexuality and vigor to blackness is rhetorically demeaning, given the slippery discursive slope that such characterizations can lead to. When Percy, or Smith, write of joyous blacks, they are doing more than caricaturing; or if they are caricaturing, they are caricaturing whiteness as much as they are caricaturing blackness. Whiteness, in these passages, becomes joyless, empty, distraught, bereft; if these points are arrived at only in their reflection off of black faces, then so be it; the point is made, and effectively: "I often conclude that the only Southerners worth talking about are the darkies." Percy, like Smith, used images of race to shore up, define, and complicate his own identity, and the identity of the white race around him.

There are also moments, famously, in Faulkner, but also in Cash, that are sharply cognizant of the unspoken practices of miscegenation and the damage these habits did even to nonparticipants. "Above all there grew up an unusually intense affection and respect for the woman of the family," Cash wrote in *The Mind of the South*.

Yet if such a woman knew that the maid in her kitchen was in reality half-sister to her own daughter, if she suspected that her husband sometimes slipped away from her bed to the arms of a mulatto wench, or even if she only knew or suspected these things of her sons or some other male of her family, why, of course she was being cruelly wounded in the sentiments she held most sacred. And even though she feigned blindness, as her convention demanded she should—even if she actually knew or suspected nothing—the guilty man, supposing he possessed any shadow of decency, must inexorably writhe in shame and an intolerable sense of impurity under her eyes. . . . And the only really satisfactory escape here, as in so many other instances, would be fiction. On the one hand, the convention must be set up that the thing simply did not exist, and enforced under penalty of being shot; and on the other, the woman must be compensated, the revolting suspicion in the male that he might be slipping into bestiality got rid of, by glorifying her. (89)

Here again, black bodies are considered "bestial," or the vehicles by which whites can become bestial. But behind this is the utter desexing of white women, who, like Percy's Aunt Fanny, must retreat into fiction, or delusions of "glory," in order to feel compensated for their physical, sexual abandonment. Cash was often brutal in his assessment of the role of black women, as Smith was not, but his acknowledgment of the ways white women were damaged by the sexual exploitation of black women was perceptive and provocative.

To Smith, black women were not merely sexual vehicles caught between the sexual lust of white men and the sexual repression of white women, and it is to another "ghost," that of black women responsible for raising white children, that I now turn. Early on in *Strange Fruit*, Tracy Deen comes upon a photograph of the black nursemaid (and mother of his playmate Henry) who raised him. Wistfully, he remembers

> her faint clean body smell like a pile of fresh-ironed sheets and he remembered her rich sweet smell on Sundays, when dressed in black silk she left the yard to go to church-meeting. He remembered her deep full breasts. There had been a time when her lap was wide enough for him and her Henry both to crawl up in. She'd sit there, knees spread wide, jogging them from side to side, singing vague sounds, breaking off, taking up after a little where she had left off, sometimes reaching for a corner of her big white petticoat to wipe one nose and the other. Knees jogging slowly, easing them back and forth, cradling them from time to time and its bitterness, glazing eyes with peace. Tune moving on, on, on, and body moving with it, and all the world no wider, no deeper, than the space her knees enclosed—no wider than that, and no colder than the heat from her breasts.
>
> There had been a time when he was sick and no food would stay in his stomach, and Mamie had fixed little odd things, and sometimes had chewed them for him and slipped them into his mouth and he had felt better. He remembered his mother used to say after that, "The child won't eat for anybody but Mamie," or when he was hurt, "Nobody can quiet him but Mamie." (107)

The sexual imagery in this passage is vivid and can perhaps be read as a kind of displaced homoeroticism—it is Mamie's body here that interests Smith, not Tracy's. But more important than this is Smith's portrait of Tracy receiving the mothering, the protection, and the nurturing from Mamie that he never received from his own mother. Mamie is highly feminized in this portrait, compared to Smith's depiction of Mrs. Deen as a cold, neurotic pious woman, incapable of comforting her own child. The image of a black woman chewing and regurgitating food for a white child is a powerful one; her very insides are issued up for the growth of the child. Later, when Tracy has decided to marry the frigid Dorothy, he listens to her describing the way they'll "make the old farm over" with a loveseat by the fireplace and a "beautiful old mahogany card table." Tracy's mind drifts from this scene directly to a memory of the old piano in the parlor where he used to go and hide and lay his head on the keys, until Mamie would "find you and hold you against her, saying half words through her crooked teeth—Old Mamie—you hadn't seen her in years—you must have been a funny little fool—a crazy kid" (185). Tracy escapes his dread of marriage to Dorothy, as he escaped his memories of a alienated mother, by imagining his youthful moments of warmth and nurturing at the knee of a black woman.

This image, with its subtle sexuality and deep longing, is mirrored in *Lanterns on the Levee*. "Southerners like to make clear, especially to Northerners, that every respectable white baby had a black mammy, who, one is to infer, is fat and elderly and bandannaed," Percy wrote.

I was a respectable and a white baby, but Nain was sixteen, divinely cafe-au-lait, and she would have gone into cascades of giggles at the suggestion of a bandanna on her head. I loved her devotedly and never had any other nurse. Everything about her was sweet-smelling, of the right temperature, and cozy. Psychiatrists would agree, I imagine, that I loved her because in her I found the comfort of the womb, from which I had been so recently and unexpectedly been ejected and for which I was still homesick. The womb may be comfortable, but I have my doubts, and, without a little first-hand information, I shall continue to believe I loved her for her merry goodness, her child's heart that understood mine, and her laughter that was like a celesta playing triplets. Chiefly I remember her bosom: it was soft and warm, an ideal place to cuddle one's head against. My earliest clear recollection is of a song she would sing me so cuddled—rather, not of the song itself, but of its effect on me. The words and tune have gone, but not what they did to me. A poor egoistic sort of memory, I know, that records nothing of the outer world, but only how certain bits of it pleased or distressed me, yet mine, and no better now than it was then, and no different. Nain would hold me in her arms and sing this song, rocking herself a little. I would try not to cry, but it made me so feel so lost and lonely that tears would seep between my lids and at last

I would sob until I shook against her breast. "What's de madder, Peeps?" she would say. "What you cryin' fur?" But I was learning not so much how lonely I could be as how lonely everybody could be, and I could not explain. (26–27)

The language here is rich: Percy's comparison of Nain's skin to a café au lait brings up his attachment to her nursemilk. When he says he loved her devotedly and never had another nurse, he sounds like a devoted husband claiming never to have cheated on his wife. His sensuous descriptions of her smell and of the psychological link to the womb from which he had recently been "ejected" speaks volumes about his own deeply wounded memories of rejection at the hands of his own parents. Rocked in the arms of his black nanny, he weeps for a loneliness that originated at the distant, alienated hands of his rarely present mother. His homesickness for love from his white family would never be gratified; he imagines himself enriched, throughout his childhood, only by blacks.

Grace Elizabeth Hale, in her incisive book *Making Whiteness: The Culture of Segregation in the South 1890–1940*, writes that the tension between black nursemaids and white women heads of households "revealed the contradictions central to the culture of segregation, the form that middle class development took in the South and in which white women reconstructed southern womanhood. . . . The mammy figure revealed, perhaps more than any other construction of the culture of segregation, a desperate symbolic as well as physical dependence on the very people whose full humanity white southerners denied and the centrality of blackness to the making of whiteness" (112).

The image of white children looking to black nannies for the rare chance to become connected to physicality, sensuousness, and joy is frequently joined in Smith's writing by the image of children, white and black, playing, questioning, and suffering together. Critics and biographers alike have tied Smith's writing to her long tenure as owner of the girls' camp in north Georgia. Some of her most vivid writing, both in *Strange Fruit* and *Killers of the Dream*, relies on images of children, often conflated with memories of her own youth. If segregation represented for Smith a bifurcation of the adult personality, then the teaching, or masking, or explaining away of segregation began this splitting at a very early age. "Neither the Negro nor sex was often discussed at length in our home," she wrote in *Killers of the Dream*.

We were given no formal instruction in these difficult matters but we learned our lessons well. We learned the intricate system of taboos, of renunciations and compensations, of manners, voice modulations, words, feelings, along with our prayers, our toilet habits, and our games. I do not remember how or when, but by the time I had learned that God is love, that Jesus is His Son and came to give us more abundant life, that all men are brothers with a common Father, I also knew that I was better than a Negro, that all black folks have their place and must be kept in it, that sex has its place and must be kept in it, that a terrifying disaster would befall the South if ever I treated a Negro as my social equal and as terrifying a disaster would befall my family if ever I were to have a baby out of marriage. (27–28)

Smith structures two chapters in *Killers of the Dream* around an allegorical conversation between herself and an inquisitive child asking about race. The child's wide-eyed fears and innocent questions have a visceral dimension that is reminiscent of Richard Wright's early reminiscences in *Black Boy*. In both cases, the racial curiosities of young children are met with severe beatings at the hands of adults who have no sensible answers. "Even its children knew that the South was in trouble," Smith wrote.

No one had to tell them; no words said aloud. To them, it was a vague thing weaving in and out of their play, like a ghost haunting an old graveyard or whispers after the household sleeps—fleeting mystery, vague menace to which each responded in his own way.

Some learned to screen out all except the soft and the soothing; others denied even as they saw plainly, and heard. But all knew that under quiet words and warmth and laughter, under slow ease and tender concern about small matters, there was a heavy burden on all of us and as heavy a refusal to confess it. The children knew this "trouble" was bigger than they, bigger than their family, bigger than their church, so big that people turned away from its size. They had seen it flash out and shatter a town's peace, and felt it tear up all they believed in. They had measured its giant strength and felt weak when they remembered. This haunted childhood belongs to every southerner of my age. We ran away from it but we came back like a hurt animal to its wound, or a murderer to the scene of his sin. The human heart dares not stay away too long from that which hurt it most. (25–26)

Here again is segregation standing in for a profound emptiness in white culture; its malevolence is haunting not only for the deprivation it causes a child or a community but for the violence that erupts at the slightest attempt to question it. This metaphor appears frequently in Percy's work as well: the unspoken, the unspeakable issue of race quickly overpowers anyone who attempts to break the silence or tries to break free of rhetorical bonds. In this passage, too, Richard Wright floats in the background like a brooding ghost; the repetition of the word "bigger" here brings up the aura of Bigger Thomas, the main character of Wright's novel *Native Son*, a work published in 1940 that shocked white audiences in its unprecedented expression of black violence and rage. Perhaps no other two writers were as powerfully evocative of the physical and spiritual violence of race.

Smith's reliance on the power of writers like Wright to evoke childhood trauma is also echoed in an allusion in *Strange Fruit* to Franz Fanon's *Black Skin, White Masks*. As a mob gathers to lynch Henry MacIntosh for supposedly killing Tracy Deen, the haunting sounds of wailing children fill the background. Sam Perry, a black friend of Henry's, encounters a white family on its way to watch the lynching.

> A child whimpered, "mommy, I'm hungry—I'm hongry," and pulled at his mother, whose face was turned toward the crowd.
>
> "Hush!" she said, not turning, "hush! They're burning a nigger. Don't you want to see em burn a nigger?"
>
> A thin spiral of smoke could now be seen rising against the late-afternoon sky. A dog barked, another took up the cry, another, another, as if a great restlessness had entered into them and would not let them go.
>
> God . . . God Jesus . . . nothing Harris can do now. . . . And you sit here and take it. . . . Yeah . . . beat your fist against a steering wheel, beat your life out against your own impotence.
>
> White women eyed him curiously, and a mill child came close to the car and stared at him. "Hit's another nigger, Mommy!" he cried, and the woman said "Shut you mouth! He might git ye and hurt ye. Don't you know that?"
>
> Every nigger a boogah man . . . under every white bed . . . It made you want to cry out to God. It made you want to laugh forever as you cried. (344)

The image "burning a nigger" is made all the more horrifying by the mother's urging her child to come see; when the child reacts to Harris by recoiling in terror, the image is complete. The lesson has been learned. The scene brings to mind Fanon's description of being fixed in the gaze of a white child, particularly in its acknowledgment of the violent, distorted childhood images of race. The child in the passage above, like the dogs that bark in the distance, is terrified by the ambiance of racial violence that it cannot see; this terror is made manifest only when a black man appears to embody that fear. Fanon's passage is equally brooding:

"Mama, see the negro! I'm frightened!" Frightened! Frightened! Now they were beginning to be afraid of me. I made up my mind to laugh myself to tears, but laughter had become impossible. . . . My body was given back to me sprawled out, distorted, recolored, clad in mourning in that white winter day. The Negro is an animal, the Negro is bad, the Negro is mean, the Negro is ugly; look, a nigger, it's cold, the nigger is shivering, the nigger is shivering because he is cold, the little boy is trembling because he is afraid of the nigger, the nigger is shivering with cold, the cold that goes through your bones, the handsome little boy is trembling because he thinks the nigger is quivering with rage, the little white boy throws himself into his mother's arms; "Mama, the nigger's going to eat me up." (qtd. in Hall, 16–17)

The enormous misinterpretation of the black man's shivering is perfectly cast; black male bodies are *only* symbols of terror, *only* threatening, *only* to be strung up and burned. Cornel West, among others, has written on this subject at length. White fear of black sexuality, he writes, is "a basic ingredient of white racism. And for whites to admit this fear even as they try to instill and sustain fear in blacks is to acknowledge a weakness—a weakness that goes down to the bone."

Social scientists have long acknowledged that interracial sex and marriage is the most *perceived* source of white fear of black people—just as the repeated castration of lynched black men cries out for serious cultural explanation.

Black sexuality is a taboo subject in America principally because it is a form of black power over which whites have little control, yet its visible manifestations evoke the most visceral white response, be it one of seductive obsession or downright disgust. On the other hand, black sexuality between blacks and whites proceeds based on underground desires that Americans deny or ignore in public and over which laws have no effective control. In fact, the dominant sexual myths of black women and men portray whites as being "out of control"—seduced, tempted, overcome, overpowered by black bodies. This form of black sexuality makes white passivity the norm—hardly an acceptable self-image for a white-run society. (86–87)[14]

It is this link, between image and action, between race and power, between rhetoric and violence, that Smith considered so central. In *Strange Fruit*, Tracy Deen flashes back to a childhood moment when he and his black playmate Henry are playing on a sidewalk as a white girl rolls by on her bicycle. Rather than move out of the way, Henry tells the girl to "Move move move yourself." The two collide; she scratches her leg on a pedal, and Henry and Tracy collapse in laughter. A strange, violent sequence follows. Mamie, Henry's mother and Tracy's nanny, sees the accident from her stoop, "takes Henry by the shirt, bent him over her knee and whipped him so hard that Tracy burst into sobs and covered his eyes from the sight though he could not make himself leave the sound of it." Importantly, it is not Henry that bursts into tears, but Tracy; here, as elsewhere, Smith uses the physical whipping of a black boy to express the psychological damage done to a white boy. If Henry is left only with a sore backside, his unjust whipping stands as a moment of horrific education in racial mores for Tracy; Henry's physical body is used as a vehicle to express the damage done to Tracy's spirit. But Smith does not end here; in the scene, the violence continues. When Tracy tries to speak to Mamie after the whipping, she bellows, "Go! Go to your *own folks*." Tracy runs home to his mother and sister, who are placidly reading a book together, and proceeds to push his sister to the ground, "expecting his mother to follow and whip him, whip him as hard as Mamie had whipped Henry. But she did not come." Tracy mistakes the reason for Henry's whipping to have been merely adolescent insolence; his awareness of the racial underpinnings come later that same evening, after he hears Mamie's husband, Ten, return home and violently reprimand her for whipping his son. "You goin to keep your hands offn him! You hear? You tetch him again count of white folks an I'll beat you till yo can't get offn da floor." Ten then grabs a blue-and-white glass vase that was "Mamie's one fine house ornament and hurled it to the floor, smashing it into a hundred fragments." Listening to the fight, Tracy and Henry crash into racial awareness.

"It means I'm white," Tracy whispered, "and you're black," eyes never leaving the shed where the two stood talking, deep shadows against the lamplighted cabin. "It means," he went on and felt a new swelling pride rising in him, "I'm always right, I reckon."

"How come?" Henry asked dully.

"Cause I'm white—you heard Mamie!"

"Do skin make the diffunce?"

"Reckon so," Tracy said, losing his confidence a little, "yep, reckon it do."

Black boy and white boy stood there in the darkness, watching the grown folks' trouble, and slowly Henry turned and went to the cabin, and slowly Tracy went to the big yellow house. (109 – 14)

Two childhood friends, one white, one black, drift into segregated neighborhoods after watching their parents explode in the violent fallout of a harmless prank. White and black are distinct traits only because of their powerful capacity to alienate, to tear apart, to split; individual spirits as well as families and communities are always vulnerable to the corrosive power of race.

CHAPTER FIVE

The Sadness Made Her Feel Queer

Race, Gender, and the Grotesque in the
Early Writings of Carson McCullers

One would get the impression that there was a rigid correspondence between color, education, income and the Negro's preference in music. But what are we to say of a white-skinned Negro with brown freckles who owns sixteen oil wells sunk in a piece of Texas land once farmed by his ex-slave parents who were a blue-eyed, white-skinned, red-headed (kinky) Negro woman from Virginia and a blue-gummed, black-skinned curly-haired Negro male from Mississippi, and who not only sang bass in a Holy Roller church, played the market and voted Republican but collected blues recordings and was a walking depository of blues tradition?

RALPH ELLISON, *Shadow and Act*

Late in Carson McCullers's 1946 novel *The Member of the Wedding*, Berenice, a black nanny, and her young white charges, Frankie and John Henry, sit around a kitchen table fancying a perfect world. Berenice dreams that "there would be no separate colored people in the world, but all human beings would be light brown color with blue eyes and black hair. . . . No war, said Berenice. No stiff corpses hanging from the Europe trees and no Jews murdered anywhere. . . . No killed Jews and no hurt colored people."

Frankie "planned it so that people could instantly change back and forth from boys to girls, which every way they felt like and wanted. But Berenice would argue with her about this, insisting that the law of human sex was exactly right just as it was and could in no way be improved. And then John Henry West would very likely add his two cents' worth about this time, and think that people ought to be half boy and half girl, and when the old Frankie threatened to take him to the Fair and sell him to the Freak Pavilion, he would only close his eyes and smile" (92).

For all three characters, and for characters throughout McCullers's work, heaven is a place where identity, particularly racial and gender identity, is fluid, changeable, amorphous. There are overt politics in this passage, for sure: the image of "stiff corpses hanging from the Europe trees" has resonances for Berenice, a black woman living in the Jim Crow South, that are far more immediate than her musings about a war across the ocean. But the scene has more intricate implications as well. McCullers, who unlike Smith or Cash never took an active role in the issues of her day, captures something beyond the political. She is writing of the irreducible complexity, or ambiguity, or indeterminacy, of human identity, and she is writing of a world in which people are both brown-skinned *and* blue-eyed, black *and* white, male *and* female. That the world as it was in the 1940s South did not allow such a polyphony of voices to exist is what causes her characters, and indeed what caused McCullers herself, such deep melancholy and isolation. In her own life, McCullers, like Smith, Cash, and Percy, was deeply ambivalent about her own sexuality and her own place in the Southern community. If Smith was more openly lesbian, Cash more sexually isolated, and Percy more obviously effeminate, McCullers, like many of her characters, both male and female, is perhaps most accurately described as androgynous. Although she married Reeves McCullers (then later divorced and remarried him), both she and her husband were drawn to members of their own sex, often in melodramatic and self-destructive ways. Carson particularly was known to countless friends and colleagues as an incorrigible flirt, who would crawl into bed with men or women without hesitation. But those who knew her best also reported that once in bed, McCullers, again like many of her characters, would simply curl up and fall asleep. Sex, to her, was violent, terrifying, spiritually isolating. As in the other chapters in this book, I will argue here that a particular reading of McCullers's life provides valuable material for reading her fiction, a body of work that deeply questioned received notions of Southern racial and sexual conduct and self-definition. Indeed, McCullers frequently used the same language to describe the isolation felt by characters "trapped" or "caught" by discourses of race and gender. "We each one of us somehow caught all by ourself," Berenice says to Frankie. "Everybody is caught one way or another. But they done drawn completely extra bounds around all colored people. They done squeezed us off in one corned by ourselves." Frankie, the tomboy, agrees: "Sometimes I feel like I want to break something, too. I feel like I wish I could just tear down the whole town" (114).

Although she was nowhere near as involved as Smith in the early civil rights movement, nor did she, according to her biographer, have many personal connections with blacks, McCullers was praised even in her day as a writer somehow intimately aware of the social and psychological complexities of race. "To me the most impressive aspect of 'The Heart is a Lonely Hunter' is the astonishing humanity that enables a white writer for the first time in Southern fiction to handle Negro characters with as much ease and justice as those of her race," Richard Wright wrote in the August 5, 1940, edition of the *New Republic*. "This cannot be accounted for stylistically or politically; it seems to stem from an attitude toward life which enables Miss McCullers to rise above the pressures of her environment and embrace white and black humanity in one sweep of apprehension and tenderness" (195).

Like several of her Southern contemporaries, notably Erskine Caldwell and Flannery O'Connor, McCullers's most evocative metaphor for expressing this "apprehension and tenderness" was the use of the grotesque, a category that included blacks and other nonwhites as often as it did the sexually or physically aberrant. Her novels are full of freak shows, carnivals, and prisons that the main characters find fascinating, familiar, and oddly comforting. In *Wedding*, Frankie, mortified by a growth spurt she fears will make her nine feet tall, visits the Freak Show to see the Giant, the Fat Lady, the Midget, the Wild Nigger, the Pin Head, the Alligator Boy, and the Half-Man Half-Woman. The Wild Nigger, who is billed as coming "from a savage island," rips the heads off rats brought to him by patrons. "Some said that he was not a genuine Wild Nigger," Frankie muses, "but a crazy colored man from Selma" (18). As we shall see, marking blacks as "freaks" allowed McCullers not only a rich opportunity for social comment but a chance to draw a link between black alienation and more broadly construed human suffering. With the notable exception of Berenice in *The Member of the Wedding* and Doctor Copeland in *The Heart Is a Lonely Hunter*, McCullers typically explored race from inside the white mind, but she did so in such a way as to break down any sense of "race" as a rigid category. Just as many of her characters are drawn as nominally heterosexual and come to an understanding of a more amorphous sexuality, so are they nominally "white" until a certain emotional epiphany, or "connection," makes them aware of their own "mixed blood." McCullers's work has traditionally been read as that of an American existentialist, marking the spiritual angst and loneliness emerging from the Second World War. But if Camus and Sartre wrote of the moral ambivalence and debasement of the midcentury, McCullers wrote more of the desperate urge to find points of human connection, even if these connections cut across "normal" lines of race or gender. She was born and raised in Columbus, Georgia, a piedmont town near the Chattahoochee River that forms the border with Alabama. To live in the South, her biographer Virginia Carr writes, was for Carson "to rot in boredom, to stagnate; yet there was ever an ambivalent pull, for home was also a balm that soothed, healed, enveloped, protected" (56). Throughout her work characters are shut off from one another by the distinctions of race and gender that prevent their fragile interiors from merging. They become instead spiritually broken, grotesque, "freaks"—not merely as social outcasts but as physical manifestations of their own isolation and suffering. Like Will Percy and many of the characters in the work of Lillian Smith, Frankie was raised not by white parents but by a black nanny, and she discovers "an unnamable connection" not with her brother and his fiancée but with "an old colored man":

> She had no sooner walked down the left side of the main street and up again on the right sidewalk, when she realized a further happening. It had to do with various people, some known to her and others strangers, she met and passed along the street. An old colored man, stiff and proud on his rattling wagon seat, drove a sad, blindered mule down toward the Saturday market. F. Jasmine looked at him, he looked at her, and to the outward appearance that was all. But in that glance F. Jasmine felt between his eyes and her own eyes a new unnamable connection, as though they were known to each other—and there even came an instant vision of his home field and country roads and quiet dark pine trees as the wagon rattled past her on the paved town street. And she wanted him to know her, too—about the wedding. (50)

Louis Rubin has written that McCullers

> focuses upon her maimed, misfitting, wounded people not as a commentary upon the complacent "normality" of the community which would term them freakish, but as exemplars of the wretched-

ness of the human condition. It isn't that freaks are commentaries or criticisms on normality; they *are* normality. Their physical grotesquery merely makes visible and identifiable their isolation and anguish; "normal" people do not confront these on quite such immediate and inescapable terms, perhaps, but they are really no better off, no happier. Everybody that is human is on the chain gang; on some the stripes and chains are merely more readily visible. . . . It wasn't enough to see and identify; she had to demonstrate that, despite the varied surfaces and individually realized characterizations, they were really all alike, and what lay at the core of each was suffering and pain derived from loneliness. One is reminded of a writer that Mrs. McCullers very much admired: Marcel Proust— significantly, a homosexual, as Mrs. McCullers was a lesbian. (145)

Rubin's conflation of the term "freaks" with life "on the chain gang" and McCullers's own sexuality is appropriate, it seems, since images of grotesquerie, race, and gender are constantly mixing together in McCullers's work. When Frankie visits the Freak Show, she is most drawn to the last booth, always the most crowded, occupied by "the Half-Man Half-Woman, a morphidite and a miracle of science."

This Freak was divided completely in half—the left side was a man and the right side a woman. The costume on the left was a leopard skin and on the right side a brassiere and a spangled skirt. Half the face was dark bearded and the other halfbright glazed with paint. Both eyes were strange. Frankie had wandered around the tent and looked at every booth. She was afraid of all the Freaks, for it seemed to her that they had looked at her in a secret way and tried to connect their eyes with hers, as though to say: we know you. She was afraid of their long freak eyes. And all the years she had remembered them to this day.
"I doubt if they ever get married or go to a wedding," she said. "Those Freaks." (18)

Frankie's move from observing the freaks to thoughts about marriage is telling: freaks don't get married, and neither will she. Freaks, for Frankie, whether they are old colored men, "wild niggers," or "morphidites," are objects of more than just curiosity or empathy. They are emblems of her own alienation, fellow travelers, soul mates. When she walked by the prison, "often some criminals would be hanging to the bars; it seemed to her that their eyes, like the long eyes of the Freaks at

the fair, had called to her as though to say: 'We know you'" (118). Similarly, in *The Heart Is a Lonely Hunter*, Biff Brannon, drawn as feminine
from the beginning and as unmistakably homosexual as the novel progresses, is described as a freak by his wife early on in the novel. When
Brannon defends his serving beer to Blount by telling his wife that he
likes "freaks," she retorts, "I reckon you do! I just reckon you certainly
ought to, Mister Brannon—being as you're one yourself" (11).

Comparing McCullers's characters to Diane Arbus photographs,
Ellen Moers writes that the images of freaks—"her drag queens, les-
bians, circus people, adolescents, lunatics, dwarfs, and the rest—look as
if they might have been designed to illustrate McCullers's fiction. Not
only the subject matter, but the tone of Arbus's work recalls McCullers:
the cold intimacy, the fear which suggests, in objective terms, the
haunted and self-hating self" (108–9).

As we shall see, the same words, "freakish" and "queer," that were
pasted on McCullers by her childhood friends became rich and dynamic signifiers in her adult fiction. According to the *Oxford English
Dictionary*, the word "queer" was first used as a reference to homosexuality by W. H. Auden in a 1932 description of "an underground cottage
frequented by the queer." McCullers never used the word so directly;
"queer" instead stands in for an ambient, often paralyzing dread that frequently accompanies feelings of isolation, loneliness, and sexual anxiety.
"To alienate conclusively, *definitively*, from anyone on any theoretical
ground the authority to describe and name their own sexual desire is a
terribly consequential seizure," Eve Kosofsky Sedgwick has written. "In
this century, in which sexuality has been made expressive of the essence
of both identity and knowledge, it may represent the most intimate violence possible" (26).

In *The Heart Is a Lonely Hunter*, when Mick throws a party for her
classmates, feelings of isolation and anxiety overwhelm any sense of
community or heterosexual energy. An "awful quietness" descends upon
the party when the boys and girls separate before a dance; boys start
punching each other, girls start giggling. "The boys thought about the
girls and the girls thought about the boys. But all that came of it was a
queer feeling in the room" (88, 93). In *Reflections in a Golden Eye*, the
silent, sexually ambiguous Private Williams lives in a barracks in which
"no one gave any thought to his oddities. There was much behavior in
the barracks far queerer than this" (82). In the story "The Ballad of the
Sad Café," Cousin Lyman, the androgynous, four-foot-tall hunchback, is
described as having a "hunched queer body." In *The Member of the Wed-*

ding, a story of a young tomboy's ambivalent search for social and sexual identity, Frankie's first spoken words in the novel are "It is so very queer. . . . The way it all just happened" (2). After Frankie tells Berenice that she will shoot herself "in the side of the head with a pistol" if the married couple does not take her along after the wedding, Berenice tells her,

> "I have heard of many a queer thing. . . . I have knew mens to fall in love with girls so ugly that you wonder if their eyes is straight. I have seen some of the most peculiar weddings anybody could conjecture. Once I knew a boy with his whole face burned off so that—"
>
> "Who?" asked John Henry.
>
> Berenice swallowed a piece of cornbread and wiped her mouth with the back of her hand. "I have knew womens to love veritable Satans and thank Jesus when they put their split hooves over the threshold. I have knew boys to take it into their heads to fall in love with other boys. You know Lily Mae Jenkins?"
>
> F. Jasmine thought a minute, and then answered: "I'm not sure."
>
> "Well, you either know him or you don't know him. He prisses around with pink satin blouse and one arm akimbo. Now this Lily Mae turned into a girl. He changed his nature and his sex and turned into a girl." (76)

The word "queer," then, appears constantly in McCullers's work, as if the uncertainty, the ambiguity, and the anxiety felt within her characters comes to color the world without. Leslie Fiedler, in *Love and Death in the American Novel*, writes that McCullers's play with gender and sexuality "were not apparent to the great audiences of the past, which would have found in any hint of female homosexuality the really unforgivable blasphemy against the conventions of womanhood. But Carson McCullers has taken full advantage of those implications, projecting her neo-tomboys, ambiguous and epicene, the homosexual's sense of exclusion from the family and his uneasiness before heterosexual passion" (325).[1]

Indeed, McCullers's work has been called the writing of pure viscera, in that it pulses with unrestrained, unalloyed (some have even said adolescent) emotion. McCullers's characters see the world outside themselves only as they experience the world of their own isolation and pain; there is rarely, with the exception of the mute John Singer, a character capable of the deep empathy for others' suffering that would constitute compassion and understanding. McCullers, then, used her "freaks" and "queers" to denote not just physically damaged people but people straining to navigate a world that is deeply antagonistic and intolerant. For McCullers, race and sexuality are simply the easiest vehicles through which to express the social alienation that is also unmistakably part of Percy's memoir, particularly when he describes some of his exploits exploring the cities of Europe. "I was always happening on a Hermaphrodite, in some discreet alcove, and I would examine the sleazy mock-modest little monster with shock and horror and fascination," he writes. "I could never imagine how it could have been created by the Greeks, usually so healthy and frank. I stumbled on the answer years later. When the Greeks practiced bisexuality, honestly and simply without thought or condemnation, they did not create these slick symbols of love divided in its objectives. It was a later, more sophisticated and prurient age, the age of the nasty *Crouching Venus* of Syracuse, that titillating and ahing [*sic*], symbolized what they understood and were ashamed of by these sentimental decadent man-woman creatures, false art and false biology" (*Lanterns*, 111).

The conflict between what her characters "understood and were ashamed of" was certainly what most concerned McCullers. In her life and in her fiction, the exploration of this conflict, particularly as it broke through accepted boundaries of racial and sexual identity, caused great upheaval to herself and those around her. Her life was short and physically tragic; after suffering three strokes and countless serious illnesses, she died at the age of fifty. But her life was also rich. Like Percy, she knew well many of the most important writers of her day; unlike Percy, who hosted most of them at his home in Greenville, McCullers bounced from Columbus to Brooklyn flat to Breadloaf to Yaddo to hospital and back again, but always seemed to find herself among the literati she so yearned to resemble. To many of these writers she was also a troubled and troublesome person to be around. Wallace Stegner considered McCullers

> young, gifted, odd, and in the view of some of the staff who watched her with interest, fey. She was a gangling, skinny girl who wore boy's white shirts and changed them three times a day. . . . I knew her only during that hectic two-week Bread Loaf session, when all of us were working our heads off, and playing tennis or drinking in every off half-hour. Louis Untermeyer called her the *fleur de mal* and predicted that she would die young. I think that was not undue prescience on his part, but an extrapolation from the amount of liquor she drank, and the hours she drank it at. Even

then, young as she was, she was drinking straight gin out of water glasses. (Carr, 112)

McCullers, as it turned out, was all of that: fey, gifted, tragic; and all of these qualities turned up in her life as in her writing. She had a singular capacity to imagine herself embodying the most deformed and alienated characters, a capacity that earned her highest artistic marks. In an essay entitled "The Flowering Dream: Notes on Writing," McCullers wrote: "I am so immersed in them that their motives are my own. When I write about a thief, I become one; when I write about Captain Pendleton (the protagonist in *Reflections in a Golden Eye*), I become a homosexual man; when I write about a deaf mute, I become dumb during the time of the story. I become the characters I write about and I bless the Latin poet Terence who said, 'Nothing human is alien to me' " (Carr, 90). It is in her life, then, that we can begin to understand her fiction. As Richard Wright wrote in his review of *The Heart Is a Lonely Hunter*, "It is impossible to read the book and not wonder about the person who wrote it, the literary antecedents of her style and the origins of such a confounding vision of life" (195).

Discussing her notions of gender and sexuality with the writer Newton Arvin in the summer of 1941, the twenty-four-year-old McCullers declared: "Newton, I was born a man" (Carr, 159). Born February 17, 1917, Lula Carson Smith as a young girl was much as she described her two most famous tomboys, Frankie Addams, from *The Member of the Wedding*, and Mick Kelly, from *The Heart Is a Lonely Hunter*. Frankie, when she decided to run away from home, could not decide whether to run to California and become a "starlet" or to New York to become a marine; Mick is described as "a gangling, towheaded youngster, a girl of about twelve . . . dressed in khaki shorts, a blue shirt, and tennis shoes—so that at first glance she was like a very young boy." McCullers was tall and awkward herself, finally leveling off at 5 feet 8 ½ inches when she was thirteen years old. "When Carson was younger, some of the girls gathered in little clumps of femininity and threw rocks at her when she walked nearby," Carr writes, "snickering loud asides and tossing within hearing distance such descriptive labels as 'weird,' 'freakish looking' and 'queer.' " She always dressed in longer skirts than her peers, preferred dirty tennis shoes or brown oxfords when others wore hose and heels, and was ridiculed for wearing slacks, straight hair, and bangs (29–30).

Although her family had nothing of the wealth or pretensions to aristocracy that Percy's did, McCullers nonetheless came from a long line of Southerners. Her paternal grandfather had settled in Union Springs, Alabama, married well, and farmed successfully until his right arm was ripped off in a cotton gin accident. Forced to abandoned his farm, he became a tax collector in Tuskegee, but he drank too much and withered away. Carson's father, Lamar, became, like the mute Singer in *Heart*, a watch repairman; afflicted with flat feet, he reportedly always looked "exhausted." The ancestors of Lula Carson, McCullers's maternal grandmother, had emigrated from Ireland and settled in South Carolina before the Revolutionary War. Lula's father, Major John Thomas Carson, had owned a 2,000-acre plantation with seventy-five slaves; during the Civil War, Wilson's Raiders ravaged the plantation, burned the cotton stores, and freed the slaves. The family that Carson was born into lived modestly but well. According to Carson's brother Lamar, "We were not rich, but we lived in a respectable, upper middle-class neighborhood and had everything we needed. Lula Carson never lacked for a thing she wanted. She did not even have to wash out her underwear" (Carr, 22).

Like Lillian Smith, McCullers was an early and prodigious reader. She was steeped in contemporary modernism particularly, reading Faulkner, Wolfe, and Sherwood Anderson as well as Joyce, Lawrence, and Stein; she claimed to reread Isak Dinesen every year. In an essay published in 1941, she wrote that she loved Dostoyevsky most of all; to her, the Russians were the original masters of the vivid and "outwardly callous juxtaposition of the tragic with the humorous, the immense with the trivial, the sacred with the bawdy, the whole soul of a man with a materialistic detail" (Carr, 33).[2]

In an important difference with Smith, who sought and received scholarly grants to visit sites of the social underclass, including sharecroppers' meetings, black universities, mental hospitals, orphanages, and homes for delinquent children, McCullers preferred the engagement of imagination over the hands-on engagement of experience. In 1949 the journalist Margaret Long offered to take Carson out in Macon and show her "some lintheads on strike, some labor leaders, some Negroes reorganizing the NAACP, some restless young people and the Council on Human relations of black and white do-gooders," but the author turned her down. Like a number of her characters, John Singer and Frankie Addams in particular, Carson did do a good bit of wandering around Columbus—including the black sections of town. As a child, she followed her mother into the town's corners on antique shopping sprees;

as an adult, she often strolled into strange neighborhoods between writing stints. Carr writes that McCullers, like Smith, was considered an odd duck by her neighbors, both in Columbus and later, after she was married, in Fayetteville, North Carolina.

In 1938–39 they knew only that a rather queer and curious girl had arrived in their town with a handsome, personable husband to whom she seemed ill-suited. They observed her prowling about their town, going out in the mornings on long tramps before daybreak or a few minutes after her husband left for work. Sometimes she stopped people in the streets to probe them about their way of life, their political views, families, and grievances. They were sure that she was "stirring up trouble, acting in some common way unbecoming to a wife whose husband is trying to engage himself as a young businessman in the town." They watched her engage blacks in earnest conversation, sympathize with them, and attempt to allay their suspicions, for they, too, wondered why she sought them out. Once the townspeople observed a black enter Carson's and Reeves's apartment, and they felt certain he was there at Carson's invitation. Surely some insurrection was at hand. After news of the incident spread about the town, no one willingly socialized with her. (Carr, 86)

In 1934, at the age of seventeen, Carson moved to New York City for the first time. She told some friends she planned to study at Juilliard, and others that she planned to take writing classes at Columbia. She returned the next year to Columbus and met Reeves McCullers, an aspiring writer himself who was just returning from four years in the army, and the two married in 1937.[3] Their marriage was to be tumultuous, mercurial, violent. Both were constantly battling sickness and an excessive dependence on alcohol; several years into their marriage, Carr reports, they were each drinking a bottle of bourbon a day (290). Soon after their wedding, the couple moved to Charlotte, where Reeves, quickly realizing the couple could not survive on two meager incomes, was forced to give up his own creative aspirations, and he found work as a credit investigator. As Carson became more serious about her fiction, Reeves became the sole domestic partner, cooking, shopping, and keeping house. Although they'd initially planned to trade off years spent writing, Carson's work immediately overshadowed Reeves's, a source of early resentment in her husband.

Reeves also quickly became aware of his wife's capacity for flirtation with members of both sexes. As the marriage progressed, Carr writes, he became "incapable of coping with his wife's sexual inclinations or of helping her to become more heterosexually oriented" (295).[4] Reeves "knew well his wife's capacity for love, knew that it was her nature to love intemperately, voraciously. Carson rarely had simple likes and dislikes; rather, she loved with passion, adoration, single-minded devotion, or she disliked with vehemence, detestation, hatred. There was no continuum, no sliding emotional scale. Reeves could put up with his wife's frequent crushes on women with stoic resignation so long as they stopped short of the bed. Now he was no longer certain of anything" (105).

In the summer of 1940, Carson and Reeves moved to New York City, just two weeks after *The Heart Is a Lonely Hunter* was published to reviews calling her one of the most exciting new literary talents of the decade.[5] But troubled by poor progress in her writing, Carson separated from Reeves in September and moved into a house on Brooklyn's Middagh Street, owned by George Davis, the editor of *Harper's Bazaar*. Among the other boarders at various times were W. H. Auden, Paul Bowles, and Gypsy Rose Lee, the burlesque dancer on whom Carson developed a crush. While in New York, Carson became friends with a group of the city's most celebrated artists, including the composers Benjamin Britten, Aaron Copeland, and Leonard Bernstein, and Salvadore Dali and his wife, Gala. Richard Wright, his wife, and their daughter, Julie, moved into the Middagh Street house in the summer of 1941. Wright, however, told friends that he was afraid for Carson's health; she appeared to be driving herself to destruction, he'd concluded, and he did not want his family around when it finally occurred. Fearing that "she might collapse at the feet of his young daughter and inflict some deep psychic wound on her," Wright's family moved away from Middagh Street and into a more private apartment in Brooklyn (Carr, 127–29).[6]

McCullers's health, at this point and throughout her life, ranged from barely stable to debilitated. Like W. J. Cash, she was beset from an early age with serious, often incapacitating illnesses that carried over in important ways into her imaginative powers. At fifteen, she was diagnosed with pneumonia (her physicians later changed the diagnosis to rheumatic fever), and she required extensive bed rest and several weeks of convalescence in a sanitarium. By the mid-1930s, she began smoking three packs of cigarettes a day and losing weight; over the next several years, she was plagued by pneumonia; a bone infection in her jaw; a kidney infection; and, before she reached thirty, three strokes, one of which temporarily affected her vision, another of which permanently paralyzed her left side. During the winter of 1946–47, Carson spent most of December in the Neurological Institute of Columbia Presbyterian Hospital in New York City; at the same time, Reeves was in a hospital drying out from his alcoholism. That spring, she spent three weeks in another institution, Manhattan's Payne Whitney Psychiatric Clinic, for attempted suicide; several years later she was treated for a broken hip, and she had her right breast removed, after being diagnosed with breast cancer. For the majority of her adult life she fought chronic depression, alcoholism, and severe pain in her useless left arm. Later photographs often show a kind of forced smile above an awkward, twisted body.

If illness provided the backbeat to her life in New York, a series of romantic attachments emerged as a kind of dark melody. After separating from Reeves in 1941, the two divorced when she learned he had begun forging checks using her account. The two reconnected and eventually remarried in 1945, but their second marriage was marked by constant separations and reconciliations. At the same time, Carson became enamored with a number of city celebrities of both sexes, particularly glamorous and assertive women like Gypsy Rose Lee and Greta Garbo, whom she "idolized as a beautifully masculine female who pulsed with sensitivity, talent, and elan vital" (Carr, 127, 129).[7] Louis Untermeyer, whom she had met and occasionally tried to seduce at Breadloaf, was aware that the strain in Carson's marriage was "due greatly to their confused sexual relations." To Untermeyer, "Carson's bisexual tendencies were obvious. . . . I did indeed visit Carson at Middagh Street. I do remember an evening there . . . a gay (in both senses of the word) occasion at which Auden and Gypsy Rose Lee were present. (Gypsy did not strip, but Auden did plenty of teasing.) Carson was more voluble than usual" (Carr, 110, 119).

During the winter of 1940, she had become obsessed with a young ballerina who was dancing with the New York City Ballet Troupe; she would stand outside the stage door just to catch a glimpse of her. George Davis finally told her, "Now look, Carson, you're simply no longer in love with that woman. She's not for you. You're not to go down and moon outside her door any longer—do you understand?" (162). But it was the wealthy friend of the exiled Thomas Mann family, Annemarie Clarac-Schwarzenbach, daughter of a Swiss silk-weaving magnate, who most turned McCullers's head. Annemarie, a thirty-two-year-old journalist, travel writer, and novelist, had come to New York to negotiate the sale of photographs to *National Geographic* and *Life* that she and a colleague had taken on expedition to Afghanistan, Bulgaria, India, Russia, and Turkey. Like Carson, Annemarie had been a precocious literary celebrity, publishing an acclaimed novel when she was just twenty-three, and six other books of autobiographical adventure and travel. By 1940, she was "the literary sweetheart of Switzerland" and "had been the object of female pursuits all over Europe" (103). She "appreciated the male image imposed upon her by her parents and did all she could to perpetuate it; she was also very much aware, and pleased, that to her admirers she was a beautiful and sensuous woman." Also like Carson, Annemarie had unending and traumatic mental and physical health problems. She had become addicted to morphine during a brief marriage to Claude-Achille Clarac while they lived in Tehran, and she was in and out of institutions for mental illness and an ongoing dependence on drugs. Unfortunately for Carson, Annemarie had romantic aspirations of her own that did not include Carson, and the two remained tied more through correspondence than physical contact.

Carson's sexual dalliances were apparent enough that many of the writers she encountered in her various stints at writer's colonies wrote about it. Edward Newhouse, a short-story writer for the *New Yorker*, met Carson at Yaddo and said,

> I never dreamed that I was at the "Table of the Sensitives"—so it had been dubbed by some presumably heterosexual wag. Katherine Anne Porter usually sat with Eudora Welty at the other end of the room. Although I had read Proust with great absorption, I must have thought he was kidding. In any case, I was not very good at recognizing a homosexual when I met him. Or her. . . . I was surprised when Colin McPhee told me about the Balinese boy he had loved, surprised that he made no bones about it. . . . I was not surprised when Carson told me about herself. She sometimes wore a man's trousers and often a man's jacket, and even I was able to make the connection. (Carr, 158)[8]

Newhouse had reason, it seems, to pay attention to McCullers's sexuality. When she met Newhouse's wife, McCullers turned to him and said, "Ah, but you never told me she was a great beauty. If I'd met her six months ago, I would have given you a run for your money.' Newhouse laughed, but Carson said gravely, 'I mean it, I could have, and I *would* have'" (Carr, 162).

According to Katherine Anne Porter, when her husband, Albert Erskine, finished reading *The Heart Is a Lonely Hunter*, he said, "Katherine

Anne, that woman is a lesbian." Indignant over such an abrupt and seemingly unjustified judgment, Miss Porter retorted: "You can't assume that—what makes you think so?" To which he replied, "I can tell from the author's mind in that novel and by what she makes her characters do and say." After this, McCullers's infatuation with Porter became too much. "I have many friends who are homosexual and the fact does not bother me at all," Porter reportedly recalled later, "but with Carson then, the thought seemed intolerable" (Carr, 155). Alfred Kazin, whom McCullers met at Yaddo in summer 1943, was perhaps the most diplomatic. "My relationship with Carson was personal without being intimate, sentimentally intense," he wrote. "She was unhappy to the point of catastrophe. . . . But we weren't together very often, actually, or very long; a deep part of her life—her sexuality—always a mystery to me and perhaps to her—was outside of my ken, as were a lot of her friends" (234).

In Paris in 1945, Carson told her friend Eleanor Clark "about her hatred of sexual intercourse with men, including her husband Reeves." In a letter, Reeves wrote to the couple's friend David Diamond: "We simply are not husband and wife any more, David. It just doesn't make sense our staying together. When I come home, she either is there or is not there, without any explanations. Sometimes she comes home early in the morning, sometimes not. After all, she sleeps with whom she pleases, sees whom she wants. I'm not her husband any longer" (Carr, 152).

In fact, no one seemed to embody the sexual ambivalences of both Reeves and Carson so much as Diamond, who found himself deeply embroiled with both of them. His diary, frequently cited in Carr's biography, provides rich detail about an emotional triangle that ranged from the intimate to the operatic. In an entry marked May 26, 1941, he wrote, "I think only of Reeves and Carson. After he left for work, I crawled into Carson's little bed and held this child, this so tender, this so great artist in my arms, felt her cracking lungs as she coughed miserably." Three days later, he wrote: "I woke early without a hangover. Reeves lay next to me." Diamond's diary entry for June 27, 1950, reads: "After Lillian [Hellman] retired to the third floor to sleep, Carson, Reeves and I sat up 'til 3:30 A.M. talking over the past and the violences in our relationship when we first met. We agreed our youth, our ambivalences, our confused seeking for happiness and security was based not on reality but falsely directed by too much alcohol and not facing the homosexual question tolerantly" (Carr, 149, 150, 372).

To be sure, Diamond wrote, Reeves seemed to feel as sexually ambiguous as his wife. In 1941, when Diamond proposed that he and Carson marry after she divorced Reeves, Carson declined after realizing it
was Reeves that Diamond really loved. She suggested that Reeves try a
fling with Diamond instead: "Why, Reeves, that's just lovely—it rounds
out your personality and has nothing to do with us, our marriage or our
love for each other. You'll have a good time together for a while, then
you'll be back." Several friends of the couple's later wrote that Mc-
Cullers's ambivalence toward her husband became intolerable to him. Si-
mone Brown, a friend of the couple, found the relationship deeply corrosive to both of them: "What Reeves did for Carson was beyond
human endurance. He loved her too much—just as we all did. Carson
had a terrible power of destruction. She destroyed everything around
her—everything she loved. Yet she also wanted to give. It was a viper-
ish thing—all involved in a rather unusual cycle of love" (Carr, 389).

This was indeed a tormented and dangerous time for Reeves. After
the check-forging incident in the summer of 1941, he moved in with Diamond. One day, while he and Diamond were strolling across a bridge,
he paused, looked over at his friend, and said "I think, David, that suicide is the only answer . . . it might be best for me." Putting his arm
around Diamond's shoulder, he said, "But don't you believe, also, that
two people who love each other as we do, David . . . should die together?" and began pulling him toward the rail. Diamond screamed and
escaped (Carr, 174).[9]

Reeves's violent and often suicidal impulses were frequent and terrifying to those closest to him. Despite their reconciliation, Carson and
Reeves had awful fights in their last years of marriage, with Reeves breaking window panes and splintering doors. While they lived in Bachvillers,
France, Reeves tried to hang himself from a pear tree in their orchard,
but the limb did not support his weight, and broke. After Carson cut
him loose, she reportedly admonished him: "Please, Reeves, if you *must*
commit suicide, do it somewhere else. Just look what you did to my favorite pear tree." Later, as McCullers told her friend Tennessee Williams,
Reeves brought Carson into a barn, showed her a length of rope and
pointed to a rafter. "See that rafter, sister," he reportedly said. "It's a
good sturdy one. You know what we're going to do? Hang ourselves
from it. I tell you, it's the best thing for us both." Several days later, driving her to the American Hospital in Paris, Carson saw two lengths of
rope in the back. "You're right, Sister. This isn't the way to the hospital.
We are going out into the forest, Sister, and hang ourselves. But first,

we'll stop and buy a bottle of brandy. We'll drink it for old times sake . . . our one last fling." When he stopped the car near a tavern to buy liquor, she fled and returned to the United States, alone.

Shortly afterward, after calling friends to say he was "going West" (an old World War I army expression describing imminent death), Reeves sent two huge bunches of flowers to his friend Janet Flanner, including one that arrived the day after his death with the note, "From the man across the Styx." He killed himself on November 19, 1953, in the Hotel Chateau Frontenac. The cause of his death was disputed; he'd been addicted to anabuse for a while, but Jack Fullilove said he'd taken a lot of barbiturates and liquor and choked on his vomit (Carr, 403). Carson at the time was visiting Lillian Smith and Paula Snelling on Old Screamer Mountain in north Georgia when she heard of Reeves's death; it was Snelling who delivered the news. At Reeves's funeral Truman Capote reportedly broke down in tears, crying out, "My youth is gone" (413).

Carson herself had a far less dramatic death. She suffered a massive brain hemorrhage on August 15, 1967, remained in a coma for forty-seven days, and died on September 29 in Nyack Hospital. She is buried in the town's Oak Hill Cemetery. In spite of a life that was both physically and emotionally trying in the extreme, McCullers managed to craft a body of fiction that both embraced a suffering she knew all too well and imagined, however subtly, a world beyond this suffering. Through her twisted, grotesque, and troubled characters she was able to conceive a world beyond the oppression of physical, racial, and sexual limitation. Patricia Box has written that McCullers's broadly conjured notions of mixed-blood race and sexual androgyny represent a kind of compassionate ideal, devoid of racial, sexual, or emotional exploitation. "Only the androgynes are guided by music, and only they are capable of lifting themselves out of the world of superficiality and creating a universe in which people genuinely care about one another," she writes. "The necessary ingredient for creating this human unity is love, not a sexual love but a love that denies sex and strives to encompass everyone equally" (117). Out of a tragic life, then, came an art that moved beyond personal boundaries and into a far broader human understanding.

Biff Brannon, the owner of the New York Café in *The Heart Is a Lonely Hunter* who has a fondness for wearing his wife's perfume, has "a special friendly feeling for sick people and cripples. Whenever somebody with a harelip or T.B. came into the place he would set him up to a beer. Or if the customer were a hunchback or a bad cripple, then it would be whiskey on the house. There was one fellow who had his peter and his left leg blown off in a boiler explosion, and whenever he came to town there was a free pint waiting for him" (18).

The "freak" to whom Biff serves the most beer is Jake Blount, a surly, besotted roustabout, who early in the novel barrels into Biff's diner. Blount is described as having hands that are "huge and very brown" and brown eyes, "wet-looking and wide open with a dazed expression. He needed a bath so badly that he stank like a goat. There were dirt beads on his sweaty neck and an oil stain on his face. His lips were thick and red and his brown hair was matted on his forehead. His overalls were too short on the body and he kept pulling at the crotch of them." Blount's race is unclear until we are shown the ferocity with which the diner's patrons object to Blount's companion, the town's only black physician, Doctor Benedict Copeland. Blount tries to bring Copeland to the counter for a drink, but Copeland, "with a look of quivering hatred," turns on his heel and walks out. Blount is then confronted by an angry white clientele:

"Don't you know that you can't bring no nigger in a place where white men drink?" someone asked him.

Biff watched this happening from a distance. Blount was very angry, and now it could easily be seen how drunk he was.

"I'm part nigger myself," he called out as a challenge.

Biff watched him alertly and the place was quiet. With his thick nostrils and the rolling whites of his eyes it looked as though he might be telling the truth.

"I'm part nigger and wop and bohunk and chink. All of those."

There was laughter.

"And I'm Dutch and Turkish and Japanese and American." He walked in zigzags around the table where the mute drank his coffee. His voice was loud and cracked. "I'm one who knows. I'm a stranger in a strange land." (16, 18 – 19)[10]

The setting of this scene—a white radical and a black activist moving toward a lunch counter in the Deep South in 1940—is evocative of archetypal civil rights battlegrounds twenty years later. But in McCullers's hands, the scene is also far richer than that. Within this passage is a deep notion of fractured racial and psychological identity that cuts sharply against the mocking voices of the other white patrons. Jake Blount, with his "thick nostrils and the rolling whites of his eyes," is part black himself, and he scoffs at efforts to categorize him more neatly. Taking her cue perhaps from writers like Twain, in *Pudd'nhead Wilson*, and Faulkner, most notably in *Absalom, Absalom!*, McCullers uses the metaphorical power of miscegenation to subvert myths of racial and personal identity. Virtually all of her characters are of "mixed blood" in that they are all marked by publicly acknowledged signs of their racial or gender opposite. In *Wedding*, Frankie's sense of the world is connected literally to blood; as a young girl she "decided to donate blood to the Red Cross; she wanted to donate a quart a week and her blood would be in the veins of Australians and Fighting French and Chinese, all over the whole world, and it would be as though she were close kin to all of these people" (21). If mixed blood is tied directly to being "close kin" with people "all over the whole world," then pure blood can only mean its opposite: alienation, loneliness, and despair.

Throughout McCullers's work, characters that draw the most empathy are the ones who either are of mixed blood or yearn for it. In *The Heart Is a Lonely Hunter*, after the mute Singer has drawn a picture of his intimate friend Antanopolous, now shut up in a mental institution, he discovers that "the picture hurt the big Greek's feelings, and he refused to be reconciled until Singer had made his face very young and handsome and colored his hair bright yellow and his eyes china blue" (4). Berenice, the black nanny in *The Member of the Wedding*, is described as "very black" but with a left eye that is "bright blue glass" and a right eye that is "dark and sad." Big Mama, the black fortune-teller Frankie consults, is described as being half white and half black: "On the left side of her face and neck the skin was the color of tallow, so that part of her face was almost white and the rest copper-colored. The old Frankie used to think that Big Mama was slowly turning into a white person, but Berenice had said it was a skin disease that sometimes happened to colored people" (119). The absurdity of marking identity strictly by skin or eye color in a country already marked so deeply by miscegenation is reminiscent of Ralph Ellison's argument with LeRoi Jones over the racial authenticity of the blues in *Shadow and Act*:

One would get the impression that there was a rigid correspondence between color, education, income and the Negro's preference in music. But what are we to say of a white-skinned Negro with brown freckles who owns sixteen oil wells sunk in a piece of Texas land once farmed by his ex-slave parents who were blue-eyed, white-skinned, red-headed (kinky) Negro woman from Virginia and a blue-gummed, black-skinned curly-haired Negro male from Mississippi, and who not only sang bass in a Holy Roller church, played the market and voted Republican but collected blues recordings and was a walking depository of blues tradition? Jones' theory no more allows for the existence of such a Negro than it allows for himself; but that "concord of sensibilities" which has been defined as the meaning of culture, allows for much more variety than Jones would admit. (252)

A "concord of sensibilities" is a close approximation of Richard Wright's comment about McCullers's "sweep of apprehension" that allowed her to write with such empathy about such a variety of characters, even as they were set against backdrops of cultural intolerance and scorn. In one scene she has Doctor Copeland wrestling with what kind of clothes to buy for his children, all of whom—Hamilton, Karl Marx, William, and Portia—bear names strikingly reminiscent of American or European icons. (In *The Member of the Wedding*, by contrast, the six-year-old white boy is named "John Henry," after the legendary black railroad worker.) In the autumn of each year Doctor Copeland

> took them all into town and bought for them good black shoes and black stockings. For Portia he bought black woolen material for dresses and white linen for collars and cuffs. For the boys there was black wool for trousers and fine white linen for shirts. He did not want them to wear bright-colored, flimsy clothes. But when they went to school those were the ones they wished to wear, and Daisy said that they were embarrassed and that he was a hard father. He knew how the house should be. There could be no fanciness—no gaudy calendars or lace pillows or knickknacks—but everything in the house must be plain and dark and indicative of work and the real true purpose. (*Heart*, 69)

The importance of plain clothing to Doctor Copeland is as important for what it stands for—a humility before the "real true purpose" of racial equality—as for what it stands against—the expressive freedom resonant of "African" dress. In this, McCullers's writing is reminiscent of Nella Larsen's in *Passing*, in which her character Helga Crane, a black woman passing as white, finds dress to be a rich way to express racial allegiances. Helga, we learn, "didn't, in spite of her racial markings, belong to these dark segregated people." While waiting to be interviewed for a job, her gaze "wandered contemptuously over the dull attire of the women workers."

Drab colors, mostly navy blue, black, brown, unrelieved, save for a scrap of white or tan about the hands and necks. Fragments of speech made by the dean of women floated through her thoughts—"Bright colors are vulgar"—"Black, gray, brown, and navy blue are the most becoming colors for colored people"—"Dark-complected people shouldn't wear yellow, or green or red."—The dean was a woman from one of the "first families"— a great "race" woman; she, Helga Crane, a despised mulatto, but something intuitive, some unanalyzed driving spirit of loyalty to the inherent racial need for gorgeousness told her that bright colours *were* fitting and that dark-complexioned people *should* wear yellow, green, and red. Black, brown and gray were ruinous to them, actually destroyed the luminous tones lurking in their dusty skins. One of the loveliest sights Helga had ever seen had been a sooty black girl decked out in a flaming orange dress, which a horrified matron had next day consigned to the dyer. Why, she wondered, didn't someone write *A Plea for Color*? (18)

When Helga finally makes her way to Denmark, a kind of icono-graphic white homeland, she proposes wearing a "severely plain blue *crepe* frock" to a party and is rebuffed by her aunt. "'Too sober,' pronounced Fru Dahl. 'Haven't you something lively, something bright?' And, noting Helga's puzzled glance at her own subdued costume, she explained laughingly: 'Oh, I'm an old married lady, and a Dane. But you, you're young. And you're a foreigner, and different. You must have bright things to set off the color of your lovely brown skin. Striking things. Exotic things. You must make an impression'" (68).

"Exoticism," as a marker of blackness, is precisely what Doctor Cope-land abhors most. Doctor Copeland is considered by his daughter Portia to be "not like other colored mens" largely because of his intellect and his skepticism about the church. His first name, Benedict, suggests both the Latin "well said" and, at some level, that he has become a traitor to his race, or to himself. He even recognizes this, late in the novel, after his re-served approach to racism has failed to stop an outburst of violence: "I be-lieved in the tongue instead of the fist," he says. "As an armor against op-pression I taught patience and faith in the human soul. I know now how wrong I was. I have been a traitor to myself and to my people" (*Heart*, 258).

This realization, in Portia's eyes, was inevitable. "This here is hard to explain," she says. "My Father all the time studying by hisself. . . . I feels sorrier for him than anybody I knows. I expect he done read more books than any white man in this town. He done read more books and he done worried about more things. He full of books and worrying. He done lost God and turned his back to religion. All his troubles come down just to that." For a black man to be full of books and worry and to have turned his back on religion is, to Portia, to be a white man. Indeed, when Mick tells Portia she doesn't believe in God any more than she does Santa Claus, Portia says, "You wait a minute! That's why it sometime seem to me you favor my father more than any person I ever knowed." To which Mick replies, "*Me*? You say *I* favor him?" "I don't mean in the face or in any kind of looks," Portia explains. "I was speaking about the shape and color of your souls" (41–42).

Examining the "color" of a soul is reminiscent of Percy's insistence that, with the Negro, "there is no relation between what you see of him and what there is of him: the only difference is a sort of hallucination in the eye of the beholder, he's a white man inside." The image of a soul having a color, or race, is hardly new, but it is interesting how Percy and McCullers use the image differently. Percy speaks with near reverence of the humility and compassion of his servants; his comment about being "white" inside is a gesture of admiration, as if whiteness carried resonances of honor, dignity, and fortitude, words he sought desperately to cultivate in himself and in the memory of his forebears. For McCullers, having Portia describe her father's soul as "white" seems quite different. She is trying to put a name to her father's distress: whiteness, to her, is alienated, godless, paralyzing in its reliance on rationality, sobriety, and industry. Doctor Copeland is an acutely intellectual and ascetic man, a vegetarian given to reading Spinoza and sitting alone in the dark. His children, he is determined, will subdue their "exoticism," which to him stands in for a kind of moral retreat, in order to lead more diligent, restrained, colorless (read: white) lives. Doctor Copeland does so much "good" for people that most of the children in town—all of whom he delivered—are named for him. But his own brand of alienation, one that speaks with ferocious determination about the education of blacks, is deeply corroded by his own acquiescence to white codes of conduct. Even as he is beaten and jailed for his insistence on dignified treatment by the law, it is his battle with the "color of his soul" that is most interesting; even as he devotes himself to "the whole Negro race," he fights down his own "black, terrible, Negro feeling."

The whole Negro race was sick, and he was busy all the day and sometimes half the night. After the long day a great weariness would come over him, but when he opened the front gate of his home the weariness would go away. Yet when he went into the house William would be playing music on a comb wrapped in toilet paper, Hamilton and Karl Marx would be shooting craps for their lunch money, Portia would be laughing with her mother.

He would start all over with them, but in a different way. He would bring out their lessons and talk with them. They would sit close together and look at their mother. He would talk and talk, but none of them wanted to understand.

The feeling that would come over him was a black, terrible, Negro feeling. He would try to sit in his office and read and meditate until he could be calm and start again. He would pull down the shades of the room so that there would be only the bright light and the books and the feeling of meditation. But sometimes this calmness would not come. He was young, and the terrible feeling would not go away with study. (69–70)

Like his literary forebear, black doctor William Miller in Charles Chesnutt's *The Marrow of Tradition*, published forty years before McCullers's work, Copeland is caught between the uneducated world of his race and the impenetrable class of white intellectuals. "There was something melancholy, to a cultivated mind, about a sensitive, educated man who happened to be off color," Chesnutt writes. "Such a person was a sort of social misfit, an odd quantity, educated out of his own class, with no possible hope of entrance into that above it" (*Marrow*, 75). While riding on a train, when Dr. Miller is confronted with a crowd of "noisy, loquacious, happy, dirty, and malodorous" blacks, he muses that "personally, and apart from the mere matter of racial sympathy, these people were just as offensive to him as to the whites in the other end of the train. Surely, if a classification of passengers on trains was at all desirable, it might be made upon some more logical and considerate basis than a mere arbitrary, tactless, and, by the very nature of things, brutal drawing of a color line" (61).

Copeland is a brooding, raging man who, despite—or because of— an education that is way out of proportion to that of the whites and blacks around him, cannot control his self-destructive fury. His feverish determination to enlighten the people of his race has resulted not only in public admiration but in private horror over the "evil blackness" of his own soul. At times, we learn, "he drank strong liquor and beat his head against the floor. In his heart there was a savage violence, and once he grasped the poker from the hearth and struck down his wife. She took Hamilton, Karl Marx, William and Portia with her to her father's home. He wrestled in his spirit and fought down the evil blackness. And eight years later when she died his sons were not children any more and they did not return to him. He was left an old man in an empty house" (122).

There are other similarities to Percy here, though perhaps more to the Mississippi writer's life itself than to his comments about his black neighbors. The alienation of the Southern intellectual—white or black —as a class is worth noting, and in this, Doctor Copeland hearkens back to the character of Chesnutt's Dr. Miller. In *The Marrow of Tradition*, Chesnutt explores the complexities of race and class conflict that exploded during the 1898 Wilmington, North Carolina, race riot; the book serves as a useful literary backdrop to McCullers's work—and Cash's, for that matter—since it so thoroughly covers both the conflicts between whites and blacks and the myriad tormenting class differences *within* the races that make the whole all the more complex.

As does McCullers, Chesnutt sets up a series of race and class binaries: on one side of the racial divide are Doctor Miller, a quiet intellectual, and Josh Green, a huge, physically aggressive man more typical of the "brute" stereotype made famous in the film *Birth of a Nation*. On the other side are Major Carteret, a pretentious aristocrat obsessed with "the value of good blood," and the villainous Captain McBane, who, as Josh Green's archenemy and literary counterpart, is cast as the stereotypically violent poor white overseer. Chesnutt's vivid description of McBane might well be considered a forebear of Cash: McBane is cast as physically revolting—as compared to the elegant Carteret—and thus quite capable of performing the violent deeds Carteret only condones:

His broad shoulders, burly form, square jaw, and heavy chin betokened strength, energy, and unscrupulousness. With the exception of a small, bristling mustache, his face was clean-shaven, with here and there a speck of dried blood due to a carelessly or unskillfully handled razor. A single deep-set gray eye was shadowed by a beetling brow, over which a crop of coarse black hair, slightly streaked with gray, fell almost low enough to mingle with his black, bushy eyebrows. His coat had not been brushed for several days, if one might judge from the accumulation of dandruff upon the collar, and his shirt-front, in the middle of which blazed a showy diamond, was plentifully stained with tobacco juice. (*Marrow*, 32)

During a train ride, McBane notices that Doctor Miller is sitting in the white car (Chesnutt's novel was published five years after *Plessy v. Ferguson*, the Supreme Court case that codified separate-but-equal train travel) and demands that Miller be moved to the black car. After a brief confrontation, Miller accedes. As interesting as the racial encounter, however, is Miller's response when the train stops to pick up a group of black riders.

> Toward evening the train drew up at a station where quite a party of farm laborers, fresh from their daily toil, swarmed out from the conspicuously labeled colored waiting-room, and into the car with Miller. They were a jolly, good-natured crowd, and, free from the embarrassing presence of white people, proceeded to enjoy themselves after their own fashion. Here an amorous fellow sat with his arm around a buxom girl's waist. A musically inclined individual— his talents did not go far beyond inclination—produced a mouth organ and struck up a tune, to which a limber-legged boy danced in the aisle. They were noisy, loquacious, happy, dirty, and malodorous. For a while Miller was amused and pleased. They were his people, and he felt a certain expansive warmth toward them in spite of their obvious shortcomings. By and by, however, the air became too close, and he went out upon the platform. For the sake of the democratic ideal, which meant so much to his race, he might have endured the affliction . . . but personally, and apart from the mere matter of racial sympathy, these people were just as offensive to him as to the whites in the other end of the train. (60–61)

Doctor Miller, it seems clear, is a direct ancestor of Doctor Copeland, in that they both find themselves caught between a white intellectual class that refuses them entry and a black nonintellectual class they do not understand or care to join. Beyond this, of course, are the active restraints under which such intellectuals find themselves placed: in Chesnutt's hands, only Josh Green and Captain McBane, representatives of their respective classes' working people, are permitted the physical expression of their rage. Carteret, as a white aristocrat, leaves the dirty work of instigating racial violence to his less refined compatriot. Doctor Miller, as a black intellectual, is not permitted to act out his rage against whites, nor is he comfortable with "his people"; like Doctor Copeland, he is compelled to seethe passively in the company of both.

Doubtless McCullers was working with ideas that drove the writing of Chesnutt, Lillian Smith, and Richard Wright to address the different kinds of rage that crash forth from representatives of different classes and demeanors within the races. Wright, in particular, relied consistently on the image of black characters putting on a smiling face even as they plotted murder. But McCullers's use of a sophisticated, highly educated black character is an interesting choice. Doctor Copeland is no Bigger Thomas, beaten down by poverty and ignorance. He is more representative of the brand of segregation that Smith speaks of in *Killers of the Dream*. "Every little southern town is a fine stage-set for Southern Tradition to use as it teaches its children the twisting turning dance of segregation," she writes. "Few words are needed, for there are signs everywhere. White . . . colored . . . white . . . colored . . . over doors of railroad and bus stations, over doors of public toilets, over doors of theaters, over drinking fountains. . . . In most towns with one fountain, only the word *White* is painted on it. The town's white idiot can drink out of it but the town's black college professor must go thirsty on a hot August day" (45).

To Nadine Gordimer, who returned to McCullers's work in a 1972 essay marking the posthumous publication of *The Mortgaged Heart*, Doctor Copeland is emblematic of a kind of educated Bigger Thomas, a character with equal rage but no more effective way to defuse it. "The shameful 'problem' was there, and one of its senseless tragedies is there, acted out, in her first novel, in the person of Doctor Copeland, an astonishingly prophetic portrait of the kind of educated black of the 'thirties to whom present-day black thinkers point as the emasculated male," Gordimer writes. "Like that of Faulkner (whom as a writer she is so unlike), her refusal to dissociate herself from, to repudiate the white South may seem to us peculiar, given her belief in the love of man. But in her work as in Faulkner's the brutality of white Southerners towards black, and the degradation of black and white through this has—I'm afraid—been brought to life more devastatingly than by any black writer so far" ("Private Apprenticeship," 137).

Indeed, if Bigger Thomas represents the rage of the laboring class of blacks, Doctor Copeland represents the rage of the black intellectual class:

> The quiet insolence of the white race was one thing he had tried to keep out of his mind for years. When the resentment would come to him he would cogitate and study. In the streets around white people he would keep the dignity on his face and always be silent. When he was younger it was "Boy"—but now it was "Uncle."

"Uncle, run down to that filling station on the corner and send me a mechanic." A white man in a car had called out those words to him not long ago. "Boy, give me a hand with this."—"Uncle, do that." And he would not listen, but would walk on with the dignity in him and be silent. . . . Because of the insolence of all the white race he was afraid to lose his dignity in friendliness. (72–73)

Doctor Copeland's insistence on silent, intellectual dignity in the face of racism, combined with an almost stylized speaking eloquence, brings W. E. B. Du Bois, the era's most articulate and polished spokesman of black psychological oppression, to mind. The mute Singer muses about Copeland thus: "He is a doctor and he works more than anyone I have ever seen. He does not talk like a black man at all. Other Negroes I find it hard to understand because their tongues do not move enough for the words. This black man frightens me sometimes. His eyes are hot and bright. He asked me to a party and I went. He has many books. However, he does not own any mystery books. He does not drink or eat meat or attend the movies" (183).

If Copeland's language and intellect do not mark him so much as "white," they certainly mark him as apart from the "black" discourse that surrounds him. Portia, who is cast as more typically "black," at one point tells her father about Willie and High Boy going down to Madame Reba's Palace of Sweet Pleasures, where Willie dances with Love Jones —"one bad colored girl"—and gets in a knife fight with Junebug. "Nearabout cut this Junebug's head off." Love Jones, Portia says, is "at least ten shades blacker that I is and she the ugliest nigger I ever seen. She walk like she have a egg between her legs and don't want to break it" (116–17).

Doctor Copeland's disdain for this talk, and the life it represents, makes him, as it makes McCullers's other primary characters, both heroic and doomed. Because he is both "black" and somehow beyond "black," he suffers a particular brand of emotional damage. "The innate love of harmony and beauty that set the ruder souls of his people a-dancing and a-singing raised but confusion and doubt in the soul of the black artist; for the beauty revealed to him was the soul-beauty of a race which his larger audience despised, and he could not articulate the message of another people," Du Bois wrote in *The Souls of Black Folk* in 1903. "This waste of double aims, this seeking to satisfy two unreconciled ideals, has wrought sad havoc with the courage and faith and deeds of ten thousand people" (6). Copeland's desperate search for a kind of intimacy with his own family is undermined by his own moral aspiration; it is as if the harder he works, the more he studies, the further he gets from the blacks around him.

This, it seems, is a typical McCullers paradox: characters pursuing an organic ideal within themselves, be it racial or sexual, find that it only distances themselves further from the people to whom they yearn to have the closest ties. In Doctor Copeland's case, this may also be read as a representation of Du Bois's notion of a "double consciousness," which forces blacks to live split emotional lives as shadows in a white society. "It is a peculiar sensation, this double-consciousness, this sense of always looking at one's self through the eyes of others, of measuring one's soul by the tape of a world that looks on in amused contempt and pity," Du Bois wrote. "One ever feels his twoness—an American, a Negro; two souls, two thoughts, two unreconciled strivings; two warring ideals in one dark body, whose dogged strength alone keeps it from being torn asunder" (5). In this, McCullers's instincts are also like those of Lillian Smith, whose novel *Strange Fruit* emerged four years after *Heart*. In that narrative, Smith depicts the black girl Bess arguing with Sam about the perils of living a double life. Nonnie, a college graduate and Bess's sister, has been having a relationship with a white boy that will inevitably lead to the novel's tragic ending.

> "Sometimes it's seemed to me, this is crazy, but it's seemed to me that Nonnie has never in her life admitted to herself that she is Negro."
>
> Sam turned, face flushed darkly. "Maybe she's never thought about it one way or another."
>
> "How could she help it! When it's rubbed in your face like something dirty every day, everywhere you move."
>
> "There's more to life than color, Bess. There's more. Lot more." He had moved to his desk now, picked up his satchel, put it down.
>
> "Oh, how can you say it!" she says. "How can we stand here and say anything—when our color has ruined our lives—yours too. Don't say it hasn't. You go around doing good to people. It's fine for everybody but you. But you inside you, you want something more. You'd like to be natural and easy and simple. It *would* be simple, Sam, to be white. I'm so tired of being two people! Sometimes I get mixed up myself," she laughed shakily, "and forget which one is me—Mrs. Stephenson's Bess, or mine." (293)[11]

This evocation of the split in Bess's identity is typical of Smith's writing, and is also appropriate to a discussion of Doctor Copeland, who also goes "around doing good to people" even as he falls into physical and spiritual malaise himself. But there is an intriguing spin on the Du Bois image that also bears mentioning. During an argument between Copeland and his daughter Portia, the two squabble over the use of the proper word for people of their "race." The scene calls to mind Du Bois's desire for a "talented tenth" of black intellectuals. But it also does something more:

"The Negro race of its own accord climbs up on the cross every Friday . . . I mean that I am always looking. I mean that if I could just find ten Negroes—ten of my own people—with spine and brains and courage who are willing to give all that they have—" . . .

"You all the time using that word—Negro," said Portia. "And that word haves a way of hurting peoples' feelings. Even old plain nigger is better than that word. But polite peoples—no matter what shade they is—always says colored."

Doctor Copeland did not answer.

"Take Willie and me. Us aren't all the way colored. Our Mama was real light and both of us haves a good deal of white folks' blood in us. And Highboy—he Indian. He got a good part Indian in him. None of us is pure colored and the word you all the time using haves a way of hurting peoples' feelings."

"I am not interested in subterfuges," said Doctor Copeland. "I am interested only in real truths." (67)

Here, then, is a slightly different image of a black intellectual whose rage and repression subvert his own efforts at heroism. McCullers allows Copeland's daughter to challenge his sense of *black* racial purity. "None of us is pure colored," she says, and this gets it just right; blacks, just like whites, are nothing if not a mixture of each other's blood, and it is the investment of such fury into preserving an illusory racial essence that Portia conjectures as the cause of her father's distress. It is this mixing, or crossing, that McCullers found to be the "real truth" of human existence, and one that transcended even racial politics.

While looking over twelve-year-old Mick Kelly one day, Biff Brannon mused that she was at the age when she looked as much like an overgrown boy as a girl.

And on that subject why was it that the smartest people mostly missed that point? By nature all people are of both sexes. So that marriage and the bed is not all by any means. The Proof? Real youth and old age. Because often old men's voices grow high and reedy and they take on a mincing walk. And old women sometimes grow fat and their voices get rough and deep and they grow dark little mustaches. And he even proved it himself—the part of him that sometimes almost wished he was a mother and that Mick and Baby were his kids. (*Heart*, 112–13)

Biff, who has passively observed the comings and goings of the small town from his perch behind the cash register, is from the beginning of the novel conceived of as androgynous. He and his wife share proprietorship of the café, but they meet each other only when they are changing shifts, and never spend any time in bed together. When she finally dies, doctors remove a tumor "the size of a newborn child," the implication being that nothing organic ever came from the couple's nonexistent sexual union. After his wife's death, Biff uncorks a bottle of her perfume and "dabbled some of the perfume on his dark, hairy armpits. The scent made him stiffen. He exchanged a deadly secret glance with himself in the mirror and stood motionless. He was stunned by the memories brought to him with the perfume, not because of their clarity, but because they gathered together the whole long span of years and were complete. Biff rubbed his nose and looked sideways at himself. The boundary of death. He felt in him each minute that he had lived with her. And now their life together was whole as only the past can be whole. Abruptly Biff turned away" (191).

There is much of Proust in this passage, certainly: the wave of memories evoked by the scent of the perfume being the most apparent. But there is also a strong Proustian notion of passive, imaginative, "inverted" sexuality as Biff slowly becomes feminized. The scent of his wife's perfume on his own body is the first sign that Biff is capable of "stiffening." Later, Biff dabs perfume on his wrist and earlobes, and when he uses her lemon rinse, he recognizes that "certain whims that he had ridiculed in Alice were now his own." He remembers when he used to sleep with other women, "and then later when suddenly he lost it. When he could lie with a woman no longer. Motherogod! So that at first it seemed everything was gone" (201). After his wife's death he sits "sewing in the room upstairs." He sews skillfully, and often: "[T]he calluses on the tips of his fingers were so hard that he pushed the needle through the cloth without a thimble." In his sister-in-law's kitchenette, he "sits with his legs crossed, a napkin over his thigh, drinking a cup of tea," and later, as he chatted, he "polished his nails on the palm of his hand," and, in response to her remorse, "clucked soothingly" (104, 106–7).

Immediately following the perfume scene, Biff encounters Jake Blount, the gruff labor agitator who declared himself "part nigger." Biff "wanted to hold him" and asks Blount what time in history he'd most like to live in. His own favorite, he confesses, would be ancient Greece, "walking in sandals on the edge of the blue Aegean. The loose robes girdled at the waist. Children. The marble baths and the contemplations in the temples." Blount responds: "Maybe with the Incas. In Peru."

> Biff's eyes scanned over him, stripping him naked. He saw Blount burned a rich, red brown by the sun, his face smooth and hairless, with a bracelet of gold and precious stones on his forearm. When he closed his eyes the man was a good Inca. But when he looked at him again the picture fell away. . . . Blount leaned over suddenly and smelled in Biff's face.
> "Perfume?"
> "Shaving lotion," Biff said composedly.
> He wanted to draw Blount out completely so that he could understand certain questions concerning him. But Blount would never really talk—only to the mute. (195)

Once the institutionalized constraints of marriage are lifted from him by his wife's death, then, Biff's own sexual imagination comes alive. He embraces his wife's femininity and immediately discovers a strong passion for a man, Blount, whose actual appearance—drunk, filthy, foulmouthed—required no small amount of conjuring to be transformed into a smooth-skinned Inca. In essence, Biff becomes sexually transformed, but only in an imaginative way; he never actually acts on his newfound impulses, he simply basks in them. In this, he is central to McCullers's aesthetic: a character who struggles under the gender restrictions of the community and then becomes imaginatively—rather than physically or actively—transformed once these strictures are removed. This image is found throughout her work. McCullers's Gothic novel *Reflections in a Golden Eye*, published in 1941, is set in an army barracks "designed according to a certain rigid pattern." Suffering within that pattern is the emasculated Captain Pemberton, who watches passively as his wife takes a lover and becomes himself violently enamored with a young army private. "Sexually the Captain obtained within himself a delicate balance between the male and female elements, with the susceptibilities of both the sexes and the active powers of neither" (8). Pemberton is referred to by his wife, whom he loathes, as "you old prissy"; he is tormented not so much by her betrayal as by the fact that he "was just as jealous of his wife as he was of her love." Late in the novel, Captain Pemberton discusses "normalcy" with his wife's lover, Major Langdon. Langdon is disgusted with his own wife's effeminate servant, who he frequently sees "dancing around to music and messing with water colors."

"You mean," Captain Pemberton said, "that any fulfillment obtained at the expense of normalcy is wrong, and should not be allowed to bring happiness. In short, it is better, because it is morally honorable, for the square peg to keep scraping about the round hole rather than to discover and use the unorthodox square that would fit it?"

"Why, you put it exactly right," the Major said. "Don't you agree with me?"

"No," said the Captain, after a brief pause. With gruesome vividness the Captain suddenly looked into his soul and saw himself. For once he did not see himself as others saw him; there came to him a distorted, doll-like image, mean of countenance and grotesque in form. (77)

Pemberton, even more than Biff Brannon, knows where to find his own "unorthodox square," but the very recognition of this makes his own self-perception "gruesome." Like Doctor Copeland, whose own demon manifested itself as a "black, terrible, Negro feeling," Pemberton and Brannon are split between an organic sense of themselves and a rigid, institutionalized structure that prevents them from fostering "any fulfillment obtained at the expense of normalcy." Marriage, in other words, is to Brannon's sense of himself what the army is to Pemberton's, and segregation is to Doctor Copeland's: socially enforced and spiritually suffocating.

Louise Westling has written of the crisis of psychosocial conflict in regard to McCullers's tomboys Mick and Frankie, but Westling's notion of the pressures McCullers's characters are subjected to seems more broadly appropriate as well. "The images McCullers associates with the crisis are the images of sexual freaks, supported by an ambiance of androgynous longings, homosexuality, and transvestitism. . . . Dresses

must be worn, manners must be learned, behavior must become restrained and graceful. As a girl the tomboy is charming; as an adult, she
is grotesque" (339). Biff Brannon, even as he comes around to his own
androgyny, must confront the "deadly secret glance" of his own image,
and Captain Pemberton must acknowledge himself not only as "doll-
like" but "mean of countenance and grotesque" as well. Here, as in
Doctor Copeland's insistence on dour clothing, Brannon and Pemberton are torn between the "charming" appearances they must adopt and
the grotesquerie of their own souls.

Given her own personal sense of sexual ambivalence, McCullers manipulated received notions of sexual and racial identity in ways that must
certainly have paved the way for writers like Lillian Smith. McCullers
was herself far more open about her own ambiguous sexuality than
Smith, and her characters, likewise, are much more apparently fragmented. If Smith wrote about the "split" mind that results from a
racially segregated society, McCullers was more interested in examining
each psychological layer for its own peculiarities. Thus, just as "whiteness" and "blackness" bubble up from members of both races, femininity emerges from within men and women, and girls are constantly
mistaken for men and boys. Characters are constantly crossing over the
usual constraints of identity. Mick feels "physically crippled by feminine
clothes," Westling writes. "The high heel shoes make her slip, and her
breath is knocked out as her stomach slams into a pipe. Her evening
dress is torn, her rhinestone tiara lost. Back at home, Mick realizes that
she is too old to wear shorts: 'No more after this night. Not any more.'
With her renunciation of these clothes, she renounces childhood and its
boyish freedom" (344).[12]

The "crippling" influence of feminine clothes for Mick, then, is simply a stand-in for the crippling influence of heterosexuality. Mick is cast
as rough-and-tumble, a girl who would "rather be a boy any day." She
has no time for the flirtations that seem to obsess the girls her own age;
confronted with a sexual advance, she muses, she would fight her way
out of it: "Some girls were scared a man would come out from somewhere and put his teapot in them like they was married. Most girls were
nuts. If a person the size of Joe Louis or Mountain Man Dean would
jump out at her and want to fight she would run. But if it was somebody
within twenty pounds her weight she would give him a good sock and
go right on" (86).[13] Later in the novel, in a scene that moves from sexual innocence to one of horror, Mick and her friend Harry Minowitz
have intercourse. Mick felt "like her head was broke off from her body

and thrown away." "I didn't like that," Mick tells Harry. "I never will marry with any boy."

The violence and terror that pour from Mick are typical of the reactions McCullers's characters have to physical sexuality, which is often portrayed as merely a spark for the loneliness, betrayal, and existential terror that inevitably follow. In *Reflections in a Golden Eye*, Alison Langdon, whose husband is having an affair with Captain Pemberton's wife, "cut off the tender nipples of her breasts with the garden shears"; she would have stabbed herself, but the shears, she finds, were too dull. In *The Member of the Wedding*, Frankie has what amounts to an identity breakdown when she learns that her older brother has decided to get married. To Frankie, the marriage, the institutionalized, heterosexual pairing off, means only that she will once again be alone, and isolated; indeed, she asks Berenice, who has been married four times herself, "Does marriage really stop your growth?" The question, given Frankie's fear of her own "freakish" height, is double-edged: she both longs to stop growing physically and dreads the constraints marriage would place on her emotionally. Violently banging her forehead on a table, she cries, "They went away and left me. . . . They went away and left me with this feeling." Her rage then turns to Berenice: "Some day you going to look down and find that big fat tongue of yours pulled out by the roots and laying there before you on the table. Then how do you think you will feel?" she says. Moments later, when Berenice kids her about having a "crush on the wedding," Frankie picks up knife and throws it, narrowly missing Berenice, saying she's "the best knife thrower in this town" (31–33). Later, Frankie describes having "committed a queer sin" in the MacKeans' garage with Barney MacKean. "The sin made a shriveling sickness in her stomach, and she dreaded the eyes of everyone. She hated Barney and wanted to kill him. Sometimes alone in the bed at night she planned to shoot him with the pistol or throw a knife between his eyes" (23). When she has a sexual encounter with a drunken soldier twice her age, Frankie is "paralyzed by horror." She violently explodes, biting down hard on his tongue and then braining him with a vase. As the soldier collapses in a bloody heap, Frankie runs from the hotel room.

Perhaps most provocatively, in the story "The Ballad of the Sad Café," Miss Amelia Evans, a six-foot two-inch, 160-pound woman with hairy thighs who "cared nothing for the love of men," ends her ten-day marriage to Marvin Macy without having slept with him; rather, she "hit his face so hard that he was thrown back against the wall and one of his teeth was broken."

Miss Evans also seems to be terrified of female sexuality. Although she is a doctor, there is one illness she will not treat: "If a patient came in with a female complaint she could do nothing. Indeed at the mere mention of the words her face would slowly darken with shame, and she would stand there craning her neck against the collar of her shirt, or rubbing her swamp boots together, for all the world like a great, shamed, dumb-tongued child."[14]

As the story progresses, Miss Amelia becomes enamored with a four-foot-tall hunchback named Cousin Lyman, who quickly falls in love with Miss Amelia's estranged husband, Macy, who is back in town after a stint in the state penitentiary. Cousin Lyman, we are told, has always been preoccupied with "each man's lower regions," and in a kind of bizarre, violent mating ritual, Miss Amelia and Macy hold a savage boxing match, nominally over the affections of Cousin Lyman. Just as Miss Amelia is about to win, the hunchback jumps from a counter onto her back, allowing Macy to win the fight.

After the boxing match, Macy and the hunchback not only run off to-gether—a kind of elopement—they steal all of Miss Amelia's valu-ables, vandalize her house, set fire to her still, and poison her food. Left alone, Miss Amelia, once a doctor of noted compassion, begins telling "one-half of her patients that they were going to die outright, and to the other half she recommended cures so far-fetched and agonizing that no one in his right mind would consider them for a moment" (69–70). Miss Amelia, in effect, is forced from her position as a compassionate an-drogyne into a violent struggle for a sexual partner. For her, the battle has been lost as soon as it is entered; she gives up the fight and is beaten and ultimately ruined, not because she lost a lover—with whom she was never physically involved—but because she was forced to compete at all. Her androgyny, once a source of innocence and stability, is, as it is in Mick and Frankie and Captain Pemberton, shattered by contact with physical sexual engagement.

Several critics have argued that McCullers, like Percy, relied upon im-ages of androgyny, or sexlessness, to personify a world beyond the "hor-ror" of sexuality, which to her represented not only the violence of desire, as it did to Cash, but artistic and spiritual shackling as well. "Sig-nificantly, only the androgynes are capable of attempting to escape the isolation of man, whereas distinct sexuality erects a barrier to human in-teraction and stifles any attempt at unity and understanding between in-dividuals," Patricia Box writes. "The sexual nature of men and women prevents them from loving everyone equally; thus when Frankie leaves the world of androgyny, she leaves behind her hopes of escape from isolation . . . no longer can she dream of a universe in which people give of themselves freely. . . . The conclusion is not optimistic: no androgynes remain to give hope to a world in need of selfless love and community" (117, 119).

As mentioned earlier, many of the friends who knew of McCullers's own ambivalent sexuality claimed that when she went to bed with a man or a woman, she primarily wanted a comforting sleeping companion, not a sex partner. This kind of childlike engagement with sex is found in many places in her writing as well. Throughout McCullers's work, characters aspiring to a kind of sexless innocence are brought to violence or heartbreak. Private Williams, the silent, sexually ambiguous object of Captain Pemberton's fascination in *Reflections in a Golden Eye*, is described as someone who did not "fornicate." He had never "been known to laugh, to become angry, or to suffer in any way. He ate three wholesome meals a day and never grumbled about the food as did the other soldiers." His erotic fascination with Pemberton's wife manifests itself only in his sneaking into her bedroom at night while she sleeps, and passively watching her. It is only when he becomes caught in a bizarre and platonic love triangle, as the object of Pemberton's own homoerotic lust, that he meets a violent end (4). In *Member of the Wedding*, Frankie convinces her little cousin John Henry to go to bed with her and proceeds to rub "Sweet Serenade" down the inside of her shirt and on John Henry as well.

> They went to bed. . . . She heard him breathe in the darkness, and now she had what she wanted so many nights that summer; there was somebody sleeping in the bed with her. She lay in the dark and listened to him breathe, then after a while she raised herself on her elbow. He lay freckled and small in the moonlight, his chest white and naked, and one foot hanging from the edge of the bed. Carefully she put her hand on his stomach and moved closer; it felt as though a clock was ticking inside him and he smelled of sweat and Sweet Serenade. He smelled like a sot little rose. Frankie leaned down and licked him behind the ear. Then she breathed deeply, settled herself with her chin on his sharp damp shoulder, and closed her eyes: for now, with somebody sleeping in the dark with her, she was not so much afraid. (13)

And John Singer, the ironically named mute at the center of *The Heart Is a Lonely Hunter*, is cast as a neutral, utterly nonjudgmental figure who, when he goes to the cinema, "never looked at the title of a picture before going into a movie, and no matter what was showing he watched each scene with equal interest" (79). Singer sits, quietly smoking, in his apartment as Brannon, Blount, Mick, and Doctor Copeland file through, telling their stories, each one seeming the more melodramatic and self-involved given the passive acceptance of Singer's own life. Singer cannot reply verbally; he simply nods his head and smiles in proportion to the emotional energy of the story he is being told. Each character leaves his presence convinced that Singer is the only one who has ever really listened to him or her; he is a priest, a wise man whose "many-tinted gentle eyes were grave as a sorcerer's." To Singer, confessors unload their most troubling tales without feàr of condemnation or reproach. Singer becomes for the other characters more than just a receptacle for their woes. He is also imagined by them as a kind of archetype of their own particular fantasies. In this respect he may stand in for McCullers's own artistic vision, in which, entering each of her characters, she found that "nothing human is alien to me."

So the rumors about the mute were rich and varied. The Jews said that he was a Jew. The merchants along the main street claimed he received a large legacy and was a very rich man. It was whispered in one browbeaten textile union that the mute was an organizer for the CIO. A lone Turk who had roamed into the town years ago and who languished with his family behind the little store where he sold linens claimed passionately to his wife that the mute was Turkish. He said that when he spoke his language the mute understood. And as he claimed this his voice grew warm and he forgot to squabble with his children and he was full of plans and activity. One old man from the country said that the mute had come from somewhere near his home and that the mute's father had the finest tobacco crop in the country. All of these things were said about him. (170)[15]

And later: "During the moonlit January nights Singer continued to walk about the streets of the town each evening when he was not engaged. The rumors about him grew bolder. An old Negro woman told hundreds of people that he knew the ways of spirits come back from the dead. A certain piece-worker claimed that he had worked with the mute at another mill somewhere else in the state—and the tales he told were unique. The rich thought he was rich and the poor considered him a poor man like themselves. And as there was no way to disprove these rumors they grew marvelous and very real. Each man described the mute as he wished him to be" (190).

Singer, then, has an identity that is perfectly malleable, suited to the whim of whomever crosses his path. He is a Jew to a Jew, a Turk to a Turk. He is a healer as well; some critics have considered him Christlike in his efforts not only to indulge his friends' stories but to unite them in a kind of brotherhood. For a variety of reasons, this does not happen. Although each character visits his room consistently throughout the novel, it is only toward the end of the novel that all four converge on his apartment at once. "Singer was bewildered. Always each of them had so much to say. Yet now that they were together they were silent. When they came in he had expected an outburst of some kind. In a vague way he had expected this to be the end of something. But in the room there was only a feeling of strain. His hands worked nervously as though they were pulling things unseen together from the air and binding them together" (179). This is McCullers's existentialism meeting her cultural critique halfway: each character is capable of empathy and confession, but only on his or her own terms. They are all withered from their battles with their own grotesquerie, and from their need to tell their own stories. Only in Singer's exclusive company are they free to give voice to their own anguish. Here, too, Singer is an appropriate stand-in for McCullers herself: a vessel through which the misshapen, the lonely, the excluded, find the means to tell their stories and navigate an inhospitable world.

Thirteen Ways of Looking at Whiteness

Scholars of African American literature have done as much as anyone to revitalize the study of the humanities in the late twentieth century, but there remains important ground to be turned in the history, literature, and rhetoric of American race relations. The relative absence of white texts in the discussion of racial discourse has allowed scholar and teacher alike to rely on black texts to shoulder the burden of race theory and race history; if a twentieth-century white text makes it into a "literature of race" classroom, it is all too often a mere caricature, a *Gone with the Wind* or, worse, Thomas Dixon's *The Clansman*. This is both unfortunate and incomplete in much the same way that caricaturing black writing or thinking was incomplete two or three decades ago. African American studies have long since destabilized notions of racial identity held *between* groups; this book hopes to challenge the stubborn idea of monolithic racial identity, in this case "whiteness," *within* a particular group.

"We can agree that the notion of a unitary black man is as imaginary (and as real) as Wallace Stevens's blackbirds are; and yet to be a black man in twentieth-century America is to be heir to a set of anxieties: beginning with what it *means* to be a black man," writes Henry Louis Gates Jr. in *Thirteen Ways of Looking at a Black Man*. "All of the protagonists of this book confront the 'burden of representation,' the homely notion that you represent your race, thus that your actions can betray your race or honor it. . . . Each, in his own way, rages against the dread requirement *to represent*; against the demands of 'authenticity'" (xvii).

The same can be said of the white authors discussed in this book. All four were white, but all four shuddered under the burden of the corrosive racial and gender discourse of their day; their ambivalences prove that this discourse also damaged members of the "majority" culture, even, strangely enough, those who compulsively perpetuated it. "The paradigm of race is the antithesis of freedom," John Edgar Wideman writes.

It locks white people in a morally and ethically indefensible position they must preserve by force. Fosters a myth of superiority they must act out: dictates to them whom they should love and hate. Since it sanctions and reinforces the idea that some people are born better than others, deserve more than others, have an innate right, even duty, to seize from others what they want, the paradigm of race is destructive to anyone not white, and ultimately also self-destructive for whites. A racist disposition towards non-whites, because it hardens the heart and rationalizes extremes of selfishness and brutality, inevitably reappears in the way whites regard and treat other whites. The pervasive violence in our society—from domestic abuse to economic exploitation to capital punishment to punitive expeditionary wars—is rooted in the paradigm of race. (xxv)

Carefully scrutinizing these texts, we can also tear apart the notion that even writers from the same race, time, and region necessarily constructed race—their own or that of others—the same way. Looking for the contradictory, disjointed, even subversive shades *within* "whiteness" —looking, for example, at the difference gender and sexuality make in the way individual writers see race—also helps keep us vigilant about psychological as well as historical and regional specificity. Just as Mississippi has everything and nothing in common with South Carolina, just as Richard Wright has everything and nothing in common with Zora Neale Hurston, so does William Alexander Percy have everything and nothing in common with Carson McCullers. As with black texts, once white texts are relieved of the need to fall into line, to be conceived of as monochromatic and uniform, we can more easily understand the contradictions and nuances of color that exist within them. It is interesting to note, for example, that Smith and McCullers seemed so much more willing to explore the psychosexual fault lines in their own minds and communities than Cash and Percy, who were otherwise so astute in their observation and analysis. Perhaps the two men were no less aware of these fault lines; perhaps they merely felt incapable of finding the courage or the language to express them. The construction of Southern masculinity has never allowed for frank discussion of emotion and sexuality, and when that discussion involves sexual ambiguity or lifelong impotence, it can only be forced underground. "White" texts—and the authors who write them—are as idiosyncratic and rhetorically variable one from the other as they are from "black" texts; indeed, Smith has more in common rhetorically with Richard Wright than she does with McCullers, who was of the same race, class, home state, and (at least in part) sexual preference.

Beyond dismantling the idea of a monolithic "white" voice, taking the next theoretical step—proving that "race" itself is merely a mirage constructed idiosyncratically in the minds of each thinker—is a relatively easy move. "Race only becomes 'real' as a social force when individuals or groups behave toward each other in ways which either reflect or perpetuate the hegemonic ideology of subordination and the patterns of inequality of daily life," writes the historian Manning Marable in *Beyond Black and White*.

> To move into the future will require that we bury the racial barriers of the past, for good. The essential point of departure is the deconstruction of the idea of "whiteness," the ideology of white power, privilege and elitism which remains heavily embedded within the dominant culture, social institutions and economic arrangements of the society. But we must do more than critique the white pillars of race, gender and class domination. We must rethink and restructure the central social categories of collective struggle by which we conceive and understand our own political reality. We must redefine "blackness" and other traditional racial categories to be more inclusive of contemporary ethnic realities. To be truly liberating, a social theory must reflect the actual problems of a historical conjuncture with a commitment to rigor and scholastic truth. (199–200)

Applying this thinking to "whiteness" helps move us in the same direction. If African American literary, historical, and legal studies have smashed the lens through which race has been viewed in this country for centuries, the study of white texts using these new reading techniques can help us take the next step. We are now aware that there are multiple voices in our communities; we must now acknowledge that there are, as it were, multiple voices in our own heads. Shelley Fisher Fishkin posits that Huck learned to speak from Jim; following Toni Morrison, we now can begin to explore how all American literature, and Southern literature in particular, has been raised by black surrogates as well as white parents. If Percy was brought up by a black nursemaid, so was his mind and the creative work that emanated from it. White sensibilities *depend* on black sensibilities; it is the relationship between the two, not so much the separate halves, that is interesting. Willie Morris, a contemporary white Mississippi writer, reveals a moment in *The Ghosts of Medgar Evers* in which a white friend from the Delta refigured his family's traditional feelings about race: "His mother died when he was little, and his father was courting again, and for all purposes he was raised by an illiterate black muledriver named Shotgun, whom he loved. 'The black people of the Delta didn't sail past the Statue of Liberty when *they* came to this country,' my friend once said to me. 'They made this place down here. They worked to death and got nothin', except just the ground itself, and it wasn't theirs either. I'd look out from my porch at night when I was a boy and wonder what they were thinking that night with their lamps blinking in the shadows. Now I know they were thinking of the same things I was'" (13).

I think of this book, then, as standing not only between Faulkner and Styron but between Charles Chesnutt and August Wilson, between Du Bois and Baldwin, between Hurston and Toni Morrison as well. Ideally, I consider all these writers' works as interwoven and interdependent; a fully realized discussion of race in twentieth-century American literature cannot stand without the consideration of all these texts bound together. Ideally, a deep understanding of race and human relations more broadly conceived will incorporate *all voices*, each validated, each distinct, each acknowledged as contributing to the conversation, both scholarly and pedagogical. "That both whites and blacks, or more broadly people of all colors, cannot truly embrace the range of North American humanity as their own, as their imagined community, is the collective cost," Grace Elizabeth Hale writes. "Making whiteness American culture, the nation has foregone other possibilities. The hybridity that could have been our greatest strength has been made into a means of playing across the color line, with its rotting distance of voyeurism and partisanship, a confirmation of social and psychological division" (10).

In my experience, using white texts in addition to black texts to explore the roots of racial discourse forces students of all races to more directly confront themselves. Once they are introduced to the rhetorical miscegenation that exists in white as well as black texts, it quickly becomes evident that students (and the texts themselves) *do not* have a different history from "the other" and never did. Black and white are and always have been inextricably linked, just as male and female have always been inextricably linked. "One of the most important results of reconceptualizing from 'objective truth' to rhetorical event will be a more nuanced sense of legal and social responsibility," writes Patricia Williams, whose *Alchemy of Race and Rights* incisively examines the racial thicket of contemporary legal discourse.

> This will be so because much of what is spoken in so-called objective, unmediated voices is in fact mired in hidden subjectivities and unexamined claims that make property of others beyond the self, all the while denying such connections. . . . In racial contexts, [this] is related to the familiar offensiveness of people who will say, "Our maid is black and *she* says that blacks want. . . ."; such statements both universalize the lone black voice and disguise, enhance, and "objectify" the authority of the individual white speaker. As a legal tool, however, it is an extremely common device by which not just subject positioning is obscured, but by which agency and responsibility are hopelessly befuddled. (11)

This is my impulse as well: to nudge scholarship and students alike to examine and take responsibility for *their own* language, *their own* racial thinking, *their own* sense of personal and cultural history, rather than treating race (and African American literature, through which race issues are most frequently taught) as a kind of localized anthropology project. "Even among left-inclined students, the idea that race is natural is so ingrained that there is an assumption that liberal and even radical education must be trying to teach that race is not very important, but nonetheless a material reality," David Roediger writes in *Toward the Abolition of Whiteness*. "When students do 'get it,' they are often tremendously enthusiastic. Seeing race as a category constantly being struggled over and remade, they sense that the possibilities of political action in particular and human agency in general are vastly larger than they had thought. They reflect on the manner in which structures of social oppression have contributed to the tragic ways that race has been given meaning. They often come to indict those structures" (2).

As uncomfortable as some white students might be to get "inside" a black text and discover a wound that "their" ancestors might have somehow "caused," looking directly at white texts to discover the racial complexity and pain there as well is an entirely different experience. Lillian Smith offers a very different reading experience than reading Richard Wright on the "same subject." White readers of Wright, for example, might find easy access to his anger, but they are still somehow capable of keeping it at arm's length; it is, after all, "his" (that is to say black) anger.

By contrast, white readers of Smith, or any of the others in this study, will find an entirely different entrance into the psychological experience of race and racism. Examining the seeds of racism in fertile ground is quite different from seeing them in full bloom.

Black readers should also find such an analytical tool useful, for it shifts the weight, or the "problem," of race from the shoulders of African American literature onto the shoulders of American literature writ large. In my experience, African American students tire quickly of African American literature being used as the only vehicle through which racial discourse can be examined; introducing white texts into this mix would certainly balance the account. Reading white texts, of course, would also force black students to complicate their own understanding of race, to realize that white racial thinking is no more simple or monolithic than black racial thinking. Reading Cash the week after reading Percy the week after reading Faulkner would certainly go some distance to proving this. Now that we have made significant strides in adding black texts to the American canon, we can encourage students to engage *all* the myriad voices threading through *all* their texts (and all their heads), be they black or white. It is, of course, as useful for black readers to understand the complexities and vagaries of the white mind as it has been for white readers to understand the vagaries and complexities of the black mind.

Historically speaking, of course, the late twentieth century offers a fascinating coda to the mid-twentieth century; who would have thought that reverse migration, among African Americans in particular, would have taken hold just a few decades after so many people left? Willie Morris discusses a 1997 *Newsweek* story in which it was reported that the reverse migration of middle-class blacks back to the South was up 92 percent over the 1980s and that "a net tide of 2.7 million—more than half of the post 1940s migration—will have headed South between 1975 and 2010." Earlier this year, black and white residents of two central Georgia counties held an art exhibit memorializing two black couples lynched in broad daylight in 1946. One oil painting, according to the *Atlanta Constitution*, portrayed two couples "first enjoying life and then . . . after their bodies were riddled with bullets." Clearly, the South is no closer to finishing its struggle with questions of race than is the rest of the country.

Eventually, of course, we will begin to understand that all these voices exist and always have existed together, as instruments in the same band. "Our ability to transcend racial chauvinism and inter-ethnic hatred and the old definitions of 'race,' to recognize the class commonalities and joint social-justice interests of all groups in the restructuring of this nation's economy and social order, will be the key to constructing a non-racist democracy, transcending ancient walls of white violence, corporate power and class privilege," Marable writes. "By dismantling the narrow politics of racial identity and selective self-interest, by going beyond 'black' and 'white,' we may construct new values, new institutions and new visions of an America beyond traditional racial categories and racial oppression" (201–2).

In a similar vein, Wideman writes in *Fatheralong* that "the implicit presence of the paradigm of race flickers just beneath the surface, offering its quasi-religious authority to the notion that problem groups are somehow fundamentally different from the rest of us, sanctioning the most drastic solutions to maintain the world as it should be. With the same blind, relentless logic of the computer whirring through the billion on/off choices of its circuitry, the Western mindset seems disposed to conquer by dividing, apprehending the world in polarized terms of either/or" (67–68).

Fifty years before Wideman, Walter White wrote of the dangers of the dualistic thinking he found so prevalent among his contemporary white Southerners. "It made no difference how intelligent or talented my millions of brothers and I were, or how virtuously we lived. A curse like that of Judas was upon us, a mark of degradation fashioned with heavenly authority," White wrote in his 1948 autobiography. "There were white men who said Negroes had no souls, and who proved it by the Bible. . . . Theirs was a world of contrasts in values: superior and inferior, profit and loss, cooperative and noncooperative, civilized and aboriginal, white and black. If you were on the wrong end of the comparison, if you were inferior, if you were noncooperative, if you were aboriginal, if you were black, then you were marked for excision, expulsion, or extinction. I was a Negro; I was therefore that part of history which opposed the good, the just, and the enlightened" (11–12).

There is something of the yin and yang in this. The cultural whole is not only made up of two complementary colors (in this case black and white); each side also has the seed of its opposite growing within it. White is defined by the existence of black, not just *opposite* it but *within* it as well, and vice versa. This, to be sure, is a radically different notion from the system of racial "opposites" we as a country (and as a Western civilization) have been cultivating for centuries, a dualism that creates hierarchies of separation flowing quickly from white/black and man/

woman to rich/poor and good/evil. One way to tear down these dualities is to reveal the complexities and "inner opposites" inherent within each of us. As Faulkner explored so intricately in *Absalom, Absalom!*, once white is revealed to *contain* and *depend upon* black, ancient myths of racial purity vanish like so much Appalachian mist. This, of course, is why the metaphor of miscegenation holds so much power in Southern literature; once black blood is found to be flowing in white veins, images of unalloyed "whiteness" can no longer be taken seriously. Hallowed portraits of pure-blooded ancestors must be removed from the walls, and reframed.

CONCLUSION

NOTES

Introduction

1. When the college students arrested in 1960 for trying to integrate a Greensboro, North Carolina, lunch counter were asked where their inspiration came from, they said Gunnar Myrdal, Gandhi, and Lillian Smith (Loveland, 197).

Chapter One

1. As Ellison has written, "Had there been no blacks, certain creative tensions arising from the cross-purposes of whites and blacks would also not have existed. Not only would there have been no Faulkner . . . there would have been no Stephen Crane . . . no Hemingway. Without the presence of Negro American style, our jokes, our tall tales, even our sports would be lacking in the sudden turns, the shocks, the swift changes of pace (all jazz shaped) that serve to remind us that the world is ever unexplored, and that while a complete mastery of life is mere illusion, the real secret of the game is to make life swing" (*Territory*, 110).

2. Half a century before Lillian Smith would explore similar issues, Charles Chesnutt wrote of the insidiousness of institutionalized segregation even at its most mundane. In a chapter in *The Marrow of Tradition*, entitled "A Journey Southward," he describes a scene in which two friendly doctors, black Dr. Miller and white Dr. Burns, are forced to sit in different rail cars: "The car was conspicuously labeled at either end with large cards, similar to those in the other car, except that they bore the word 'Colored' in black letters upon a white background. The author of this piece of legislation had contrived, with an ingenuity worthy of a better cause, that not merely should the passengers be separated by the color line, but that the reason for this division should be kept constantly in mind. Lest a white man should forget that he was white,—not a very likely contingency,—these cards would keep him constantly admonished of the fact; should a colored person endeavor, for a moment, to lose sight of his disability, these staring signs would remind him continually that between him and the rest of mankind not of his own color, there was by law a great gulf fixed" (56).

3. Lynching frequently involved torture and not merely hanging. As Hazel Carby has pointed out, "The institutionalized rape of black women has never been as powerful a symbol of black oppression as the spectacle of lynching. Rape has always involved patriarchal notions of women being, at best, not entirely unwilling accomplices, if not outwardly inviting sexual attack. The links between black women and illicit sexuality consolidated during the ante-bellum years had powerful ideological consequences for the next hundred and fifty years" (39).

4. Lillian Smith, in *Killers*, put it more bluntly: "Many a man went into politics, or joined the KKK, had a nervous breakdown or forged checks, got drunk or built up a great industry, because he could no longer bear the police-state set up in his own home. But this would have been a hard thing for these good mothers and wives to believe, and for the men also" (150).

5. The Agrarians' position also left several of the writers wide open to race criticism. Donald Davidson wrote, "What did a few lynchings count in the balance against the continued forbearance and solicitude that the Georgian felt he exercised toward these amiable children of cannibals?" Allen Tate wrote that "the white race seems determined to rule the Negro race. . . . I belong to the white race; therefore I intend to support white rule" (King, 59–60).

6. City life offered some advantages to poor Southerners, but in truth, the cities were little more than oversized country towns where the problems of employment, health, education, and safety were often just as acute as in the rural areas. The largest city in the South in 1930 was New Orleans, with 459,000 people; half a dozen others had between 200,000 and 300,000, and a mere ten more topped the 100,000 mark.

7. "Most lynch mobs killed swiftly. The typical victim, after being hoisted with a rope tossed over a tree limb, trestle, or utility pole, would have his death throes ended by a fusillade of bullets. But some lynchings involved prolonged torture and fire" (Ferris and Wilson, 175).

8. In this climate of fear and hate, William Alexander, the director of the Commission on Interracial Cooperation, traveled through the South to avert bloodshed where racial violence appeared imminent. When he asked one elderly white minister whether there was any local trouble with Negroes, the man answered, "No we had to kill a few of them, but we didn't have any trouble with them" (Sosna, 21).

9. The success of black athletes during the 1930s and 1940s gave the anxieties of white demagogues something to latch onto. In 1936, Jesse Owens won four gold medals in Berlin. A year later, Joe Louis knocked out James J. Braddock to become only the second black heavyweight champion. The uproar surrounding Jackie Robinson's venture into the heart of the segregated American pastime was emblematic of country torment over race generally. "The history books will have to record that Jackie Robinson's triumph, so widely publicized and admired, enormously furthered acceptance for the Negro in many fields of American life," Eric Goldman writes. "They will also have to record a more important fact. The revolutionist in a baseball suit was the flashing symbol of an era in the national life when, for all minority groups, for all lower-status Americans, the social and economic walls were coming tumbling down" (52).

10. Racial liberals, including Smith, tried to convince other whites that lynching harmed whites as well as blacks, although their rhetoric at times ran to the extreme. "The wrong that [lynching] does to its wretched victims is almost as nothing compared to the injury it does to the lynchers themselves, to the community, and to society at large," reported the Southern University Race Commission in 1916. The Georgia educator and minister Atticus Haygood admitted that lynchings were barbarous, but he apologetically said they usually resulted from black sexual assaults upon white women. "Though he did not directly condone mob justice, Haygood argued that the torture suffered by a ruined woman was greater than that of a burning black man. However, the continuation and increasingly brutal nature of lynching—bodies were often mutilated—ultimately led racial liberals to condemn it under any circumstances" (Sosna, 31).

11. Lillian Smith took lynching as a central theme of the misplaced rage and ignorance of the white South. In *Killers*, she notes that for the 3,148 lynchings be-

tween 1882 and 1948, no member of a lynch mob was ever given life sentence or the death penalty.

12. It should be noted that the racial ideology of even groundbreaking sociologists evolved as the decades passed. Odum, in his 1910-11 dissertation study of black folk music, reflected racial attitudes then prevalent: "It will thus be seen that the songs of the most characteristic type are far from elegant," he wrote. "Nor are they dignified in theme or expression. They will appear to the cultured reader a bit repulsive, to say the least. They go beyond the interesting point to the trite and repulsive themes. Nor can a great many of the common songs that are too inelegant to include be given at all. But these are folk songs current among Negroes, and as such are powerful comment upon the special characteristics of the group" (Sosna, 44).

13. The transition to an integrated military was not smooth. In December 1941, Gen. George Marshall wrote War Secretary Stimson that "[t]he settlement of vexing racial problems cannot be permitted to complicate the tremendous task of the War Department, and thereby jeopardize discipline and morale" (Bergman, 494). In 1948, Randolph formed the League for Nonviolent Civil Disobedience Against Military Segregation, threatening to urge blacks to resist induction unless segregation and discrimination in armed services was ended. Finally, in July, President Truman's Executive Order 9981 barred segregation in armed services and created the President's Committee on Equality of Treatment and Opportunity in the Armed Services.

14. The Republican platform in 1940 read: "We believe that racial and religious minorities have the right to live, develop, and vote equally with all citizens and share the rights that are guaranteed by our Constitution. Congress shall exert its full constitutional power to protect these rights." Walter White called this plank "a mere splinter."

15. The Democratic National Committee nominated Truman and Alben Barkley, a U.S. senator from Kentucky; the ticket won with 24.1 million votes; Dewey was second with 21.9 million; and Strom Thurmond finished a distant third with 1.2 million.

16. *Atlanta Journal*, Sept. 3, 1948.

Chapter Two

1. Appropriately enough, Clayton writes that Cash admired Joseph Conrad and his "haunting tales of wandering, displaced white men living in distant corners of the world among half-caste and oppressed men and women of different races" (123).

2. Lynchings were about "strengthening the culture of segregation, creating a new southern future in which an expanding consumer culture created and maintained rather than blurred and transformed racial difference," Grace Elizabeth Hale writes. "Lynching ensured that a black man or woman was not just, as Du Bois had stated, 'a person who must ride Jim Crow in Georgia,' but also someone who could be publicly tortured and killed, prevented even from being a person." Lynchings also indirectly put black bodies back on the market, as grim photographs of burned bodies and other ghastly trinkets circulated as souvenirs. Hale reports on one case in which a lynch mob in Texas skinned a black man named "Big Nose" George and

made the tanned "leather" into a medical instrument bag, razor strops, a pair of women's shoes, and a tobacco pouch. The Rawlins National Bank displayed the shoes for years in a front window (Hale, 229). Cash, like many other white liberal Southerners of the time—Lillian Smith being a notable exception—opposed a federal antilynching law, saying its passage would incite whites to violence and thus do blacks more harm than good.

3. From the Civil War to the present day, the suicide rate in the South has in fact been far lower than the national average, and the homicide rate much higher. See Escott, 39.

4. Cash's grave is in Shelby, North Carolina, around the corner from his parents house, where he wrote *Mind*. His simple, flat stone, increasingly hard to read, says: "A great mind, a sweet nature, a scholar, author, and editor. He loved the South with intensity and was to all a friend. 'God's finger touched him and he slept.'" Across the road, a six-foot granite monument marks the grave of Thomas Dixon Jr., paid for by his friends when they realized he was broke. It called him "the most distinguished son of his generation" (Clayton, 1).

5. The day before Cash was born, his biographer Bruce Clayton discovered, Gaffney switched on the town's first electric streetlights. "They are the very latest design and give a splendid light," the local paper wrote. "We have now been ushered from darkness into light" (Clayton, 3).

6. When President Woodrow Wilson saw *The Birth of a Nation*, D. W. Griffith's 1916 film version of *The Clansman*, he exclaimed that the film "was history written with lightning."

7. Cash conflated the image of poor whites with that traditionally reserved for blacks in other ways as well. In one passage, he sexualizes poor whites in a way he never does when describing the wealthy. On any given Saturday night, he writes, poor Southerners "let off steam with the old hunting yell; maybe to have a drink, maybe to get drunk, to laugh with passing girls, to pick them up if you had a car, or to go swaggering or hesitating into the hotels with their corridors saturated with the smell of bichloride of mercury, or the secret, steamy, bawdy houses; maybe to have a fight, maybe to end whooping and singing, maybe bloody and goddamning, in the jailhouse—it was more and more in the dream and reality of such excursions that the old romantic-hedonistic impulses found egress, and that men and women were gratefully emptied of their irritations and repressions, and left to return to their daily tasks stolid, unlonely, and tame again" (*Mind*, 296).

8. Such a conflation of race and class is all too easily accepted by traditional white thinking, writes David Roediger in *The Wages of Whiteness*. "The point that race is created wholly ideologically and historically, while class is not so created, has often been boiled down to the notion that class (or the 'economic') is more real, more fundamental, more basic or more *important* than race, both in political terms and in terms of historical analysis," writes Roediger, arguing that "working class formation and the systematic development of a sense of whiteness went hand in hand for the U.S. white working class" (8).

9. It should be remembered, as Clayton points out, that although the Charlotte paper for which Cash wrote "had taken several steps away from the racist language that had characterized southern newspapers for decades," it still held to the sacred line of segregation. "Darkey cartoons appeared now and then and editorials and articles lapsed into darkey language on occasion. It was a different day, to be sure, and

dialect or the word *nigger* could be used, as Cash did regularly, for effect, often in a way intended to expose racism" (143).

10. Fantasies about "pure women," as Lillian Smith recognized, are a natural outgrowth of fears of sexual impotence; women placed outside the world of flesh and desire are less sexually threatening. Cash has been justly criticized for leaving women almost entirely out of *The Mind of the South*; like blacks, the women in the book serve only to mirror the desires and anxieties of the white men who largely populate it.

11. After a brief stint working for the *Chicago Post*, Cash began work for the *Charlotte News* in 1926. It was around this time that he also wrote a "blood and thunder romance" that he later destroyed; a manuscript left in his desk at the newspaper was described by Katherine Grantham, the paper's book editor, as "centering pretentiously on a beautiful young white goddess of a primitive South Sea people. If published, this potboiling novella would scarcely have enhanced Cash's reputation" (Joseph Morrison, 42).

12. For a complete chronicling of Cash's depression and its effect on his writing, see Bertram Wyatt-Brown's essay, "W. J. Cash: Creativity and Suffering in a Southern Writer," in Paul Escott's collection *W. J. Cash and the Minds of the South*.

13. As a writer, Cash most admired Thomas Wolfe, who he memorialized after Wolfe's death in 1936 as "undoubtedly the ablest novelist of his generation"; he also admired Erskine Caldwell for his frankness about poverty. But Cash prodded other Southern writers to move beyond the imaginative paradigms set by these two literary monoliths. In the February 12, 1939, issue of the *Charlotte News*, he wrote, "I am pretty sick of detailed photographs of nigger lynchings which are exactly like the other 211 I have read. I'd like to see my poor whites through some other eyes than Caldwell's—and I'd like to see the country represented as being populated by somebody besides those poor whites and the coons."

14. In "A Fanatic Menaces Civilization," Cash wrote: "The Western World faces now what it should have realized long ago—that Nazism is no civilized philosophy made a little grotesque by a few wild aberrations, but a system invented by a gang of criminals for the deliberate purpose of taking a whole nation back into barbarism, and using it as an instrument to carry barbarism over the whole earth. . . . The thing that is at issue now is precisely whether or not we shall all be Nazified, whether we shall return into barbarism, or whether civilization shall survive—whether men shall retain some dignity as men or revert to blood-drinking beasts" (qtd. in Joseph Morrison, 258–59).

15. Cash got himself under control enough to deliver his speech in Austin, but for some reason he ad-libbed it rather than reading from a prepared text. The university recorded the speech, which remains perhaps the only recording of his voice; the recording is available through the Southern Historical Collection at the University of North Carolina, Chapel Hill.

16. Joseph Morrison questions the drama of Key's statement: "But how many suicides, exactly, did Professor Key tabulate and thus consider a 'depressingly high rate of self-destruction'? His principal assistant in composing *Southern Politics*, Alexander Heard, put this question to his senior and has since informed me that Key had named exactly three: one whose name Heard could not recall; then Clarence Cason, and finally W. J. Cash. Since the incidence of three suicides cannot rigidly be construed as a 'depressingly high rate of self-destruction,' Key's

engagingly written generalization must be set down as artistic license, no more" (140).

17. King quotes a Sylvia Plath scholar on this subject, and I think it works well for an analysis of Cash: "For the artist himself, art is not necessarily therapeutic; he is not automatically relieved of his fantasies by expressing them, A. Alvarez is quoted as writing. 'Instead by some perverse logic of creation, the act of formal expression may simply make the dredged-up material more readily available to him. The result of handling it in his work may well be that he finds himself living it out'" (158).

18. Cash's frequent invocation of violence served a deeply ambivalent purpose that both revolted and intrigued him. Etienne Balibar says: "I shall therefore venture the idea that the racist complex inextricably combines a crucial function of *misrecognition* (without which the violence would not be tolerable to the very people engaging in it) and a 'will to know,' a violent *desire for* immediate *knowledge* of social relations. These are functions which are mutually sustaining since, both for individuals and social groups, their own collective violence is a distressing enigma and they require an urgent explanation for it. This indeed is what makes the intellectual posture of the ideologies of racism so singular, however sophisticated their theories may seem. Unlike for example theologians, who must maintain a distance (though not an absolute break, unless they lapse into 'gnosticism') between esoteric speculation and a doctrine designed for popular consumption, historically effective racist ideologues have always developed 'democratic' doctrines which are immediately intelligible to the masses and apparently suited from the outset to their supposed level of intelligence, even when elaborating elitist themes" (19).

Chapter Three

1. Even Percy's original title, "Jackdaw in the Garden," called up medieval imagery; he was apparently "thinking of the jackdaws in his volumes of English literature, who had a reputation for loitering about old castles and cathedrals and mimicking human voices to no one in particular." Percy's editor feared such a title might become a self-fulfilling prophesy and suggested the change (Baker, 169).

2. If Percy struggled with his sexuality, particularly given his cultural surroundings, he never felt comfortable discussing it publicly. Wyatt-Brown mentions the "unspoken code" that existed between Percy and the rest of his family regarding his refusal to marry, and he writes of Percy's "shame at his own sexual feelings for which the Church had no more sympathy than had his parents or Greenville society" (223). Both before and after World War I, Percy became involved with a group of Englishmen calling themselves the "Uranians," who "celebrated in verse the merits of young male beauty in the nude. For the Uranians, chaste aestheticism was the ideal." Percy became particularly friendly with a man named Norman Douglas, known for his "Uranian proclivities, as the gays of that time used the term" (Wyatt-Brown, 219).

3. Percy's adult library was steeped in the classics of both Roman and Victorian literature, particularly Matthew Arnold, that he read and re-read. "Not even his distinguished contemporaries and fellow Southerners, the Nashville poets Allen Tate, John Crowe Ransom and company, met his Edwardian tastes," Wyatt-Brown writes. "Yet he had a variety of nineteenth-century stories of adventure and romance upon which his young cousin [Walker Percy] voraciously fed" (276).

4. "Indeed if I know Will Percy," Walker Percy wrote, "I judge that in so far as there might be a connection between him and the Northumberland Percys, they, not he, would have to claim kin. He made fun of his ancestor Don Carlos, and if he claimed Harry Hotspur, it was a kinship of spirit. His own aristocracy was a meritocracy of character, talent, performance, courage, and a quality of life" (*Lanterns*, xviii). Percy's fascination with his ancestry is mirrored by Captain Pemberton in McCullers's novel *Reflections in a Golden Eye*: "Captain Pemberton had never known real love." He "was a Southerner and was never allowed by his aunts to forget it. On his mother's side he was descended from the Huguenots who left France in the seventeenth century, lived in Haiti until the great uprising, and then were planters in Georgia before the Civil War. Behind him was a history of barbarous splendor, ruined poverty, and family hauteur. But the present generation had not come to much; the Captain's only male first cousin was a policeman in the city of Nashville. Being a great snob, and with no real pride in him, the Captain set exaggerated store by the lost past" (50).

5. Despite his poetic leanings, Percy apparently enjoyed being a lawyer; when a guest asked him how he had fused reality with poetry, and pointed out that Coleridge had done so with opium and Poe with alcohol, Will replied, "And I am a lawyer" (Baker, 156).

6. Cash astutely marked the closing of the aristocratic ranks: "And so it happened that while the actuality of the aristocracy was drawing away toward the limbo of aborted and unrealized things, the claim of its possession as an achieved and essentially indefeasible heritage, so far from being abated, was reasserted with a kind of frenzied intensity" (*Mind*, 127).

7. The statue was completed by the end of 1933; the artist was aware of a statue Henry Adams had sculptor Augustus Saint-Gaudens create in 1885 for the grave of his wife.

8. Percy's anxieties might have been appeased had he been able to read his own obituary. The January 22, 1942, edition of the *Memphis Commercial-Appeal* was impressed "that any man of his relatively few years could have accomplished so much in such a variety of worth-while fields. . . . Born into a family with a long and unusual record of personal distinction and public service, Mr. Percy lived up to his heritage and made a most useful and constructive thing of that tradition. He was a student, a teacher, a landowner, a soldier, an economist and author, and it was the crown of his abilities that he owned and employed an excellent literary imagination and a coherent style."

9. After *Lanterns* was published in the spring of 1941, Percy visited the hospital for high blood pressure in August; doctors told him he had the oldest body they had ever seen for a man his age. He soon afterward suffered a cerebral hemorrhage that impaired his speech, and he finally died on January 21, 1942, at the age of fifty-six.

10. "If it is necessary every Negro in this state will be lynched, it will be done to maintain white supremacy," Vardaman once said (Wyatt-Brown, 179). Leroy was beaten badly in the general election; he came in third, with just 15 percent of the vote. The loss rocked the Percy family.

11. Hodding Carter, in *Where Main Street Meets the River*, says Percy had a "sensitive mouth about a fighter's jaw"; later, as a student at the all-male University of the South, Percy would show his prudishness in a public objection to the "smut" he found in *Othello* (Wyatt-Brown, 199).

12. Will believed that blacks' simpler way of life led to a greater spiritual awareness than that found among whites, and he was more than willing to point this out to his neighbors. On Easter morning 1938, over 3,000 people gathered at a river for a sunrise service. Percy was among them, and though he was impressed by the spiritual hunger of the crowd, he was disappointed by the service. In a letter to the local newspaper, Will wrote that those who had arisen before dawn and braved uncertain weather had received only "a few perfunctory prayers, uttered apparently to catch the ear of the audience, but not God, some execrable, listless singing and the worst playing ever done by the un-uniformed Greenville Public School Band. The only saving grace was the singing of a song spiritual by the timid negroes—their sole participation in the service—and even their habitual fervor was dampened by the apathy of the white participants" (Baker, 158).

13. The Percy family had also long boasted of employing the best cook in town, Wyatt-Brown writes. Louisa's fried chicken, beaten biscuits, and other delicacies were locally renowned. Will Percy christened her "the Queenly Woman" because of her memorable proportions of three hundred pounds, regal dignity, and fierce temper. Yet for reasons of some unknown "malady of the spirit," as David Cohn recalled the matter, Louisa became so thoroughly demoralized and probably alcoholic that her food became inedible, her kitchen management slovenly. With heavy heart, Percy finally called her in to give her notice. "And so it was that this once majestic figure, a canker at her heart, left the household," Cohn recounted. She was replaced by "the gentle Theresa who remained as long as Will lived" (Wyatt-Brown, 265).

14. Like Faulkner, Cash was also aware that rampant miscegenation had a way of both subverting and energizing racist ideology. He would later write: "Stay awhile in any town of the land and presently some gentleman native to the place will point you out a shuffling, twisted specimen, all compact of tangled hair, warts, tobacco stains, and the odor of the dung heap, and with a grandiloquent wave of the hand and a mocking voice announce: 'My cousin, Wash Venable!' What he means, of course, is what he means when he uses the same gesture and the same tone in telling you that the colored brother who attends to his spittoons is also his cousin—that you will take him seriously at your peril. What he means is that the coincidence of names is merely a little irony of God, and that the thing he says is clearly not so" (*Mind*, 28).

15. Percy's appreciation of black dialect runs throughout his book. At the front during World War I, he stumbles across a black battalion (the 92nd) and finds himself overwhelmed with gratitude to have found someone from home, "[n]ot knowing whether to laugh or cry. . . . Next morning I felt at home when upon asking a Negro orderly for some warm water he averred there warn't none and you couldn't git none. I suggested borrowing from the house across the street. He sighed and commented: 'Lawd, that woman ain't seen no warm water since the last time she cried'" (*Lanterns*, 197).

16. Percy's opposition to mechanizing his farm apparently went beyond economic considerations. He told Hodding Carter, "We've got to think of the human side. The tenants have their homes and their roots here, and I'm not going to pull them up" (Baker, 156). Yet his noblesse oblige comes forth throughout his text; in response to the carping of opponents, he said: "Our plantation system seems to me to offer as humane, just, self-respecting, and cheerful a method of earning a living as human beings are likely to devise. I watch the limber-jointed, oily-black, well-fed,

decently clothed peasants on Trail Lake and feel sorry for the telephone girls, the clerks in chain stores, the office help, the unskilled laborers everywhere—not only for their poor and fixed wage but for their slave routine, their joyless habits of work, and their insecurity. . . . Share-cropping is one of the best systems ever devised to give security and a chance for profit to the simple and the unskilled" (*Lanterns*, 280, 282).

17. Before becoming the senior member in his firm, Will had been christened "little Jesus" by local blacks for his passionate defense of a black man who claimed that he could cure the lame and blind by baptizing them in a nearby stream. Will argued that since the man gave credit to Christ for doing the actual healing, he was not making excessive claims, and he added that if Christ came back to earth, he too would be considered an impostor. Will's client was acquitted, though he was arrested again later for shooting at a planter who came to the spring to fetch his tenants home to tend their crops (Baker, 156).

18. The writer Jonathan Daniels, who was a guest in the Percy home, wrote that Percy's love of Negroes "is the feudal lord's love for his serfs. . . . He is not concerned for the black man's morals. Indeed, he holds that the Negro is to be judged by entirely different ethical standards than those supposedly applicable to white men. I had the feeling that Percy loved Negroes as another gentleman might love dogs, and that somehow the fiercer the beast the more he might prefer it" (173).

19. A marked element of cultural insecurity also surely marked the burgeoning mythology; the region's intellectuals had been stung with H. L. Mencken's famous —if oddly racist itself—essay titled "The Sahara of the Bozart" in 1917, which mocked Southern literary pretensions: "Nearly the whole of Europe could be lost in that stupendous region of worn-out farms, shoddy cities, and paralyzed cerebrums: one could throw in France, Germany and Italy, and still have room for the British Isles. And yet, for all its size and wealth and all the 'progress' it babbles of, it is as sterile, artistically, intellectually, culturally, as the Sahara Desert. There are single acres in Europe that house more first-rate men than all the states south of the Potomac; there are probably single square miles in America. If the whole of the late Confederacy were to be engulfed by a tidal wave tomorrow, the effect upon the civilized minority of men in the world would be but little greater than that of a flood on the Yang-tse-hiang. It would be impossible in all history to match so complete a drying-up of a civilization" (Mencken, 184).

20. Balibar continues: "The new racism is a racism of the era of 'decolonization,' of the reversal of population movements between the old colonies and the old metropolises, and the division of humanity within a single political space. Ideologically, current racism, which in France centers upon the immigration complex, fits into a framework of 'racism without races' which is already widely developed in other countries, particularly the Anglo-Saxon ones. It is a racism whose dominant theme is not biological heredity but the insurmountability of cultural differences, a racism which, at first sight, does not postulate the superiority of certain groups or peoples in relation to others but 'only' the harmfulness of abolishing frontiers, the incompatibility of life-styles and traditions" (21).

21. After a local Klan member's attempt to abduct his father senator, William went to the local Cyclops and said, "I want to let you know one thing: if anything happens to my Father or to any of our friends you will be killed. We won't hunt for the guilty party. So far as we are concerned the guilty party will be you" (*Lanterns*, 236).

Chapter Four

1. Lewis Allen was the pen name of Abel Meerpol, who also wrote "The House I Live In," a plea for racial and religious tolerance sung by Frank Sinatra in a 1945 movie short of the same name. Meerpol and his wife adopted the sons of Julius and Ethel Rosenberg after they were executed in 1953 for allegedly passing atomic secrets to the Soviet union (White, *Billie Holiday*, 50).

2. By some accounts, the song "Strange Fruit" marked a turning point in the career of Billie Holiday as well. Previous to her recording, "she had been singing mostly the cheerful banalities of Tin Pan Alley, alchemizing June-moon trash into gold. Now she had a song that was strong, if obvious, material. Billie became an actress assuming a role. During the instrumental introduction she stood in a single spotlight, motionless, eyes closed. When she began to sing, she delivered the words rather in the style of a recitative. It was a brilliant, definitive performance. Aside from her, few but the late Josh White dared to touch the song. But *Strange Fruit* possessed her too. She became serious in a new, not altogether suitable style. 'Overnight,' said one observer, 'she changed from being a marvelously talented club singer to "La Grande Chanteuse."' With *Strange Fruit* Billie was becoming the Dark Lady of Songs, with the white gardenia that became her trademark glowing in her black hair. Gradually she imprisoned herself in her own myth. 'The more conscious she became of her style, the more mannered she became,' John Hammond said; artistically, *Strange Fruit*'s success was 'the worst thing that ever happened to her'" (Melvin Maddox, liner notes to *Billie Holiday* in the Time-Life *Giants of Jazz* series, Alexandria, Va.: Time Life Books, Inc., 1979).

3. Holiday's recording had been banned by the BBC, but not in the United States. The use of the word "fuckin" (twice) got Smith's novel outlawed in Boston and created an aura of "dirty book," which helped sales. The Boston ban was challenged by Bernard DeVoto, who bought a copy from Abraham Isenstadt in the presence of two police officers. DeVoto was found not guilty, but Isenstadt was fined $100; his appeal was upheld by the state supreme court, and because it was never brought to the U.S. Supreme Court, the book is still technically banned in Boston (Blackwell and Clay, 38). The book sold openly in Atlanta and Birmingham. *Strange Fruit* has since sold upwards of 3 million copies and has been translated into sixteen languages.

4. A stage version of *Strange Fruit*, directed by Jose Ferrer and starring Walter White's daughter Jane in the lead role, opened in Montreal, then Toronto, Boston, and Philadelphia, and it finally opened on Broadway on November 29, 1945.

5. Smith claimed to have first heard the song in 1942, a year after "Two Men and a Bargain" was published. Originally submitted as a manuscript entitled *Jordan Is So Chilly* to ten publishers, the novel *Strange Fruit* was rejected by all ten. Smith wrote to Walter White, the executive secretary of the NAACP, that the manuscript's poor reception was due to "my complete frankness about the racial ambivalence of the South." In 1943, Frank Taylor, an editor with Reynal and Hitchcock, asked to see the manuscript, accepted it four days later, and asked her to change the title.

6. The title for *Killers* came to Smith while she was writing the novel *Julia*; in it, she wrote about the suicide note of a preacher, who used the phrase "I have killed my dream." She realized "the killers of the dream are ourselves as well as 'the others' and we kill our dreams on so many levels of being" (Loveland, 97).

7. In 1938, following the death of her mother, Smith traveled to Brazil with Paula Snelling. Perhaps inspired by the comparatively free movement of different races there, it was in Brazil that she wrote much of *Strange Fruit*.

8. Faulkner published "A Letter to the North" in *Life* magazine in March 1956, in which he said that although he had long opposed segregation, he was disturbed at the violence that had recently accompanied forced integration. He would, he wrote, "go on the record as opposing the forces outside the South which would use legal or police compulsion to eradicate that evil overnight." Although *Life* did not accept Smith's reply to that letter, she did have a piece accepted at *Time* arguing with a speech by the editor of the *Louisville Courier-Journal* that equated the NAACP and segregationist U.S. senator James Eastland, calling them both "radical."

9. King was driving her to Emory Hospital in Atlanta for a checkup when a police officer, seeing them together, pulled the car over; when King's Alabama license was found to have been expired, he was fined $25 and given a year's probation. When he violated that probation on October 25, 1960, he was sentenced to four months of hard labor, and it took the Kennedy administration to get the judge to reverse his decision.

10. The ways cultural discourse damages both sides of the racial divide is also evocative of Faulkner's *Intruder in the Dust*: "All he requires is that they act like niggers. Which is exactly what Lucas is doing: blew his top and murdered a white man—which Mr. Lilley is probably convinced all Negroes want to do—and now the white people will take him out and burn him, all regular and in order and themselves acting exactly as he is convinced Lucas would wish him to act: like white folks; both of them observing implicitly the rules: the nigger acting like a nigger and the white folks acting like white folks and no real hard feelings on either side (since Mr. Lilley is not a Gowrie) once the fury is over; in fact Mr. Lilley would probably be one of the first to contribute cash money toward Lucas' funeral and the support of his widow and children if he had them. Which proves again how no man can cause more grief than that one clinging blindly to the vices of his ancestors" (48–49).

11. Smith grew up just miles from the Okefenokee Swamp, the "Land of the Trembling Earth," and part of the region that inspired the folklore of Zora Neale Hurston.

12. The name Pusey conjures up a vulgarity that, according to the *Oxford English Dictionary*, was first used in 1879–80.

13. Catherine Clinton reminds us that this cult of fragile womanhood dates back to the earliest years of the plantation culture. She quotes from an 1817 letter from C. A. Hull to his niece Sarah Thomas as she prepares to leave home to begin a teaching job: "I view you on the pinnacle of an awful precipice. . . . Peculiarly delicate is the crisis, and one false step forever blasts the fame of a female. . . . Malevolence is so predominant in the human heart, that in all, it displays the devouring jaws of a mighty Maelstrom ready on every touch to destroy the vessel that perchance may be cast into the whirlpool" (110).

14. It is precisely this loss of control among whites, then, that leads from displaced sexual desire to cultural and physical oppression, particularly as it is manifested in the lynching of black men. Indeed, the rage contained in the word "nigger" in Smith's and Fanon's passages above is evocative of Faulkner's *Intruder in the Dust*, published in 1948, just four years after *Strange Fruit*. In that novel Lucas Beauchamp, a self-possessed black man, is lynched not for a crime but because his

"arrogance" offended local whites; the fury (and the underlying impotence) he inspires "hung nightly in the black abyss of rage and impotence: *If he would just be a nigger first, just for one second, one little infinitesimal second*" (Faulkner, 22).

Chapter Five

1. Fiedler considers the post-Faulkner era of McCullers and O'Connor to have been full of a "sensitive and Satanic . . . quite frankly homosexual" style, whose violence and grotesquerie was cultivated by magazines catering to wealthy women. "It was not until the female intermediaries had begun the grafting of Jamesian sensibility onto the Southern gothic stem, that the true Magnolia Blossom or Southern homosexual style could be produced: pseudo-magical, pseudo-religious, pseudo-gothic" (451).

2. Also like Lillian Smith, McCullers was a gifted musician as a child and was encouraged from an early age to pursue an extensive study of the piano. She often practiced three hours before school and three to five hours after school. The most important creative influence in her life, her piano teacher Mary Tucker, moved away with her husband in 1934, leaving the young prodigy feeling artistically bereft for the first time in her life.

3. Reeves had an insecure childhood. Born August 11, 1913, in his grandfather's home in Wetumpka, Alabama, he moved as child to Jessup, Georgia. His father, James "Bud" McCullers, had been a drugstore clerk, telephone lineman, penitentiary guard, unsuccessful farmer, and railroad man. His mother, Jessie Winn, was the daughter of John T. Winn, a gentleman farmer who sold farm implements and animals through his own company. The elder Winn agreed to set the couple up on some of his land, but Bud ended up hiring blacks to do all the work while he played baseball and worked as a lineman with Postal Telegraph Company. Bud later became a brakeman on the Atlantic Coast Line Railroad, a job that ended a year later when he fell from a coal car and had his leg crushed. With the settlement money he received from the railroad, Bud opened a bakery, which failed. He then started drinking and eventually abandoned his family.

4. Reeves had his share of physical trauma as well; during the war, he took shrapnel to his body and badly fractured his hand. He received the Silver Star and three Bronze stars, a presidential unit citation, and a Purple Heart.

5. McCullers was awarded a Guggenheim Fellowship in 1942 along with, among others, John Dos Passos and W. H. Auden, and she won another in 1946. She was given a $1,000 grant by the American Academy of Arts and Letters and National Institute of Arts and Letters in 1943. In 1947, a weekly newsmagazine called *Quick* called her one of six best postwar writers in the country. Her short story "A Tree. A Rock. A Cloud." was included in the O. Henry Prize Stories of 1942, and her story "The Ballad of the Sad Café" made it into the *Best American Short Stories* in 1944. For her dramatic adaptation of *The Member of the Wedding*, with Ethel Waters as Berenice and Julie Harris as Frankie, she won a New York Drama Critics Circle Award in 1949, the year in which *South Pacific* was given the Pulitzer Prize. *The Member of the Wedding* grossed over $1.1 million from a fourteen-month, 501-performance Broadway run alone and went on to a successful road show. On January 15, 1951, McCullers was named as one of fourteen people to win lifetime admission to the National Institute of Arts and Letters, along with her friends Tennessee Williams

and Newton Arvin; Eudora Welty and Henry Steele Commager; and the poet Louise Bogan.

6. It was through Auden, who at the time was married to Erika Mann, that Mc-Cullers was to meet Annemarie Clarac-Schwarzenbach, a Swiss writer with whom she became romantically infatuated. Erika, Thomas Mann's oldest child, was trained in the theater, had been divorced from the actor Gustaf Grundgens, and remarried Auden in 1935 in a marriage of convenience so she might have British citizenship and be free to travel.

7. Early in 1945 Middagh Street was razed to make way for a wider automobile approach to the Brooklyn Bridge.

8. The Yaddo writer's colony was named by four-year-old Christina Trask in 1881; her family had been "shadowed" by a number of recent bereavements, and when her mother asked her what they should name the place, the child answered, "Shadow, Yaddo—Yaddo, shadow. Call it 'Yaddo,' Mama. It sounds like shadow, but it's not going to be a shadow any more, is it?" (Carr, 153).

9. Eight years later, in front of a group of guests at Sullivan's Island, off the coast of South Carolina, Reeves asked his friend Harrell Woolfolk, "Come on Harry, how would you like to sleep with Carson and me tonight?" (Carr, 397).

10. The description of Blount's hands is found on p. 45.

11. The image of Du Bois also seems to arise when, toward the end of Mc-Cullers's novel, two black friends of Copeland's offer their own opinion about the best way to handle the imprisonment of Willie. Their rhetoric, in marked opposition to Copeland's, seems a virtual mirror of the debate between Du Bois and Booker T. Washington over the most appropriate way to navigate black life in a white world. One of the men, Marshall Nicholls, says, "Naturally we have discussed this matter *extensively*. And without doubt as members of the colored race here in this free country of America we are anxious to do our part toward extending *amicable* relationships." "We wish always to do the right thing," says John Roberts. "And it behooves us to strive with care and not endanger the amicable relationship already established. Then by gradual means a better *condition* will come about." Nicholls soon replies, "We members of the colored race must strive in all ways to uplift our citizens. The Doctor in yonder has strived in every way. But sometimes it has seemed to me like he had not recognized fully enough certain *elements* of the different races and the situation" (*Heart*, 251–52).

12. Amusingly enough, there is even "crossing" among McCullers's animals. In *The Member of the Wedding*, there is a cat that answers to both "Charles" and "Charlina." In *The Heart Is a Lonely Hunter*, there is a mule that will not plow unless he is wearing a straw hat, and in *Reflections in a Golden Eye*, Major Langdon says, "Only two things matter to me now—to be a good animal and to serve my country."

13. The only boy Mick feels comfortable with is Harry Minowitz, the only boy not completely dwarfed by her size. Harry, "a Jew boy" with "a red, droopy sty" on one of his eyes, is presumably the son of one of the town's "quick, dark little Jew men." When Mick begins humming a song by Mozart, Harry asks if the composer is "a Fascist or a Nazi" and starts angrily punching the air. Mick says that Nazis are new and Mozart has been dead a long time. "It's a good thing," Harry says. "Because I hate Fascists. If I met one walking on the street I'd kill him." Harry wants to tell Mick about the Nazis, but she doesn't have time, and returns to the party, which

by now has descended into chaos. She is oblivious to Harry's anxiety; when the two meet later on, she throws up her arm and shouts "Heil!" as a joke.

14. The "horror of female identity" is as often used to fill out the psychological complexity in McCullers's men, many of whom fear women even as they imagine themselves cross-dressing. In *Reflections in a Golden Eye*, Private Williams, we learn, was taught from an early age "that women carried in them a deadly and catching disease which made men blind, crippled, and doomed to hell. In the army he also heard much talk of this bad sickness and was even himself once examined by a doctor to see if he had touched a woman. Private William had never willingly touched, or looked at, or spoken to a female since he was eight years old" (13).

15. The interpretability of Singer's language brings to mind Edgar Allan Poe's early grotesque story "The Murders in the Rue Morgue," in which a variety of "ear" witnesses claim to have heard the grunts of a murderer during a killing. Each witness, a native of a different European country, asserts that the voice heard was that of a Russian, an Englishman, a German, a Frenchman, or an Italian. The culprit was, in fact, a gorilla, presumably without developed language skills.

BIBLIOGRAPHY

Andrews, William L. "In Search of a Common Identity: The Self and the South in Four Mississippi Autobiographies." *Southern Review* 24 (1988): 47–64.

Appiah, Anthony. *In My Father's House: Africa in the Philosophy of Culture*. New York: Oxford University Press, 1992.

Arendt, Hannah. *Eichmann in Jerusalem: A Report on the Banality of Evil*. New York: Viking Press, 1963.

Ashmore, Harry. *Civil Rights and Wrongs: A Memoir of Race and Politics, 1944–1994*. New York: Pantheon Books, 1994.

———. *Hearts and Minds: The Anatomy of Racism from Roosevelt to Reagan*. New York: McGraw-Hill, 1982.

Ayers, Edward L. *The Promise of a New South*. New York: Oxford University Press, 1992.

Baker, Lewis. *The Percys of Mississippi: Politics and Literature in the New South*. Baton Rouge: Louisiana State University Press, 1983.

Balibar, Etienne. "Is There a Neo-Racism?" *Race, Nation, Class*. New York: Verso, 1991.

Berg, Barbara. *The Rememberer Gate: Origins of American Feminism, the Woman and the City, 1800–1860*. Oxford: Oxford University Press, 1978.

Bergman, Peter. *The Chronological History of the Negro in America*. New York: Harper and Row, 1969.

Blackwell, Louise, and Frances Clay. *Lillian Smith*. New York: Twayne Publishers, 1971.

Box, Patricia S. "Androgyny and the Musical Vision: A Study of Two Novels by Carson McCullers." *Southern Quarterly* 16 (1978): 117–24.

Bragg, Rick. *All Over But the Shoutin'*. New York: Pantheon, 1997.

Branch, Taylor. *Parting the Waters: America in the King Years, 1954–1963*. New York: Simon and Schuster, 1988.

———. *Pillar of Fire: America in the King Years, 1963–1965*. New York: Simon and Schuster, 1998.

Carby, Hazel. *Reconstructing Womanhood: The Emergence of the Afro-American Woman Novelist*. New York: Oxford University Press, 1987.

Carr, Virginia Spencer. *The Lonely Hunter: A Biography of Carson McCullers*. Garden City: Doubleday, 1975.

Carruth, Gorton, ed. *The Encyclopedia of American Facts and Dates*. 7th ed. New York: Harper and Row, 1956.

Carter, Hodding. *Lower Mississippi*. New York: Farrar and Rinehart, 1942.

———. *Where Main Street Meets the River*. New York: Rinehart, 1955.

———. *The Winds of Fear*. New York: Farrar, Rinehart, 1944.

Cash, W. J. *The Mind of the South*. New York: Vintage, 1960.

Chesnutt, Charles. *The Marrow of Tradition*. Ann Arbor: University of Michigan Press, 1969.

Clayton, Bruce. *W. J. Cash: A Life*. Baton Rouge: Louisiana State University Press, 1991.

Cliff, Michelle, ed. *The Winner Names the Age: A Collection of Writings by Lillian Smith*. New York: W. W. Norton, 1978.

Clinton, Catherine. *The Plantation Mistress: Woman's World in the Old South*. New York: Pantheon, 1982.

Cohn, David. "Eighteenth Century Chevalier." *Virginia Quarterly Review* 31 (1955): 561–76.

———. *God Shakes Creation*. New York: Harper Bros., 1935.

———. *Where I Was Born and Raised*. South Bend: University of Notre Dame Press, 1967.

Conkin, Paul. *The Southern Agrarians*. Knoxville: University of Tennessee Press, 1988.

Cook, Sylvia Jenkins. *From Tobacco Road to Route 66: The Southern Poor White in Fiction*. Chapel Hill: University of North Carolina Press, 1976.

Cowdrey, Albert. *This Land, This South: An Environmental History*. Lexington: University of Kentucky Press, 1983.

Cox, Oliver. *Race Relations: Elements and Social Dynamics*. Detroit: Wayne State University Press, 1976.

Daniels, Jonathan. *A Southerner Discovers the South*. New York: The Macmillan Company, 1938.

Dixon, Thomas. *The Clansman*. New York: Grosset and Dunlap, 1905.

Du Bois, W. E. B. *The Souls of Black Folk*. New York: Penguin Books, 1989.

Eagles, Charles W., ed. *The Mind of the South: Fifty Years Later*. Jackson: University of Mississippi Press, 1992.

Egerton, John. *Speak Now against the Day: The Generation Before the Civil Rights Movement in the South*. New York: Alfred A. Knopf, 1994.

Ellison, Ralph. *Going to the Territory*. New York: Random House, 1986.

———. *Shadow and Act*. New York: Random House, 1953.

Escott, Paul, ed. *W. J. Cash and the Minds of the South*. Baton Rouge: Louisiana State University Press, 1992.

Escott, Paul, and David R. Goldfield, eds. *The South for New Southerners*. Chapel Hill: University of North Carolina Press, 1991.

Faulkner, William. *Intruder in the Dust*. New York: Random House, 1948.

Ferris, William, and Charles Reagan Wilson, eds. *The Encyclopedia of Southern Culture*. Chapel Hill: University of North Carolina Press, 1989.

Fiedler, Leslie. *Love and Death in the American Novel*. New York: Criterion Books, 1960.

Foster, Frances Smith. *Witnessing Slavery: The Development of Anti-bellum Slave Narratives*. Westport, Conn.: Greenwood Press, 1979.

Frederickson, George. *The Black Image in the White Mind*. New York: Harper Torchbook, 1972.

Friedman, Lawrence. *The White Savage*. New York: Harper and Row, 1971.

Gaines, Kevin K. *Uplifting the Race: Black Leadership, Politics, and Culture in the Twentieth Century*. Chapel Hill: University of North Carolina Press, 1996.

Gates, Henry Louis, Jr. *Race, Writing, and Difference*. Chicago: University of Chicago Press, 1986.

———. *Thirteen Ways of Looking at a Black Man*. New York: Random House, 1997.

Gerster, Patrick, and Nicholas Cords, eds. *Myth and Southern History.* Urbana: University of Illinois Press, 1989.

Gladney, Margaret Rose. *How Am I to Be Heard? The Letters of Lillian Smith.* Chapel Hill: University of North Carolina Press, 1993.

Goldfield, David. *Black, White, and Southern: Race Relations and Southern Culture, 1940 to the Present.* Baton Rouge: Louisiana State University Press, 1990.

Goldman, Eric. *The Crucial Decade—and After: America, 1945–1960.* New York: Vintage, 1956, 1960.

Gordimer, Nadine. "A Private Apprenticeship." *London Magazine* 12 (1972): 134–37.

Grantham, Dewey W. *The South and the Sectional Image.* New York: Harper and Row, 1967.

Gray, Richard. *The Literature of Memory: Modern Writers of the American South.* Baltimore: The Johns Hopkins University Press, 1977.

Halberstam, David. *The Fifties.* New York: Villard Books, 1993.

Hale, Grace Elizabeth. *Making Whiteness: The Culture of Segregation in the South, 1890–1940.* New York: Pantheon, 1998.

Hall, Stuart. "Ethnicity, Identity and Difference," *Radical America,* June 1991.

Higginbotham, Evelyn Brooks. "African-American Women's History and the Metalanguage of Race." *Signs* 17 (1992): 251–74.

James, Judith Giblin. *Wunderkind: The Reputation of Carson McCullers.* Columbia, S.C.: Camden House, 1995.

Jefferson, Thomas. *Notes on the State of Virginia.* Chapel Hill: University of North Carolina Press, 1954.

Kazin, Alfred. *Bright Book of Life: American Novelists and Storytellers from Hemingway to Mailer.* Boston: Little, Brown & Co., 1971.

Key, V. O. *Southern Politics in State and Nation.* Knoxville: University of Tennessee Press, 1984.

King, Richard H. *A Southern Renaissance.* New York: Oxford University Press, 1980.

Kneebone, John. *Southern Liberal Journalism and Issues of Race.* Chapel Hill: University of North Carolina Press, 1985.

Larsen, Nella. *Quicksand and Passing.* New Brunswick: Rutgers University Press, 1986.

Lawson, Lewis A. *Another Generation: Southern Fiction Since World War II.* Jackson: University Press of Mississippi, 1984.

Lemann, Nicholas. *The Promised Land.* New York: Alfred A. Knopf, 1991.

Loveland, Anne C. *Lillian Smith: A Southerner Confronting the South.* Baton Rouge: Louisiana State University Press, 1986.

Lukacs, Georg. *The Historical Novel.* London: Merlin Press, 1962.

McCullers, Carson. *The Ballad of the Sad Café and Other Stories.* New York: Houghton Mifflin, 1951.

———. *The Heart Is a Lonely Hunter.* New York: Houghton Mifflin, 1940.

———. *The Member of the Wedding.* New York: Houghton Mifflin, 1946.

———. *Reflections in a Golden Eye.* Boston: Houghton Mifflin, 1941.

McDowell, Margaret B. *Carson McCullers.* Boston: Twayne, 1980.

McGovern, James R. *Anatomy of a Lynching: The Killing of Claude Neal.* Baton Rouge: Louisiana State University Press, 1982.

Marable, Manning. *Beyond Black and White: Transforming African-American Politics.* London: Verso, 1995.

Mencken, H. L. *A Mencken Chrestomathy.* New York: Knopf, 1949.

Mitchell, Juliet, and Jacqueline Rose. "Introduction II." *Feminine Sexuality: Jacques Lacan and the école freudienne,* ed. Juliet Mitchell and Jacqueline Rose, trans. Jacqueline Rose. New York: W. W. Norton, 1982.

Moers, Ellen. *Literary Women.* Garden City: Doubleday & Co., 1976.

Morris, Willie. *The Ghosts of Medgar Evers.* New York: Random House, 1998.

Morrison, Joseph. *W. J. Cash: Southern Prophet.* New York: Alfred A. Knopf, 1967.

Morrison, Toni. *Playing in the Dark: Whiteness and the Literary Imagination.* Cambridge: Harvard University Press, 1992.

Nelson, Richard. *Aesthetic Frontiers: The Machiavellian Tradition and the Southern Imagination.* Jackson: University Press of Mississippi, 1990.

Nossiter, Adam. *Mississippi and the Murder of Medgar Evers.* Reading, Mass.: Addison-Wesley, 1994.

O'Brien, Michael. *The Idea of the American South, 1920–1941.* Baltimore: The Johns Hopkins University Press, 1979.

Omi, Michael, and Howard Winant. *Racial Formation in the United States.* New York: Routledge Press, 1986.

Percy, William Alexander. *Lanterns on the Levee: Recollections of a Planter's Son.* Baton Rouge: Louisiana State University Press, 1941.

Perry, Constance. "Carson McCullers and the Female *Wunderkind.*" *Southern Literary Journal* 19 (1986): 36–45.

Powdermaker, Hortense. *After Freedom: A Cultural Study in the Deep South.* New York: Russell and Russell, 1939.

————. *Stranger and Friend.* New York: Norton, 1966.

Quarles, Benjamin. *The Negro in the Making of American Life.* New York: Macmillan, 1964.

Ransom, John Crowe, et al. *I'll Take My Stand: The South and the Agrarian Tradition.* New York: Harper & Brothers, 1930.

Raper, Arthur, and Ira Reid. *Sharecroppers All.* Chapel Hill: University of North Carolina Press, 1941.

Roediger, David R. *Toward the Abolition of Whiteness: Essays on Race, Politics, and Working Class History.* New York: Verso, 1994.

————. *The Wages of Whiteness: Race and the Making of the American Working Class.* New York: Verso, 1991.

Roper, John Herbert. *C. Vann Woodward, Southerner.* Athens: University of Georgia Press, 1987.

Rose, Arnold. *The Negro in America: A Condensed Version of Gunnar Myrdal's "An American Dilemma."* New York: Harper and Row, 1944.

Rubin, Louis D. *A Gallery of Southerners.* Baton Rouge: Louisiana State University Press, 1982.

Said, Edward. *Culture and Imperialism.* New York: Vintage Books, 1993.

Sedgwick, Eve Kosofsky. *Epistemology of the Closet.* Berkeley: University of California Press, 1990.

Seidler, Victor. *Rediscovering Masculinity: Reason, Language, and Sexuality.* London: Routledge Press, 1989.

Silver, James. "William Alexander Percy: The Aristocrat and the Anthropologist." Unpublished paper presented at Southern Historical Assoc., 1955.

Singal, Daniel. *The War Within: From Victorian to Modernist Thought in the South, 1919–1945*. Chapel Hill: University of North Carolina Press, 1982.

Smith, Lillian. *The Journey*. Cleveland: World Publishing Co., 1954.

————. *Killers of the Dream*. New York: W. W. Norton and Co., 1949, 1961.

————. *Memory of a Large Christmas*. New York: W. W. Norton, 1962.

————. *Now Is the Time*. New York: Viking, 1955.

————. *One Hour*. New York: Harcourt, Brace & Co., 1959.

————. *Our Faces, Our Words*. New York: W. W. Norton, 1964.

————. *Strange Fruit*. New York: Reynal and Hitchcock, 1944.

Sosna, Morton. *In Search of the Silent South*. New York: Columbia University Press, 1977.

Stone, Albert. *The Return of Nat Turner*. Athens: University of Georgia Press, 1992.

Sullivan, Margaret. *A Bibliography of Lillian Smith and Paula Snelling*. Memphis: *Bulletin of the Mississippi Valley Collection*, Memphis State University, Spring 1971.

Sundquist, Eric. *To Wake the Nations: Race in the Making of American Literature*. Cambridge: Harvard University Press, 1993.

Tindall, George B. *The Emergence of the New South, 1913–1945*. Baton Rouge: Louisiana State University Press, 1967.

Tolson, Jay. *Pilgrim in the Ruins: A Life of Walker Percy*. Chapel Hill: University of North Carolina Press, 1992.

Treat, John Whittier. *Writing Ground Zero: Japanese Literature and the Atomic Bomb*. Chicago: University of Chicago Press, 1995.

Van den Berghe, Pierre. *Race and Ethnicity*. New York: Basic Books, 1970.

Waldron, Ann. *Hodding Carter: The Reconstruction of a Racist*. Chapel Hill: Algonquin Books, 1993.

Warren, Robert Penn. *John Brown: The Making of a Martyr*. New York: Payson and Clark, 1929.

————. *The Legacy of the Civil War*. Cambridge: Harvard University Press, 1983.

————. *Who Speaks for the Negro?* New York: Random House, 1965.

Webster, Yehudi. *The Racialization of America*. New York: St. Martin's Press, 1992.

Welter, Barbara. "The Cult of True Womanhood, 1820–1860." *Dimity Convictions: The American Woman in the Nineteenth Century*. Columbus: University of Ohio Press, 1976.

West, Cornel. *Prophesy Deliverance!* Philadelphia: Westminster Press, 1982.

————. *Prophetic Fragments*. Grand Rapids: Eerdmans, 1988.

Westling, Louise. "Carson McCullers's Tomboys." *Southern Humanities Review* 14 (1980): 339–50.

White, Helen, and Rudding A. Sugg, eds. *From the Mountain: An Anthology of the Magazine Successively Titled Pseudopodia, the North Georgia Review, and South Today*. Memphis: Memphis State University Press, 1972.

White, John. *Billie Holiday: Her Life and Times*. London: Omnibus Press, 1987.

White, Walter. *A Man Called White*. New York: Viking Press, 1948.

Wideman, John Edgar. *Fatheralong*. New York: Vintage, 1995.

Williams, Patricia. *The Alchemy of Race and Rights*. Cambridge: Harvard University Press, 1991.

Williamson, Joel. *The Crucible of Race*. New York: Oxford University Press, 1984.
Wilson, Edmund. *Patriotic Gore: Studies in the Literature of the American Civil War*. London: The Hogarth Press, 1962.
Woodward, C. Vann. *American Counterpoint: Slavery and Racism in the North-South Dialogue*. Boston: Little, Brown & Co., 1964.
———. *The Burden of Southern History*. 3rd ed. Baton Rouge: Louisiana State University Press, 1993.
———. *The Future of the Past*. New York: Oxford University Press, 1989.
———. *The Strange Career of Jim Crow*. New York: Oxford University Press, 1955, 1966.
Wright, Richard. *Black Boy*. New York: Harper Perennial, 1993.
———. "Inner Landscapes." *New Republic* 103 (1940): 195.
———. *Native Son*. New York: Harper Perennial, 1993.
———. *Uncle Tom's Children*. New York: Harper and Row, 1965.
Wyatt-Brown, Bertram. *The House of Percy*. New York: Oxford University Press, 1994.
Young, Thomas Daniel. *The Past in the Present: A Thematic Study of Modern Southern Fiction*. Baton Rouge: Louisiana State University Press, 1981.
Zangrando, Robert L. *The NAACP Crusade Against Lynching, 1909–1950*. Philadelphia: Temple University Press, 1980.

INDEX